T0088176

The Doryman's Reflection

A Fisherman's Life

Paul Molyneaux

Seahorse Publishing

Seahorse Publishing books may be purchased in bulk at special discounts for sales promotion, corporate gifts, fund-raising, or educational purposes. Special editions can also be created to specifications. For details, contact the Special Sales Department, Skyhorse Publishing, 307 West 36th Street, 11th Floor, New York, NY 10018 or info@skyhorsepublishing.com.

Seahorse Publishing ® is a registered trademark of Skyhorse Publishing, Inc.®, a Delaware corporation.

Visit our website at www.skyhorsepublishing.com.

10 9 8 7 6 5 4 3 2 1

Library of Congress Cataloging-in-Publication Data is available on file.

All photos used courtesy of the author unless otherwise noted.

Cover design by Tom Lau
Cover photo credit: Neal Parent

Print ISBN: 978-1-944824-22-8
Ebook ISBN: 978-1-944824-23-5

Printed in the United States of America

To Jim Molyneaux

CONTENTS

PART FOUR: LIVING IN THE EYE OF THE STORM

PART FIVE: CLOSING

APPENDICES

Part One

NO REFUGE

One

NO REFUGE

You stand in an unfamiliar place, in motion. You see a steel door with six handles; it shifts, and you shift, leaning first one way then another. The door is not in a wall, it's in a bulkhead. You don't go downstairs here; you go down below. You don't go upstairs—you go above, on deck; higher still and you are aloft in the swaying rigging. And all the time you are being lifted and dropped. You look at a man, your dorymate, and the gray line behind his head that ceaselessly rises and falls in shifting angles: the horizon. You are flexing and leaning to keep from falling down and it gets to where you stop noticing, so much so that after ten days you come ashore and you can barely stand up. You are still rising and falling, leaning and flexing, being lifted by waves that have rolled into your body, but not this far ashore. You grab for your dorymates, laughing and stumbling toward the bar.

Next thing you remember you are waking up in a motel room and half the crew is there and the captain is banging on the door. Somebody lets him in and he hands out your shares, and they're less than you figured, and yours is half of what everybody else gets cause you're new and you only get a half share while the rest of the crew divides your other half. And they keep telling you next trip'll be full share.

You think maybe you could find another boat, but before you do you are throwing the lines again, headed out for another ten days. You are on a scalloper out of Cape May, New Jersey, wondering where the glory is.

Since you're shorthanded the watches are split, which means you don't get to sleep much and you go on deck when they tell you to and stay there till you're limp, wet, and bleary eyed, then you go below into the stinking fo'c'sle, and eat a little, and sleep a couple of hours until somebody comes and wakes you and says "Come on."

On deck, the dredges, fifteen-foot-wide triangles of welded steel bars, trailing long chain bags, and weighing tons, are swung out on each side of the boat. They rest heavy on the rails, each held by a single pelican hook until "knocked out" on the downward roll. The bell rings, you swing, and the steel pelican hook that you put on wrong whips past your face when you hit it, and your hammer goes over with the dredge.

The boat rolls on through the night under the winter stars, and people keep yelling at you and telling you what to do and how not to get hurt. They say to you repeatedly not to put your hand on the rail when the dredges are in the water, because on every roll of the sea the cables run up and down the sides of the boat like great big scissors, but you don't get it till one night you put your hand on the rail, and the tips of the fingers of your glove get clipped off.

Another night you are hauling back and the dredge comes rising from the darkness and banging alongside. You hook the tackle to it and the winch man hoists it up high over the rail. It swings in over your head, big chain bag full of tons of rocks and sea bottom dripping in the halogen glow of the deck lights, but it's too rough to land it and when it swings out again the tackle parts and the whole works goes crashing into the sea. The cable screams out through the bollard behind you; you can feel it whizzing past the backs of your legs, but you are not getting hurt so you stand still, calculating the odds.

You are too small to reach the tackle when the dredge is on the rail so you climb out over the empty space to unhook it. You can hear the water a few feet beneath you, rushing past the hull, and just as you are jumping back aboard the pelican hook breaks. You push off and fall on deck as the dredge slides into the sea—the suction would've taken you to bottom with it. They tell you that if that ever happens to hang on and they'll get you back. And you look at them and wonder.

And this is how you started fishing. But it's not. You started on the bank of a Pennsylvania farm pond with your brother and grandfather. And they smiled at every gleaming fish you caught.

Two

KERR'S POND

My grandfather made me a fisherman before anything else. He held the strands of a barbed wire fence apart so my older brother Jimmy and I could get into the pasture. He passed us a bucket and our rods, and stepped over the fence after us. The rising sun burned through the morning haze, and a dozen knock-kneed Black Angus steers looked up, chewing their cuds as we walked from the roadside to the pond. We avoided looking straight at the huge cattle; it always prompted them to move toward us. Instead we looked at them sidelong, and kept an eye on the ground ahead. "Cow pie," Jimmy warned, pointing at it with his rod.

Standing on the red clay bank of the pond, we watched our grandfather as he slipped the delicate line through the eye of a hook. He rolled the shank between his nicotine-stained fingers, twisting the monofilament before he tucked it back in on itself and pulled it tight. He leaned his head back as smoke drifted up into his blind eye and around the frayed bill of his cap; then he took the cigar out of his mouth, knocked the ashes off, and carefully touched its glowing end to the excess line, burning it off close to the knot.

"What are you doing that for?"

"So the fish won't see it. Get yourself a worm there, Jackson." He called us that sometimes and it made us laugh.

He tied on Jimmy's hook while I pawed around in a Styrofoam cup full of shredded newspaper and worms. "They're not in here."

"Keep looking—they're in there."

Jimmy reached for the cup, but I turned away. "I got it," I said, and he let me go.

The worms had twined themselves into a squirming ball in the bottom. I pinched off the tough end of one, the head, and held it as it struggled between my fingers. "Here." I handed Jimmy the cup and he took the other piece.

"Go ahead and put them on your hooks," our grandfather told us.

I watched Jimmy slip the open, bleeding end of his worm over the point and around the shank of his hook, and I did the same, pulling my worm around the steel hook like a sock until the brown segmented head just hid the barb. The half worm dangled from the end of my rod, and writhed above the calm water of the pond.

"Alright, try casting it out," said my grandfather.

I cocked back my rod and whipped it forward, holding on to the release button a little too long. The hook landed in the algae mat that rimmed the edge of the pond. I considered it a moment, before lifting it out to clean the slick green coat off my bait.

"Try again, Paul, and see if you can get it out farther."

My second shot barely made it out into the muddy water beyond the algae. I started to reel it in again.

"That's alright, leave it there," my grandfather said.

"It's too close."

"You never know—try it for a while."

He opened a brown paper bag he had pulled from his pocket and passed me a Sugar Daddy. Jimmy got one too, and walked to a spot farther around the bank. I watched him cast his line into deep water, and from our perches, we watched our grandfather pick up his long black spinning rod. The tapered end bounced with each step as he walked around to where the water spilled out of the pond. He stood high on the bank, and from there he cast. We watched his spinner arc through the air and hit the water with a little splash more than halfway across the pond. We heard the bail on his reel click, and the spinner rose to swim back to him. He made it stop and go, like a tadpole, or an injured minnow. Jimmy and I stared at the lure moving erratically through the water. We'd seen it before; our grandfather would catch a bass, he always did.

I squatted in the red mud and held my rod, watching for signs of a bite. The clear nylon line lay in loose coils across the surface of the pond, and disappeared beneath it. I imagined, almost willed, the slow unwinding of those coils, followed by the tightened line moving back and forth through the water—the frantic pull of a fish jerking my rod down.

But the line sat there; water bugs rowed past it; dragonflies inspected it. As the day warmed, the smells of cattle dung and rotting algae rose around me. I looked at the animal card from my candy wrapper, a buffalo. At the other end of the pond my brother stood holding his pole, Sugar Daddy hanging out his mouth, feeling for a bite with his right hand. A black steer moaned out in the field, but Jimmy focused intently on the spot in front of him. We each wanted that first fish.

Beneath the surface, a small sunfish skirted through the cloudy water along the shadowed edge of the algae mat. It swam cautiously, always ready to dart into its green sanctuary. Its lateral lines registered pulses—the electric charge of motions in the water: the distant hum of catfish, a larger sunfish fanning her eggs in a gravel depression, and the slight splash of water striders paddling above.

The shadow of a barn swallow, swooping low over the pond's surface, drove the little fish into the algae, where it turned and watched for several minutes before re-emerging. As it swam on in cautious spurts, the fish caught the scent of blood in the water. With a quick snap of its tail it dashed ahead. It felt a weak signal, no threat. The form of a worm loomed out of the murk, twisting slowly. The hungry fish charged forward and sucked it in. It swallowed deep, felt the bone, and tried to spit it out. Synapses fired alarms through its simple brain; the line tugged against its lip; the hook twisted in its fragile guts as the sunfish made a frantic dash for cover—too late.

Overpowered, it felt itself torn out of the water. It burst into the open air, warm and dry. Naked and shorn of the cool pressure that had encased and supported its body, it sailed across the sky, flipping fiercely as it crashed down onto creased stones and sharp grass. All the weight the fish had never known: the sky, its own three ounces, bore down on it, pressed it into the earth. Bright sun baked one eye; dark gravel drove into the other. The fish gasped and flipped, air burned across its gills.

"I got one, Granpop! I got one!"

The fish lay up in the field at the end of my line. Fresh out of the water its colors shone glossy in the sunlight: orange belly, blue tinged gill plates, and spotted silver sides. Bits of grit and grass clung to it.

The steers moaned at the commotion. Jimmy and Grandpop put down their rods and walked over to inspect my catch. When they got close I lifted it up by the line to show them. My grandfather dipped his hand in our bucket and gently combed the fish's spines back as he took hold of it. "Always wet your hand," he told us, "so if you have to throw the fish back you won't hurt its slime coat." Jimmy looked at the trembling sunny measured across our grandfather's hand, and made the call. "Too small."

My grandfather nodded in assent. "But he swallowed the hook. We'll have to keep him." He burned off the line with his cigar and dropped the fish into the bucket.

"I didn't mean to pull back so hard. It went right over my head, did you see it?" I squinted up at him; his head framed against the pale blue sky, cigar clenched in his teeth.

"I saw it."

Jimmy looked into the bucket; the fish swam around in circles on its side, bleeding from the gills, a bit of line hanging from its mouth. "What's he doing Granpop?"

Our grandfather looked in the bucket and said nothing. He was not fond of seeing animals suffer, not even fish.

We fished, and gnawed down our Sugar Daddies. I caught more sunnies. Jimmy caught the prize, a smallmouth bass: a keeper. Granpop caught bass and let them go, and I wandered around the pond with my rod, looking for a better spot.

"You won't catch fish with your hook out of the water," my grandfather said.

"Where's a good spot?"

"Anywhere, you just need to be patient."

I stopped to look at him.

Over where the pond spilled into a small stream, the bow of a sunken skiff poked out of the mud, the last flakes of green paint peeling from its bleached wood. I leaned out until I fell toward the boat. Catching hold, I hung there with my body suspended over the murky pond, trying to figure out the next move to get aboard.

"Now Paul, don't get on that," my grandfather called over to me.

"I just want to get on it."

"You'll get wet. Come on out of there. I think it's time to go home." I shoved myself back and stood on the bank again.

Back at our grandparent's farm, Jimmy and I played on the concrete step outside the kitchen—squishing fish guts on half wet newspaper while our grandfather carried seven cleaned sunnies and the bass inside. We poked the eyes out of fish heads, and played with the smooth organs: the deep brown livers, the earth red hearts. Jimmy pulled something out of a fish stomach, and held it up.

"Look, your hook."

"Boys! Don't get that everywhere," our great-grandmother Ludy scolded us.

Ludy sat on a porch swing hung from the sprawling apple tree in the backyard where she smoked cigarettes in a black cigarette holder. She called to my brother and me, and we climbed up and sat on either side of her. She held us close, touched her feet to the ground and gently rocked us with her stories of life growing up on Michigan's Upper Peninsula in the late 1800s.

"Indians would come to our house to trade furs," she said. "They would always give me presents." We looked at her lean wiry arms, the deeply wrinkled skin of her hands and face. She was a different kind of animal than us, but she connected us to a vanished world where people lived off the land and in the wild. We embraced that spirit as our grandfather called us it to eat the fish.

Kerr's Pond overflowed into a stream that fed Skippack Creek, and the Skippack snaked slowly through Montgomery County, past the east boundary of our grandparents' farm. Jimmy and I walked down and sat underneath the iron bridge that spanned the broad shallow creek. We saw no farther than that visible stretch of gentle water; time began and ended in each moment. Straddling the girders, we stared into the water fifteen feet below. An occasional car crossed the bridge, rattling over the wooden planks a foot above our heads, but our attention stayed on the creek.

The broad shadow of the bridge cut a swath across the mirror surface of the water, and in that shadow we could see the cobble bottom. We scanned it carefully, searching for fish in their secret places. Jimmy had the eye.

"I see one."

"Where?"

"Right there." He pointed down at the maze of muddy rocks, but I could see only a mix of undulating shadows, appearing and disappearing.

"Where?"

"There. See it?"

"I think so."

He climbed along the side of the bridge, hanging on to the iron rails until he reached my girder, and slid down behind me. He put his hand on my shoulder and ran his arm past the side of my head. I looked down his arm beyond the outstretched finger.

"See it? It's moving now."

A dark silhouette moved diagonally across the current.

"I see it!"

We watched the fish for a while, guessing whether it was a bass or a sunny as it idled in the current, swimming just enough to keep its place. After a while we grew bored. We climbed up onto the bridge, gathered some stones, and threw them at the fish until it disappeared amid the splashes.

"Come on." Jimmy slid down the bank to where red slate flaked into the mud. We chose small flat stones, always searching for the perfect one, and skipped them across the creek, waiting for one to skip back. But they never did.

"It's Skippack, not skip back," our Uncle Donald had explained one day. "It's a Leni Lenape word—means 'slow moving.'"

Somebody had made a raft out of two oil barrels lashed together with a few boards on top, and it lay grounded on a sandbar downstream from the bridge. Cicadas rattled in the heat, and Jimmy and I stood on the bank, both of us sticky with creosote and sweat.

"Let's get out on that raft."

"No. Come on, Paul, let's go home."

The Skippack flowed into the Perkiomen Creek, and the Perkiomen into the Schuylkill River. After a weekend on the farm, our mother would drive us home to Drexel Hill, in the Philadelphia suburbs, passing through Valley Forge on the way.

In Gulph Mills, a few miles from the old camp of the Continental Army, a relic of those times jutted out over the road: the rock that had knocked George Washington's hat off. When we crossed the bridge over the Schuylkill, our mother would tell us to get ready, and we would stare at it as we passed—a huge crag overhanging the road.

After the disasters at Brandywine, White Marsh, and Paoli, George Washington led his men up the Schuylkill, and into winter quarters at Valley Forge. In November of 1777, on the road through Gulph Mills, he passed under the overhanging rock that brushed his hat off. Already humbled by the events of the year, he regarded his plumed black hat behind him in the fallen leaves. He started to dismount, but one of his subalterns retrieved it and held it up to him.

"Your Excellency."

The hopes of the American Revolution never looked as bleak as they did when the wind blew across the frozen ground of that plateau twenty miles west of Philadelphia. The battered and barefoot troops shivered in their drafty cabins around fires of green wood that offered more smoke than heat. Every morning fewer men turned out for roll call. "No meat, no soldier!" they chanted from their huts. Pneumonia, scurvy, and dysentery all took their toll; but the sense of being forgotten brought morale to its lowest ebb.

The nascent Continental Congress, sitting in York, faced its own struggles. Mired in political squabbling and subterfuge, it could hardly attend to itself, let alone the basic needs of its hungry soldiers. When it did, corrupt provisioners and teamsters often looted food and clothing en route to the winter camp. In the bitter month of February, when 10,000 British feasted in Philadelphia, the Army's numbers dwindled to a little over 4,000 troops. Magnetic leaders such as the faux Prussian General, Baron Von Steuben, the Marquis de Lafayette, Alexander Hamilton, and Washington himself, could barely stem the tide of desertion and resignation; but where human effort fell short, other forces prevailed.

The Schuylkill empties into the Delaware River, and the Delaware into the Atlantic Ocean. Popular legend has it that in the spring of 1778, while Washington brooded, huge schools of shad, fat with roe, began their annual migration from the sea. The anadromous shad (*Alosa sapidissima*), which live in salt water but spawn in fresh, ascended the Delaware, then the Schuylkill, and swam on, into the midst of the starving army.

Historians writing long after the events reported that the schools appeared in late March like a rippling tide moving upstream. The soldiers are said to have charged into the water, heedless of the icy current, and using branches, pitchforks, and their bare hands, tossed fish onto the bank. One chronicler writing a hundred years later tells of the cavalry riding their horses into the ford upstream to hurry the fish back toward camp.

In the book *The Founding Fish* (2002), author John McPhee's careful research seems to have debunked the story of the shad arriving to save the Continental Army in March 1778. McPhee acknowledges that shad may have been an important part of the soldiers' diet, augmenting their salt meat rations, but not the lifesaver many claim.

But those of us raised on the myth still believe that it may have been so. If not, one could argue that while the soldiers may have had bellies full of old preserved foods, it was not until the shad arrived that they were truly fed and invigorated. And while the role shad played at Valley Forge may be doubted, the role that fishermen played in the Revolution has been well documented. New England fishermen for instance—Marbleheaders— had gotten Washington and the army across the Delaware to defeat the Hessians in 1776, and throughout the war, fishermen from along the Atlantic coast kept Washington's intelligence network informed as to the movements of the British fleet. When the Continental Army left Valley Forge in late spring of 1778, it took to the road well fed, and confident of the enemy's disposition. On July 3, at Monmouth Courthouse, New Jersey, it ran the British Army from the field.[1]

Jimmy and I sucked up the stories of Valley Forge. Real or imagined, they offered fodder for our imaginations. But for us history happened in a nebulous time called "before you were born." We did not see ourselves as characters in later chapters of the same ongoing tale, though the shad were our link to the past.

On Fridays in the springtime, our mother would cook up one or two of the shad descended from the schools that fed the Continental Army. Jimmy and I wished the soldiers had eaten them all, as we picked the flesh off the bony shad. "This tastes like the creek smells."

Our fish came from the lower Delaware. Few shad swam up the Schuylkill in our time, and the fish traps on that river had disappeared. Industry and agriculture had combined to turn the river into a toxic,

---

[1] After the Revolution, fishermen reaped the rewards of their service. The new United States government valued the fishing fleet, which provided a lookout off America's shores and trained potential sailors for the Navy. In 1792 Congress subsidized the industry with direct payments to boat owners. When Congress curtailed those subsidies after the Civil War, the men and women who fished for cod, porgies, herring, and other species off the northeast coast, continued to act as North America's first distant early warning system. During World War II the US Coast Guard equipped fishermen with VHF radios and instructions on how to identify German U-boats.

anoxic sluice. Fish and fishermen forgotten, the Schuylkill had become a means of disposal rather than supply.

With our grandfather, Jimmy and I touched the tendrils of fresh water far from the coast. Intimate with a few shallow places, we seldom considered the oceanic depths. If we did think of the sea, we could hardly have made sense of what was happening out there.

In the 1960s, American fishermen watched helplessly as foreign boats invaded the country's coastal waters again, this time unchallenged. In the first half of that decade, foreign fishing vessels off the New England and Mid-Atlantic states increased exponentially in number and size—from twenty-six boats in 1959 to 354 in 1965, with a third of the new boats exceeding 300 feet in length.

The arrival of the distant water fleets in the 1960s set a chain of events in motion that by the end of the century would leave few fish stocks or fishing families unscathed. When fishermen raised the alarm, the State Department appeared unwilling to confront the problem. Over the course of that turbulent decade the government, which considered the fish stocks to be infinite, responded by pouring money into modernizing the American fleet. Expectations, which had exceeded the available resources, were ratcheted up, and while high tech fleets from Russia, East Germany, and Spain plundered North America's fisheries, often within sight of shore, rather than chase out the foreign factory trawlers and fish sustainably, the US built up its capacity to replace them.

In 1967, my brother and I saw it firsthand. In the heat of August the denizens of suburbs of Philadelphia fled to relative coolness of the Jersey shore. Under the shade of the maple in the front yard, our dad would load our blue Chevy Malibu wagon, and when he had it jammed full, our mother would take the helm. With, my brother, two sisters, and me in the back she'd steer her laden craft for Sea Isle City.

The summer of '67 we rented we rented an apartment with a view of the bay, and every morning around 8 we watched the deep sea fishing boats chug down toward Townsends Inlet, bound for the open ocean. With a pair of binoculars we could read their names—the *Cap'n Chum* and the *Miss Sea Isle.* Taking turns with the glasses we studied them. Fishing rods leaned against the rails, and people moved up and down the deck, looking busy. Both boats had signs on top: Deep Sea Fishing, twice daily. On rainy days we drew pictures of the boats from memory.

Jimmy and I begged our father to take us out deep sea fishing. Fishing was not exactly his thing, but he humored us, and one sunny morning, instead of going to the beach, he drove us down to the wharf where the deep sea boats tied up. While he paid our fare, Jimmy and I ran down the dock and took our first up close look at the *Miss Sea Isle,* a sixty-foot boat, painted all white, with her name in red and black letters on the bow and across the stern.

With trepidation and excitement we looked across the treacherous space between the dock and the boat and looked down at the soupy harbor water, laced with scum and bits of garbage. Stepping awkwardly across the gangplank we leapt one after the other to the *Miss Sea Isle's* deck.

Before our father got aboard we forgot him, and began exploring. Benches lined the rails and a long cabin ran the length of the boat. The smell of salt and rotten bait hung in the cool shadows. Inside the cabin, two toilets jammed into narrow closets offered dubious comfort for "buoys" and "gulls." We looked them over, and peeked inside.

"Whew, that stinks, I'm not going in there."

"Me neither."

Confusion ruled the deck as the boat pulled away from the dock. People found their places and prepared for the morning's fishing. Expectancy buzzed in the air. Old timers sorted through their tackle boxes and set up multiple hook rigs. Two young crewmen handed out rental rods, already rigged with two hooks and a lead sinker.

"How do you cast these?" Jimmy asked, looking at the broad boat reel, so unlike our spinning reels.

"You don't," said the crewman and moved on.

We poked at the bait, hunks of cut-up surf clam in the kind of red-and-white-checked paper french fry tray that the burger joints used for French fries. The clams looked appetizing too, but we didn't taste. Some people brought their own bait: minnows, swimming around in little buckets. We motored down the bay and everywhere we looked something new bedazzled us.

"I wonder if they'll open the bridge," I asked Jimmy as the boat turned toward the inlet.

"I don't think so," someone offered, overhearing us.

We passed through the shadow of the bridge between Sea Isle and the neighboring town of Avalon. For a brief second the echo of the engines blasted off the concrete and steel. Then we broke free, out into the sunshine with the whole sparkling Atlantic before us. A quarter mile out, where the ebbing bay water mixed with the ocean tide, waves churned in a boiling uproar. Jimmy and I ran to the bow and sat as far up on it as the captain would let us go. He tooted his horn and waved us back from hanging over the edge.

A wave lifted the boat with a rush. The bow shot off the crest, and we held tight as it dropped out from under us and plunged into a cushion of spray and foam. The boat became a roller coaster, and after a few minutes several people vomited, but we laughed. No ride on the boardwalk could have matched the action on the bow of *Miss Sea Isle* that morning.

Six miles offshore the waves died down, and the sea rolled easy. Someone said we were over a wreck in eighty feet of water. I tried to imagine the wreck, visualized fish swimming around an intact sunken battleship, and wondered if we'd snag our hooks. Our father had found spaces for us along the starboard rail. We baited with the slices of clam, dropped our hooks into the water, and let our lines unspool, clicking off our reels as the lead weights plummeted toward bottom.

"Let them touch bottom and then reel them in a little," said the crewmen on our side of the boat. "Then lift them up and down."

We looked the sun-blond teenager over, closely. In matters of fish, we only trusted our grandfather, but we did what the boy said. I hooked the first fish and reeled it in. "Looks like a big sunfish," I said when I lifted the squat silver fish over the rail and landed it on deck.

"That's a porgy," said the teenager. He offered to take it off the hook.

"I can do it," I said, wetting my hand in a puddle on the rail.

Its sharp dorsal spines poked out, but I combed them back the way our grandfather did, and held the fish so I could take the hook out of its mouth. We caught more, and started getting choosy about what we kept.

"What are you doing?" a man asked Jimmy after he'd seen him throw a fish overboard.

"Throwing back the small ones."

"I'll take them if you don't want them."

"Dad, is that really the first fish you ever caught?" I asked as he boated a porgy.

"Yeah," he said, smiling behind his sunglasses and cigarette. He let Jimmy take it off the hook for him.

Further offshore big ships dotted the horizon—dark hulls with tall masts.

"They're Russian trawlers," someone said. "Spying on us," said another.

We watched the hazy forms for a while. By noon everyone seemed drowsy in the heat and the *Miss Sea Isle* headed home. Passing through the breakers again we ran to the bow, but on the flood tide the wave action had died down to some mild bumps.

We went out on the deep sea boats at least once a year for several seasons after that, and the sense of adventure never failed. Back at the dock Jimmy and I would clean our own fish, and in the apartment our mother cooked them for dinner. Tired from the sun and the sea, we sat at the Formica table and proudly ate our porgies. It wasn't that we liked the taste that much, but that we had caught them.

One evening, the whole family went out to dinner at a harbor side restaurant down on Forty-Second Street. I knelt on my chair and looked out the window at a boat; ropes looped down from the dock to the boat, rising and falling as the big wooden hull, painted dark green with black trim, drifted in and out. Its reflection swirled in the oily harbor water, a Coke bottle bobbed nearby. On deck, men talked to each other and worked at moving things around.

"What are they doing?"

"I don't know. That's a fishing boat," said my mother.

I looked at her, then back at the boat.

"Where are their fishing rods?"

"It looks like they fish with nets. Sit down."

"Paul, sit down," my father added for emphasis.

"Can we go see it later?"

"If it's still light."

By the time we left the restaurant and walked over to the docks the men had gone. The boat sat squat on the water, its deck crammed with nameless objects of wood, steel, and wire. It did not look as inviting as the *Miss Sea Isle,* but more self-possessed—confident. Windows wrapped around the pilothouse and looked out over the deck. I tried to see inside, but the glass reflected the sunset and my own image looking back at me.

"Come on Paul," my father said. "Let's go."

Ten years later, sound filtered in through the frosted window panes of our house in Drexel Hill: the hydraulics of a trash truck whined as it crushed torn packages and garbage; afterward came the hollow clatter of a trash can toppling into the street. A car passed, its engine slowed, and revved again on its journey from nowhere to nowhere in a maze of residential streets. As it drove down the block I listened to the fading sound of its tires singing on the frozen asphalt.

I sat on the worn green carpet in the room I had shared with Jimmy; he had moved to California. My grandfather was dead. I was alone with a large book on the floor in front of me: the paintings of Edward Hopper. My mother had given it to me for Christmas.

Turning a page, I saw two paintings that struck me. Difficult to recognize at first, one showed a cropped view of the deck of a fishing boat, the beam trawler *Osprey,* lying alongside a wharf. On the facing page another print showed the bow of the beam trawler *Widgeon.* The vacant boats appeared quiet under the high summer sun—two quickly executed water-colors capturing details of people's lives: a length of chain dropped on deck, a rope coiled on the mast.

The rusty iron and slanted wooden decks looked familiar. *Rockland 1926* it said in the corner of each painting; but what Hopper painted of the *Osprey* looked almost identical to the boats I had seen at the Jersey shore. I wanted to get on those boats.

I wonder if some people are born to callings that no longer exist. Technology and economic systems may have outpaced evolution, leaving the celestial navigators and masters of the wind with no way to express their true talents. These people, disposed toward skills thousands of years old, may be the ones who sometimes say they wish they had been born in a different, earlier era—before the continuity of their reason for being was broken.

I might have been one of them—the image of those men working on the trawler's deck in Sea Isle City stuck in my mind like a beacon. Hopper's paintings offered a clue to where it led; but Rockland, Maine, was far off. I needed to get my foot in wherever I could—the doors on the old fishing culture were closing fast.

Three

THE STRATTON REPORT

*The goal of domestic fisheries management must be the development of a
technically advanced and economically efficient fishing fleet with a minimum
number of units required to take the catch over a prolonged period of time.*
—Commission on Marine Science,
Engineering and Resources, Our Nation and the Sea,
also known as the Stratton Report, of 1969

Most of the US boats that fished off New England and the mid-
Atlantic in the 1960s, even the most modern, still bore a resemblance
to the old schooners. The trawlers of that era, known as "eastern rigs," carried their wheelhouses aft, where the helmsmen of the sailing vessels once
stood. The boats' keels plunged deep below the surface; and their rails
swept down from the bow close to the water before rising slightly to the
stern. The eastern rigs hauled their nets aboard over the side and retained a
classic form that recalled the language of wind and waves. But the policies
guiding US fisheries—the commercial harvest of seafood—had changed
since the early days of nationhood when Congress had subsidized every
boat on the coast. The new global economic model called for fewer fishermen and did not view eastern rigs as part of the "advanced fleet."

Although the US fishing fleet had modernized rapidly following World War II, the eastern rigs had grown technologically obsolete

compared to the three-hundred-foot Russian and eastern European factory trawlers that dominated North Atlantic fisheries in the late 1960s. In 1967, growing alarm at the decline of the US position in world fisheries—from second place in 1959 to sixth in 1967, and continuing to slide—prompted Congress to establish the Commission on Marine Science, Engineering and Resources, commonly known as the Stratton Commission, after its chairman, Julius Stratton. Congress directed the commission to formulate a policy that would increase the competitiveness of the US fleet.

In 1969, the year that saw Woodstock and the moonwalk, came the Stratton Report, which has guided fisheries policy ever since. The Stratton Report carried in it the DNA of Breton Woods, a post WWII agreement by wealthy nations to create a new global economy. The Stratton Commission laid groundwork for a technologically advanced, economically efficient US fishing fleet, and new institutions to manage it, leading to the formation of the National Marine Fisheries Service (NMFS) in 1970, and passage of the Magnuson Fishery Conservation and Management Act in 1976. The Commission's primary recommendation, which called for achieving the highest net profit from marine resources, has been reasserted in fisheries legislation ever since, and implemented through privatization schemes that range from individual fishing quotas to industrial scale aquaculture.

Chaired by Julius Stratton, former president of MIT and one-time chairman of the Ford Foundation, the nineteen-member commission strongly recommended privatization of fisheries in order to secure investments that would lead to a modernized fleet. In an about-face from the centuries-old policy giving fishermen free access to fisheries in the open ocean, the waters beyond twelve miles offshore, the report advocated the equivalent of an "enclosure act" on the high seas: a delineation and allocation of rights to harvest wild fish stocks.

In 1969, however, the International Commission for the Northwest Atlantic Fisheries (ICNAF, "ick-naff") held jurisdiction over Georges Bank and all the waters beyond twelve miles from the US coast. As a first step toward privatization, the commission recommended national transferable fishing quotas. The report called for establishing quotas for all fisheries and dividing those quotas among the thirty-three ICNAF member countries. Each country would have a fixed allowable catch based on its past landings. After the initial allocation, quotas would become transferable; they could be bought, sold, or leased among countries—a system that would allow the market to determine future allocations.

The ICNAF commissioners believed ownership of a fixed percentage of the quota would eliminate the risk for investors who might be unwilling to build new boats if the resources were being gobbled up by foreign fleets. The commission also believed that privatization would promote conservation, and prevent overcapitalization: "fishing rights" owners would reduce their fleets to the "minimum number of units required to take the catch over a prolonged period of time."

Exclusive rights to the fisheries off the Northeast US had not been sought since 1621, when Sir Ferdinando Gorges received a charter to all the fish between New Jersey and Newfoundland. When Gorges's emissaries tried to collect fees for fishing rights, they met stubborn resistance, and gave up. In a resource rich environment they had no leverage. Thus began the longstanding tradition that the fruits of the sea belonged to no one and everyone. But the Commission identified that tradition in its report as an "institutional barrier to a more efficient and expanded harvesting of the ocean's food resources."

The long accepted standards of North American fishing culture did not fit the new vision of striving for the highest net return from the available fish stocks. The fishermen who went to regulatory meetings in the late 1990s screaming, "you're putting us out of business," should have read the Stratton Report. Then they would have understood that that was the intent, and it started with limited access. As early as 1971 the fledgling National Marine Fisheries Service identified free access to fisheries resources as a major problem.

Speaking at the Museum of Science in Boston that year, NMFS Northeast Regional Director, Russell T. Norris, reiterated the views of the Stratton Commission: "One element of this institutionalized setting [aka tradition] which is particularly guilty of creating problems is the common property basis for allocating fisheries resources" Russell went on to rehash the tragedy of the commons and explain how open access led to overcapitalization and resource depletion: "It was for some of these same reasons that we broke away from this concept in agriculture, and created private property rights as a means of allocating land, grazing rights, and water. For these same reasons, in my view we are going to have to break out of this tradition in allocating fishery resources."

The Stratton Report, however, had acknowledged the difficulty of dismantling institutions, especially when it would disrupt a long established way of life:

Fishing is an ancient business, and its practitioners are less concerned with economic efficiency than with the simple fact of making a living from the sea. Fishermen may be perfectly aware that a half a dozen modern, efficient ships could harvest the permissible crop with high monetary return, but they still may prefer a system under which a number of families can eke out what, to them, is an adequate living of the kind they prefer. Because fishing communities form the constituencies of important elements in state legislatures, their desire to maintain the status quo has a strong influence on fishing legislation and on regulations of State agencies.

The commissioners noted that it would take time to eliminate an entrenched culture, particularly in New England.

The Commission recognizes that needed changes must be made, in the interest of simple equity, at a pace which does not compel individuals to leave an established way of life.

In short, rather than rip apart the social fabric of fishing communities, the goals of fisheries management would be to unravel it slowly; severing fisheries production thread by thread from its past, and binding it to what they called a "rational" model, which would seek the highest net economic return from the resource, and nothing else. If the commission's recommendations had been implemented immediately, there would have been little left of traditional fisheries by the time I made it to the sea.

But as the commissioners expected, the policies they advocated met with fierce resistance, particularly in New England. Thanks to state legislators, the existing fleet endured while federal regulators laid the groundwork for the modern fleet. The sense that the old and new boats could exist together had been fueled by a skewed interpretation of the Stratton Commission's estimates of abundance, which represented the fundamental flaw in the report. In a time when the world's annual seafood production stood at fifty million tons annually, and many experts, including some on the commission, contended that it could no more than double, the report predicted a tenfold increase:

It is realistic to expect a total annual production of marine food products (exclusive of aquaculture) to grow to four hundred million to five hundred million metric tons before expansion becomes excessive. Even this estimate may be too conservative if significant technological breakthroughs are achieved in the ability to detect, concentrate, and harvest fish on the high seas and open ocean.

In 2003, James Crutchfield, a fisheries economist from the University of Washington, and a former Stratton Commission member recalled: "There were a couple of people around at the time, Wib Chapman and Milner Schaeffer, who came in with those numbers. Chapman, the principal proponent of the five-hundred-million-metric-ton sustainable yield ceiling, was laughed out of the room by the fishery people. His projection was based on some fanciful estimates of total biological production of all types. I remember pointing out at the time that this was equivalent to estimating total agricultural production by including weeds, grasses, and trees," said Crutchfield.

"Realistic estimates of sustainable harvest of potentially usable proteins from the sea ranged from 100 to 150 million metric tons, and this would include working down the trophic scale to produce items which could reasonably expect to find markets."

In spite of Crutchfield's and other's objections, Stratton embraced Chapman's estimates.

"I don't know how those ridiculous figures emerged in the final report," said Crutchfield. "Having written a good deal of it I had no desire to do more of the final review, and I guess it slipped by. I wrote most of the report and they weren't in the copy I submitted." Crutchfield noted however, that Chapman was a close friend of Julius Stratton's. "Chapman was very well connected, and that may account for the change. A number of other changes were made without the express approval of the commission members."

Crutchfield did not believe the wild estimate had an impact with scientists and academics, but it did among fishing interests—and their representatives in Congress. In the 1970s, headlines often repeated the mantra of the blue revolution: "Millions of Tons of Seafood from the Ocean," but few people read the fine print that this estimate included things like plankton and many other underutilized species.

Fishermen and politicians eager to promote economic growth in their regions managed to link the ideas of inexhaustible resources with lucrative, but already overcapitalized, fisheries. Promoters of fisheries development selectively presented the numbers that supported their agenda and completely ignored the Stratton Commission's recommendations to guard against overcapitalization.

"They told us we were going to feed the world," is what most fishermen remember from those times.

When Congress kicked the foreign factory trawlers out of US coastal waters, it added a variety of subsidies to the existing programs aimed at new vessel construction, and the scene was set for a massive buildup of fishing effort. The Stratton Commission had advocated against extending national jurisdiction beyond twelve miles, because the US shrimp and tuna fleets often fished that close to South American and Latin American countries. But many small countries had already extended their jurisdictions, and the US, along with most other countries, followed suit. In 1976 Congress passed the Magnuson Fishery Conservation and Management Act, and while incorporating many of Stratton's recommendations, the legislation established a fisheries conservation zone extending two hundred miles from all US coastlines. The US suddenly held a Fishery Conservation Zone (later called the Exclusive Economic Zone) of 3.4 million square miles, more than any other country in the world. Policy makers envisioned a fleet that could tap the theoretical abundance of those seas, and Congress subsidized building it.

The Stratton Report inadvertently bolstered belief in the inexhaustibility of fish stocks at a time when harvesters in many areas were already passing the limits of sustainable production. In spite of Stratton's warnings, the institutionalized fallacy of the ocean's abundance undermined all efforts to prevent overcapitalization of the fishing industry. As the cataclysmic combination of political, economic, and environmental forces converged on the US fisheries, the Stratton Commission provided a weather report predicting sunny skies.

The unfortunate circumstances, which would lead to seemingly endless fisheries battles, provided aspiring but unlikely fishermen, such as myself, an entryway into the business. The US owned the ocean, and, though the fish stocks were getting hammered, new boats needed crew.

Four

MIDWIVES

The Stratton-inspired Magnuson Stevens Fisheries Conservation Act of 1976 made room for new blood in the fishing industry. With the foreign boats gone, the domestic fleet in the Northeast expanded rapidly. Statistics showed that in the final months of 1977, one new boat entered the fishery in the region every four days. There could not have been a better time for a wayward youth to find a home in the fish business than the spring of 1977, and so, like Melville's Ishmael, I headed for the coast.

Like most people without a sponsor of some sort, I entered the fishing industry on the bottom rung of the ladder, an unskilled unit of labor in a business increasingly driven by an economic equation that looked at dollars, but not sense. I came to the business with no solid fishing tradition, and was easily molded to the new industrial model.

I started in a processing plant, and the black women on the docks of Cape May, New Jersey, became my second fishing family, after my grandfather and brother. They acted as the midwives to my birth as a fisherman, and they helped set me on that course.

Outside Lund's Seafood, a packing house in the backwaters of Cape May, New Jersey, tractor trailers lined up in the parking lot, their refrigeration units running hard under the August sun. Some had come all the way from Provincetown, on Cape Cod, full of scallops still in the shell. Inside, the din drowned almost all thoughts. The smell of cooked scallops swirled around us in the steam from the shucking machine as we worked amid the rolling belts and the clatter of scallop shells. In my rubber boots, a pair of cut-down hip waders from the farm, I splashed around the concrete floors hefting forty-pound baskets of shucked scallop meats. Three of us, Greg Clements, P. J. Neil, and I stood out among the crew, the only white cogs on a predominantly black wheel.

Emma Shockley ran the floor. As matriarch of an extended family that comprised the bulk of Lund's employees, her shout, "Clarence!" and a pointed finger would smooth any wrinkle in the flow of work. Clarence would hustle to shut down a conveyor belt, or grab people and set them moving right.

For my part I swung baskets from the shucking machine to the picking table, where women picked off bits of guts the machine had missed; from the picking table to the chlorine bath, and from there to the packing table.

Pulling a basket of ivory colored scallops out of the washtub, I dumped them onto the stainless steel packing table in front of Emma's daughter. She picked them up and let the creamy white medallions slip through her fingers into cans, and when she flashed her smile at me I smiled back. We worked like that all week, sometimes around the clock as the trucks backed up in the parking lot and boats rafted out from the wharf.

On Friday a steady rain blew in from the south. The big doors of the packing room opened out to the harbor. Outside, raindrops bounced on the rail of an old scallop boat rocking gently against the dock at high tide.

At ten o'clock the shucking machine broke down. I went to smoke a cigarette and look at the boat. It was wood, the hull painted the same dark green as the sunken skiff in Kerr's Pond. In front of the white wheelhouse two welded pipe triangles, one on each side of the boat, lay folded across the deck. The piles of chain that lay beneath them, and spools of cable behind them, all dripped rust in the warm rain.

A guy in coveralls holding something in a greasy rag came out from behind the wheelhouse and spoke up the ladder to a man inside. The man came to the door and looked down at the greasy rag.

He seemed to be making a decision. He put on a black Greek fisherman's hat, the kind with a short bill and a bit of braid across the front, and climbed down out of the wheelhouse. The two men crossed the wet deck, stepped up onto the boat's rail, and onto the dock.

"How ya doin'?" I said to the man from the wheelhouse.

"Could be better," he said back, distracted.

"You need any help?"

He stopped and looked me up and down. "Nah. I guess we're all set." He turned away. The guy in coveralls followed him.

Greg came up beside me. "Did you ask him for a site?"

"A site?"

"A job."

"Yeah, he said he's all set."

"We're punched out, the machine is fucked."

"Cool."

The rain had let up by the time we hitched into town. We bought a six-pack of Miller at the Anchorage Inn and took it down past Cold Springs dock. In the parking lot at the edge of the water Greg leaned against a blue Chevy truck with a Gerald Ford bumper sticker on it, and P. J. sat on top of the short piling.

We drank and admired the new boats, big bright-colored steel stern trawlers—most of them rigged for scalloping. "I heard those guys make like four grand a trip."

"Jesus man," I said, "I wonder how the hell you get on one."

"I could get on one back home, but fuck that," said Greg. He tossed an empty bottle into the harbor, and we watched it bob on the surface.

"You're crazy man, I thought you wanted to go fishing." I picked up a stone and threw it at the bottle. We started bombing it with stones until Greg broke it.

"Not scalloping man, too many things can happen. There was a boat from Maine, the *Snoopy;* they caught a torpedo in the dredge. Coast Guard told'm to leave it over the rail until they got there. Next thing, kaboom! Blew them all to fuck. They didn't even find any bodies."

"Man." P. J. shook his head.

"I'm going back to autobody repair school this winter," said Greg. "Fuck fishing."

"Wait a minute, I thought I rescued you from autobody school back in Woods Hole. You wanted to travel and work the docks. You said you wanted to go fishin.'"

Greg looked at me. "I don't want to go fishing anymore, and I don't want to spend the winter sleeping on Charlie's porch."

"We could go south. I worked on the docks down there in 1975. You get a nickel a pound for snapping heads off shrimp in Key West. I seen these black women down there making like forty dollars a day."

P. J. laughed, "How much did you make?"

"About seven. I didn't have the right gloves. The shrimp got my hands all infected. But those women, they'd be going with both hands just whaling on'm."

"Fuck it, I'm going home at the end of this week. Charlie said he'd drive me up there."

"Huh."

At that juncture, P. J. broke the news that his uncle Charlie was evicting me from the porch.

Greg left and P. J. stopped coming to work. After a weekend on the street I stashed my stuff in the back room of the Anchorage Inn and went to work alone. At Lund's a flight of stairs descended from a locker room to the big packing room. At the base of the stairs workers congregated around the time clock—the boundary, between our time and Lund's.

Tony Shockley, Emma's sister-in-law, punched her card and stood there; she passed the long strings of her plastic apron behind her back and tied them in front of her belly. "You know what my name is?" she asked me out of the blue.

She was my height, and I smiled at her. I knew her name was Tony, but I looked over at her card, and read it. "Natoma."

"Right," she said. "You know what kind of name that is?"

"Sounds like an Indian name."

She nodded proudly. "That's right," she said, then asked, "Where's your mama?"

I paused for a second. "Far away."

"Well, I'll be your mama."

It surprised me that anybody would say something like that to me, and I wondered what it meant. "Git to work," she said.

Instead of the machine starting up, Clarence waved me over to a pile of baskets brimming with unshucked scallops.

"What's going on?"

Clarence leaned back and looked at me like he needed to spit. "We gotta shuck all the scallops the machine didn't do."

Emma, Tony, and the other women stood around the big stainless steel packing table with scallop knives in hand. Clarence and I each dumped two baskets of scallops in front of them.

"You know how to shuck scallops?" Tony asked me from across the table.

"No." I looked at all the women already starting to cut the shells apart.

"Show him what to do," she said to the woman standing next to me.

"Getcha some gloves and a knife," said the woman, without looking at me.

Clarence pointed to a pile of knives and gloves on a bench near the time clock.

I came back with a pair of rubber gloves and one of the short twisted knives. The woman next to me picked up a scallop and held it upside down in the palm of her gloved hand. I looked at the white circle of the shell, with a square hinge on the edge. She drove her knife into the small opening near the hinge. "You turn the knife like this and cut the meat offa the top," she said as she demonstrated the motion. "An' flip the shell off." She flung the shell into an empty basket. "Put your knife under the guts like this and roll'm off." A ring of guts went into the basket. "Then you got just your meat there, see? An' cut it into the bucket." She cut the white medallion of muscle into the bucket.

I mangled a lot of scallops getting the hang of it. Trying to go fast, I threw guts into the bucket and meats into the gurry basket.

"First you learn it right, then you learn it fast," said Tony.

With the machines off, the women could talk, and they did. It was not their words—the gossip, teasing, and practicalities—but the cadence and tone of their language that drew us all together. I fell into the rhythm after a while, shucking scallops steadily to the patchwork music of their voices amidst the clatter of shells.

At lunchtime Emma sent Clarence out for fried chicken.

"You want some chicken?" she asked me.

"I don't have any money."

She nodded and turned away. When Clarence came back with the food everyone went out to sit in the sun. I started to wander off, but Emma held up a little two-piece box for me. "Come on, have some chicken." She handed me the box.

"I didn't know if you wanted white meat or dark," she said, and some of the women from the packing table snorted, turning away laughing.

When we got paid I took off for Wildwood and partied with the college kids until my money ran out. I showed up back at Lund's on a Wednesday morning. My boots were gone from my locker.

"They stunk," said the foreman in the office, a white guy named Bob. "You guys think you can just work whenever you want, and not show up when you want. I don't need ya, forget it, you're all done."

Back in the locker room I looked around for my stuff, but found only lockers full of other people's clothes. When I came downstairs no one looked up from their work. The shucking machine hammered and clanged. Tony had her back to me; I almost tapped her on the shoulder to say goodbye, but changed my mind.

I walked out the door of Lund's with one gift: Tony's words—she would be my mama. It seemed a small thing at the time, but opened a door for me into the fishing industry. I tried other jobs but always gravitated back to the boats and the docks. A lot about the commercial fishing industry appealed to me: the boats, the intense work followed by long breaks, and the people.

From the late 1970s to the early 1980s I explored the coasts, from Key West to Alaska, Cape May to California, and finally Maine. Gradually I found my way aboard the boats and bit by bit I established a history, one that coincided with a new fisheries regime under the Magnuson. My early years traveling around in the fish business amounted to a survey of its transition from an artisanal occupation to an industrial enterprise intended to be competitive on a global scale.

It left a lot of people behind, but they did not go away.

August 12, 2003:

Went fact checking down in Cape May and stopped to see Natoma. She had remarried and was living in a little house in Rio Grande with her husband Bob Ramsey. She had quit Lund's.

"I was cutting bluefish: me and four men. I could cut as fast as any of them and they all got raises so I went to Bob—the white foreman at Lund's— and told him it was about time for me to have a raise too, and he said no. So I went to Mr. Lund and I told him I could fill a box of sea bass headed and gutted, in ten minutes, and I could do a box of porgies in twenty minutes. I said it's about time I got a raise too, and he said, 'Talk to Bob,' and I said, 'I talked to Bob.'

"He said, 'Well you have to listen to your foreman.' I said, 'Well I listened.' And I took off my gloves."

"Clarence was a two-faced ass," she said. "He's dead."

"My kids all done good. I got more grandkids, great-grandkids, I got more people call me mama."

"Including some white boy from out of the past," I said, and told her about the other two white guys, Greg and P. J., how they both committed suicide, within a month of each other. I told her how I thought she maybe saved me from the same fate with just a few endearing words. But she didn't say much to that.

"This is funny, a lot of people I ain't seen in years keep showing up. Maybe it means I'm going to die soon."

"Maybe you got something they want."

"Well, I wish they'd give it back, 'cuz I could use it 'bout now. I got asthma, high blood pressure, and I had a heart attack.

"I drink more now than I ever did," she said. "I'm tired of people. I seen too much."

Five

VOYAGER

SEPTEMBER 1978, THE *KAYNELL*, MOSS LANDING, CALIFORNIA

A year after I left Cape May I walked down the shell-covered road that skirted the harbor of Moss Landing, California. The industry was changing fast, but a lot of old timers kept at it.

"Hey! You a seaman?"

I looked at the tangle of masts and rigging sprouting from the boats rafted out into the harbor. A gray bearded face stuck up just above the edge of the dock.

"Are you a seaman?" he asked again and waved me toward him.

I considered him a moment. "Yeah."

"I thought so," he said as he climbed up onto the dock. "Good. I'm going out tonight and I need a man. My daughter don't want me going out alone anymore." He wore a faded denim jacket over a gray sweater, and loose navy blue pants tucked into his socks. He looked me up and down; I was dressed about the same, gray sweater and jeans. He stuck out his hand. "Virgil McDowell."

"Paul." We shook hands.

"You been fishing before, Paul?"

"Yeah," I lied.

"Where?"

"Off New Jersey."

"New Jersey. What'd you fish for in New Jersey?"

"I was scalloping."

He looked at me, and motioned brusquely toward the boat. "Come aboard and look her over."

He took my pack and I followed him down the ladder. I stretched my leg across to the rail of the boat and made the leap onto the deck.

"What're ya fishing for, Virgil?"

"Albacore."

"What's albacore?"

"It's a tuna, about yeh big," he said stretching out his hands about three feet. "I'll tell you about it on the way out." I waited for the tour, but he seemed preoccupied, so I stumbled around, tripping over hatches and bolts in the deck, looking—wondering how all the arcane equipment worked.

Virgil lived onboard when he was fishing and moved about comfortably like an old monkey in a tree. His long arms reached everywhere, and his quick eyes checked every inch of his craft. The boat had been fueled and ready since morning; now he had his crew. He offered me a drink from a half-pint bottle and I took a long pull. His daughter stopped by just before we left and looked at me skeptically as I finished her father's whiskey. Late in the afternoon we tossed the lines.

"Coil'm and stow'm in the lazerette," said Virgil.

I looked confused. Virgil pointed to the back of the boat. "Down that hatch aft there," he said, and turned back to the wheel, steering the boat through the narrow channel out of Moss Landing Harbor.

"What's the name of your boat?"

"The *Kaynell*."

She was a classic wooden troller in the West Coast style—forty-two feet long with a deep draft, wheelhouse set forward over a high bow. She had a Caterpillar engine, which model I never knew. A few miles out into Monterey Bay, Virgil pulled a lever that engaged the autopilot, and took me out on deck.

"We fish thirteen lines," he said, as he let down the outriggers, twenty-five-foot-long poles made from young fir trees. Six lines hung from each and led to the stern. "Six off each pole, and one off the boom. Each is a different length."

"Why?"

"It makes them fish at different depths." He picked up a bright yellow rubber squid about three inches long and rolled it over to expose a hook hidden in the tentacles. "We use a barbless hook; when you get a fish you have to keep a strain on it or it'll come out."

He lifted big steel triangles out of slots near the rail on each side, and dropped them overboard, where they hung by chains. "Stabilizers," he said. "Cuts down on the roll."

Back in the wheelhouse he showed me the electronics. "This is Loran A. You line up these little squares . . ." he tuned it until the squares on the screen melded, "then you line up these triangles. . . ." He melded the triangles, and flipped a switch. "And those numbers give you your position."

"Huh."

"They got Loran C now, and you don't have to tune it in, but I can't afford it. Ain't been catching'm like we used to"

"Where are we going?"

"About two hundred miles out. Here." He swept his hand over an area on a chart crisscrossed with colored lines, and a thin strip of land along the eastern edge.

We sailed west, chasing the sun down. Over the stern the Diablo Mountains remained visible until dark.

"That's your bunk." Virgil nodded toward a narrow slot that disappeared under the console. "Not much room. But it'll fit you," he laughed.

By dawn the mountains in the east had vanished.

Virgil flipped the hooks out over the rail. Each line attached to a long spring, which stretched and contracted rhythmically with the roll and pitch of the *Kaynell*.

We stood in a well at the stern. "If you see one of those springs stretch out and stay that way it means you've got a fish, haul in on this," he said lifting a tagline that ran from the stern to the fishing line. He showed me how, by pulling on the appropriate tag line, I could get my hands on the fishing line.

He had a hydraulic hauler on the transom. "Only use it if we get into a lot of fish," said Virgil. "If they're coming one at a time haul'm by hand."

We hit a school right off. Virgil hauled in the first fish in, his long gnarled arms dragging in lengths of line as he leaned back with each pull.

"Go ahead, get the next one," he said as he pulled his fish up and landed it on the deck.

I struggled to drag the fish through the water. The monofilament dug into my bare fingers, but the fish came steadily toward me. I could see it when it popped out of the waves. My arms ached. Virgil watched.

"It's been a while since you been fishing."

I grunted. The fish slid heavily toward the stern.

"Okay now grab him, be quick."

I hauled the fish over the rail, and let it drop into the tangle of line at my feet.

"Get him out of there!"

I grabbed the thrashing fish and tossed it onto the deck next to the other. Its skin shone blue and silver in the morning sun; long black fins stretched along its sides. The two albacore shivered frantically, battering the deck.

"Watch your feet."

Virgil paid out the line carefully, making sure it did not tangle.

Turning to look at the fish with me he pointed to the long fins. "That's how you can tell an albacore. No other tuna has fins that long."

The sporadic strikes continued all day and by nightfall I could barely move my arms. The fish never came in bunches, always one at a time.

"Haul'm by hand," he had said, but when Virgil seemed occupied in the wheelhouse I used the hauler.

On deck the fish piled up. Their shivering ebbed as the life left them, and their hot blood cooled. At dusk Virgil sent me into the hold and instructed me from above on how to ice the fish.

"Pretty good pile of fish," I said when I had them packed away.

"Shit," said Virgil. "This time a year we ought to be getting ten times that. This is nothin' compared to what we used to do out here."

Our second day out the seas turned gray and a swell grew from the northwest. Virgil worked into it shifting to the east a bit. The fish had bunched up. I ran the boat from a steering station atop the wheelhouse, and headed us toward some jumping baitfish. Passing through the school the lines went stiff again, almost in unison. Virgil stood in the stern reeling a dozen of them aboard with the hauler.

He turned laughing. "Can you do that again?" By night the seas grew steeper and the wind backed around counterclockwise. Virgil bent over his chart table, working his dividers and parallel rulers across the yellowed paper.

"Where we going?"

"We're heading in."

"Why?"

"'Cuz she's gonna blow."

"We going back to Moss Landing?"

He shook his head. "We can't." He pointed to the chart, still open on the table. "We're heading for Sausalito."

In late September of 1978, a low pressure system rolling down out of the northwest collided with the fast moving remnants of a hurricane blasting in from the southwest. The two systems became the "Gale of '78," one of the most devastating storms to hit the West Coast in the twentieth century. Virgil steered northeast toward the only safe harbor within reach.

By dawn the wind had increased to fifty knots, according to the weather report. The *Kaynell* burrowed into the northwest swells and surfed along on the twenty-foot seas rolling in out of the southwest.

Coming off a wave she rolled down hard and all the galley works sprung loose and flew across the wheelhouse: plates, cups, and pans crashed into the far wall, and then tumbled onto the floor as we rolled down the other way. Virgil started tossing everything that came loose down forward and I joined the fun as we ran for the Golden Gate, our only chance of escape.

Off to the west a boat followed us a quarter mile away. In amazement I watched it come flying off a wave. The boat hung in the air, its red bottom and cooling pipes exposed, before it tumbled down and buried itself, seeming ready to capsize at any minute. It occurred to me that we must look like that.

"What would it take to roll us Virgil?"

"A hell of a lot more than this."

I looked at him standing there braced at the wheel—his long gray beard, his ease on the water—and took him at his word.

Out on deck I played. I hung in the shrouds as we slid down the steep seas, and kicked at the waves when they ranged up over the rail. The springs on the outriggers stretched out tight, so I made my way to the stern where I tested one of the lines: heavy. I hauled in a fish, its mouth nearly torn out. I shouted to Virgil but he couldn't hear me, so I kept pulling in fish; by the time I finished eight albacore slid around on deck in their death shivers.

Virgil looked out. "Hey, you been fishing again," he hollered from the cabin. "Why didn't you tell me? I'd have slowed down."

"I tried yelling." I hollered back.

"Are they still biting?"

"Not now."

"Bring the lines in then."

Back in the cabin the radio crackled with Coast Guard messages I could not quite understand: Maydays, vessels missing. It did not really register with me that boats could really sink, that the distress calls came from our immediate vicinity.

All around the gray seas blocked our view when we dropped into the troughs. We watched the sky disappear as the rollers passed by the cabin windows. Atop the waves we scanned geography in motion, an endless expanse of spindrift topped mountains and treacherous valleys.

I felt privileged to be there, to see the ocean in such a wild state of madness. Perfectly safe, I thought.

All day we struggled through the storm, sometimes in the company of other boats, usually alone. As we headed into another night, all Virgil could do was keep on the course he'd plotted.

After dark I stood braced in the back of the wheelhouse watching Virgil. "See that?" He held his finger to the radar. On the screen two masses of red connected by a thin red line appeared and faded with every pass of the revolving bar. "That's the Golden Gate Bridge."

"Huh." I stared at it for a while, then crawled into my bunk and fell asleep.

Two hours later Virgil grabbed my foot and shook it. "Get up."

The engine cover stood open; in the bilge the old Caterpillar sat unnaturally silent. "Hold this," he said and handed me a metal cylinder and glanced at the hatch cover. "Hold that so it doesn't fall." Virgil worked with more urgency than I had ever seen.

"What's the matter?"

"Filter's plugged."

Out the window I could see waves crashing into the great pilings of the bridge. Leaning over to get a better view, I could see the lights and hear the roar of traffic above us.

"When those freighters come through here they don't stop," he said as he reached up and plucked the filter from my hand. "Here, toss this." He handed me an oily used filter. I flung it out the cabin door and it disappeared over the side. Virgil spun on the new filter and jumped out of the engine box. He pushed a button on the console and the Cat roared back to life.

"Get the birds up!"

I could not pull the heavy steel stabilizers out of the water, and Virgil jumped aft, cursing me. He pushed me aside and hauled on the chains. With the birds aboard he dove back into the wheelhouse, slapped the boat into gear, and got underway. A tanker plowed past off our port side.

"Can you see that boat ahead?" He pointed to a small white light rising and falling ahead of us.

"Yes."

"Follow it." He went below to his disheveled bunk and poked his head out the companionway one last time. "Wake me if anything happens."

Virgil collapsed into his bunk, and I followed the light. It disappeared in the waves and rain occasionally but always reappeared; holding the spokes of the wheel I struggled to keep it in sight. After a while the quality changed, but I still followed it. All seemed well until I looked in the radar, a large red blip lay dead ahead: Alcatraz.

"Virgil. Hey Virgil, wake up."

JANUARY 1979, THE *ELIZABETH R.,* CAPE MAY, NEW JERSEY

Virgil put me ashore in Sausalito. The season was over he said, and I hitched back east. I went back to working the docks in Cape May, lumping—unloading the fish out of boats—cutting fish, and shucking scallops. At night I made my way out to a shack on top of a half sunk barge at the edge of the harbor, where I squatted as winter came on.

The expanding fleet continued to require crew, but none of the new boats had a place for me. The Stratton Commission had recommended a program to scrap old boats as new ones entered the fishery. But that idea did not fly politically. Instead, the worst old boats kept fishing, and that is where I finally found a site.

Joe Musgrove looked at me across the bar at the Anchorage Inn. "Have you been scalloping before?"

"No. Just tuna fishing off California."

"How long did ya go out for?"

"We were about two hundred miles offshore for five days."

"But you can't get a site here, eh?"

"Not yet."

"Can you shuck?"

"Yeah."

"Well you can go out with us if you want," he said. "For a half share." He took a drink from his glass and turned to his girlfriend.

Two days later I stepped aboard the *Elizabeth R.,* a 105-foot wooden eastern rig. Holding my sea bag ahead of me, I pushed through the doghouse, the shelter over the entry to the fo'c'sle, and climbed down the ladder into what would be my home. Narrow bunks lined the sides of the dark compartment and converged at the bow. A triangular table filled the space between. Lockers between the bunks and table served the dual purpose of storage and seats.

"Where should I put my stuff?" I asked the cook.

"That one there's empty, and that one, and that one," he said in a southern drawl, and pointed to different bunks.

I tossed my bag into the lower foremost bunk on the port side and went back on deck.

With the price of scallops still around $4 a pound, and crew members sometimes earning as much as $5,000 per trip, we threw the lines. Passing the breakwater at dusk, we steamed hopefully through the January night, and started fishing at dawn.

The first time we set out our dredges, Matt, the mate, told me to just stand by and watch.

"You'll have plenty of chances later," he said.

As the sun rose on that cold morning, the two winch men hoisted the fifteen-foot-wide steel dredges up over the rail and lowered them so that the chain mesh bags hung in the water, and the triangular frames, the "bails," rested on the port and starboard rails, each ready to be "knocked out." I watched as foam washed over the bag dragging off the starboard side, and the hookup man snapped a quick release pelican hook onto the bail. The winch man let the weight of the dredges come onto the pelican hook, and the hookup man unhooked the tackle from the bail.

We stood ready to set out. Matt waved me back by the wheelhouse.

"Watch what he does," he said pointing to the hookup man standing by the starboard dredge, who at that moment was taking the safety pin out of the pelican hook. "When the bell rings he'll knock 'er out."

Joe's hand came out of the wheelhouse window. He jerked the clapper of a small bell hanging there. *Ding-ding.* As the boat rolled down the hammer came up and slapped the pelican hook open. The hook dropped limp to the deck and the two-ton dredge rumbled off the rail, disappearing with a rush. As the boat rolled the other way I heard the other dredge go.

"Always hit it on the downward roll," Matt said above the slapping of wire spinning off the big drums of the free rolling winches. "Otherwise it'll turn upside down." The wires of each dredge whipped forward through heavy pulleys on deck—the bollards—then through blocks on the forward gallows, heavy steel frames, and back along the sides of the boat beating and slapping the hull before vanishing under water.

"Keep'm even," Joe shouted out to the winch men. "A hundred and twenty-five fathoms at the bollard."

The winch men spun the steel-spoked wheels that tightened the brakes on the drums; asbestos dust filled the air as the wires slowed. Eventually the winch men stopped them, tightening the brakes down with a last turn. Barely visible bits of rope that had been wound between the strands marked 125 fathoms, and I looked at them as the tense wires vibrated between the winches and bollards. On every roll the wires outside the boat slid like a giant scissors along the steel sheathing that capped the gun'll, the two-foot high rail around the deck. Below in the engine room, the 12–71 GM hammered louder as the dredges dug in and the boat slowed to its task. Her bow lifted easy on the dark blue winter sea, and as the sun rose the rigging cast its shadows across our gold-lit faces.

We stood on deck for a moment, silently drawing on our cigarettes. All the usual complaints: wet boots, cut fingers, constipation, and the rum jitters, forgotten in that celestial moment.

"Can you shuck?" Matt asked.

"Oh yeah."

We five of the mate's watch went below for breakfast. Before we turned in some of the guys explained to me how things worked.

We'd be out for ten days, they said, weather permitting, and January weather did not always permit. When we sold our scallops the owners would take 50 percent off the top. All trip expenses: fuel, oil, ice, and bags (for the scallops) would come out of what was left. Whatever remained would be split evenly among the crew—except for me. Because of my inexperience I would get a half share and the rest of the crew would divvy up my other half.

"Say we stocked $40,000," said Matt, illustrating the share system. "The owners take $20,000. Fuel and ice and all would cost about $4,000; that leaves us $18,000."

"$16,000."

"Okay, so grub's two grand then you got $14,000. Divide that thirteen ways and you got a little over a thousand dollars per man, except you, but you'd still have over five hundred, and that ain't bad for somebody who don't know shit."

"Plus you get a full share of the shack," another guy said, leaning over the table.

"What's shack?"

"It's the lobsters, headfish, and whatever else we catch that ain't a scallop. The crew shares that up among themselves."

"How much is that?"

"Never know, could be a couple hundred."

I crawled into my bunk and lay there being lifted and rolled as the dredges plowed through the gravel bottom below us. The motion left me feeling a bit queasy, but I thought with eager anticipation about having $700 in my pocket all at once; I'd be good for two months or more.

It did not occur to me to wonder why the pay system on fishing boats worked the way it did, using the archaic system of shares found in no other trade. A number of factors kept the system in place: but it boiled down to risks and rewards. The losses owners could face paying a crew fixed wages motivated them to share the risks of the enterprise, and consequently the rewards, with the crew. For most crewmembers the rewards exceeded the risks they took, though the work could kill a person more easily than any other. Shares also offered fishermen a level of social justice found in no other industry. *A Theory of Justice* by John Rawls, which I read many years later, articulates an ancient philosophy that workers need a sense of justice in order to "pursue their conception of good with zest and to delight in its fulfillment." Aboard a boat fifty miles offshore in winter, people need to care a great deal about their enterprise, and the vessel that makes it possible.

But the zest in the fo'c'sle of the *Elizabeth R.* was purely theoretical at eleven o'clock, when the cook woke us for lunch. We crawled out of our bunks, ate cheeseburgers, and stumbled out on deck. The four men of the captain's watch looked grateful as we stepped into the shucking houses, plywood shelters on either side of the wheelhouse, and helped them finish up.

On deck, Matt helped me tape up the handle of my knife and put the proper bend in the blade. I picked up my first scallop, held it upside down and poked the tip of the knife into the little slot by the hinge. I slid the blade in, turned it, and cut back across the top, peeling away the shell. Matt grabbed the shell I was about to toss and showed it to me.

"Look at that."

A small medallion of scallop meat about an eighth of an inch thick clung to the shell.

"That adds up," he said and tossed the shell over. He picked up a scallop and cut the shell off, and showed it to me. The pearly iridescence was pure, not a scrap of meat remained.

"Like that. Go slow and get it right, then go for your speed," he said, and slapped my shoulder.

A scallop boat bears more resemblance to a floating factory that any other type of fishing vessel, and it took a while for me to learn the fine points that kept the production flowing smoothly. The trials began immediately. Trying to stand on a bucket to reach the shucking box, I fell when the boat rolled violently.

My dorymate, the winch man I would hook up for, gave me a pair of scallop rings, each had a slot cut in it and a short length of rope between them. He showed me how to pass the rope behind my back and slip the rings over the edge of the box, binding myself to it so that **I** could not be thrown.

Joe rang the bell. "Haul back," several guys repeated. We jammed our knives into slots over the shucking table and headed out on deck. As the big Hathaway winch wound our dredge toward the surface, my dorymate gave me a pep talk.

"Stay away from it until I land it," he said. "If it starts to slide, jump on it."

I tried to imagine why I would want to jump on a moving dredge.

"Why not just get out of the way?"

"Cuz it could pin you."

The dredges broke the surface, dark wet steel glinting in the light as the winch men hoisted them up to the gallows frames. I leaned out and hooked the tackle from the starboard boom to the thick steel ring at the end of the bail.

"Heyup!" I shouted, but nothing happened.

I turned to look. My dorymate pointed up and indicated a twisting motion with his wrist. I looked up confused.

"Your tackle's twisted," he hollered, and he watched as I unhooked, turned the heavy tackle, and turned its steel hook until the ropes ran straight.

After I hooked it back onto the bail, he nodded in approval, then wrapped the rope around the winch head and took the strain on the tackle. He held the rope with one hand and eased off the winch brake. The steel dredge, dripping with mud, rose higher and higher out of the sea until the bottom of the bulging bag cleared the rail. He quickly lowered it to the deck. As soon as the bail dropped somebody shouted at me. I looked over at the hookup man on the other dredge, watching what he did. Following his example, I unhooked the tackle and rehooked it to the bottom of the bag. The moment I stepped away the winch hoisted the bag again, upside down, and its contents spilled out on deck.

The winch man dropped the dredge again, and nodded at me to hook up the bail so that he could set it on the rail again.

"There," he said, pointing to a slot on the middle bar of the bail.

Holding the tackle, I stepped between the closest bar on the bail and slipped the hook into the slot he pointed to. In the cold air a foreign smell hung about the deck: the rare aroma of sponge and deep water bottom mud, full of marine life and decay.

Again the drag lifted and he set it out on the rail. I put the pelican hook on the way they'd shown me, wrapping the hinged shackle around the bail, and slipped in the flat steel pin that held it closed. A chain hung from the hook and was bolted to the deck. As my dorymate loosed the brake, the dredge slipped down and the chain took the strain. I had to climb out over the dredge to unhook the tackle. I felt the emptiness beneath me, saw the white foam roaring around the empty chain bag as it dragged through the water, and saw the softness of the sea; it seemed more peaceful out there than on deck, but I jumped back.

I took the knock out hammer from its hook on the winch and stood ready. My stomach churned. The bell rang. The boat rolled down, I hesitated; then swung the hammer up. It struck the pelican hook, but I had not taken out the safety pin. Nothing happened. I heard the other drag roll off the side on cue. Matt jumped down out of the wheelhouse and took the hammer from me. In a flash he slipped the pin out and on the next downward roll, knocked the dredge out.

He handed me back the hammer, and said nothing. In the next few days I lost three hammers, caught and carried over the side as I knocked out the dredge. When they had all taken the plunge I had to use a rock.

"You'll be lucky if we don't drop you down to a quarter share boy," Matt said in the fo'c'sle later.

The work became a familiar and constant routine. As soon as the dredges disappeared beneath the surface we started clawing through the pile of sea bottom, picking out the scallops and tossing them into wire bushel baskets that weighed around eighty pounds when full. They told me not to put my hand on the rail to steady myself, or the wire would cut it, but I did not listen until the wire cut off the tips of my glove.

The plates that closed the scuppers, large holes in the gun'll, would not open, so once we had picked out the scallops, lobsters, and headfish, rather than push the rocks, mud, and empty shells out those holes we shoveled them all over the side. Some rocks needed the help of the whole watch to lift them over the rail. Others we wrapped in old netting and lifted with the winch.

We dragged the full baskets back to the shucking house and dumped them into our boxes. With luck we'd get the scallops all cut before the next haul back, and have time to cut the headfish and smoke a cigarette.

My dorymate showed me how to cut the headfish, known also as monkfish, goosefish, and anglerfish, and to scientists as *Lophius americanus.* They were all head and a little tail, and spent most of their time sitting on bottom with their wide jaws agape waiting to snap up anything that came to investigate the glowing worm at the end of an appendage that sprouted from between their eyes. They were among the ugliest of the underutilized species the Stratton Report had advised developing markets for, but we cut the slimy tails from the giant heads and few buyers ever knew what the whole fish looked like.

"We used to throw these overboard," said my dorymate. "Now we get thirty-five cents a pound for'm. If we had market for the livers we'd save them too. But they ain't buying right now," and he tossed the head trailing a string of guts over the side.

From noon until six, and midnight to dawn, the mate's watch manned the deck. I struggled to lift the eighty-pound baskets, bulldoze through the rock piles, and keep clear of the machinery. Over and over we hauled our dredges and picked the pile: trancelike we weaved back and forth at the boxes, shucking scallops in a monotonous meditation during the wee hours of the morning.

"I seen you rockin' back and forth at the box," said my dorymate. "That's a good sign, man; you're in the groove."

At first light the captain's watch straggled out of the fo'c'sle. They pissed over the rail or on deck, lit cigarettes, and sauntered back to the shucking house.

While I worked, my torn gloves slick with scallop guts, one of the captain's watch, a guy named Steve, put a cigarette in my mouth and lit it.

"Thanks," I nodded.

"Were you up in Woods Hole a couple years ago?" he asked.

"Yeah, for a little while. Me and my friend Greg came across from the Vineyard, and lumped a boat out there in the middle of the night."

"I remember you," he said. "I was aboard her."

"No shit." I looked at him trying to recall his face, but couldn't. "What are you doing down here?"

He laughed, his cigarette dangling on his lip as he started shucking. "Making a few transit trips until swordfishing starts," he said.

I nodded, and we talked for a while. I told him about Greg losing it and blowing his brains out, and he said he'd heard.

"I know his brother." He told me some stories about swordfishing, and his job as the doryman, gathering up the fish.

Down below after my watch, I laid in my damp bunk. Water dripped into the fo'c'sle when the weather got rough, and after five days the whole place stank of mildew. We still had not caught enough scallops to pay expenses, and the weather had deteriorated. Matt, the first mate, began to harass me for all my mistakes, threatening to sodomize me in my sleep, among other things. I wanted to go home. I prayed to God that if I could just get off that boat I would never go fishing again.

We steamed to new grounds through twenty-foot seas, and as the waves pressed against the big rudder it took two of us to hold the wheel.

"Be careful if it gets away from you," said Matt. "It could break your arm."

My dorymate and I stood our two-hour wheel watch, holding tight on either side of the big wooden wheel, keeping our chins clear of the spokes which threatened an uppercut or a slam in the temple. On the new grounds our luck got worse, misfortune followed misadventure; the dredges came up full of empty shells and one mishap piled on the next. Among other things, a towing wire broke and we lost a dredge.

On the seventh day we rested—broke down and dead in the water—rolling side to side in the waves. The boat drew twelve feet, so we didn't worry about going over, but the deck leaked like a sieve and with the scuppers plugged water tended to slosh around between the bulwarks before it found its way overboard or ran below.

We made our ignominious return to Cape May under tow from the Coast Guard and found our way back to the dock at Cold Springs. Joe gave us each a $50 advance on the shack, and told us to come back in the afternoon. We took out the lobsters and divided them up. As I went over the rail with my basket one of the owners came by and asked if he could have a couple. He took half. I sold the weak and dying lobsters for two dollars a pound and wound my way up the dock unsteadily, still feeling the waves in my legs and back. Easy now, I said, laughing.

In the bar that night, we sat drinking. Joe had given us each another hundred and fifty dollars. "This is it," he had said. "There's no half shares."

Steve asked me how I liked scalloping.

"S'alright."

"You going out again?" he asked.

"Maybe."

MAY 1979, A NAMELESS STEEL BOAT UNDER CONSTRUCTION, MOSS LANDING, CALIFORNIA

As the rest of the country slid into recession, the boatbuilding boom of the late 1970s covered all the coasts, and enabled me to keep working wherever I went. Back in Moss Landing, I found work fiberglassing fish holds—the worst job imaginable. But five dollars an hour was twice minimum wage in those days, and a man had to hide if he didn't want to work.

I sat at the kitchen table of a two room cabin I rented near the harbor, sipping a beer. Hugh Emmanuel opened the door without knocking and stood there looking at me. He had the face of a big sad-eyed hound. His unshaven jowls hung alongside his half open mouth, big belly framed by red suspenders, a little flowered welder's cap, and his inquisitive raised eyebrows.

"You comin' to work or not?" Hugh owned one of several boats under construction around the island and competition for labor was stiff. He had seen me in a bar in San Francisco, remembered me from the survivors' party in Sausalito after the storm the year before, and "rescued me," he said.

I drained my beer. "I'm comin.'" Early afternoon on the steel boat, I put on the face mask, started the vacuum cleaner that blew fresh air into the mask, and climbed into the fish hold. Hugh passed me the chop gun and rollers. Down in the hold with no peripheral vision I aimed the gun at the walls and pulled the trigger, and watched fine chopped bits of fiberglass mixed with resin shoot against the wall. After covering a small section I had to put down the gun and roll the air bubbles out of what I had sprayed. For hours I worked down there in the gray light with the screaming of the vacuum cleaner and the chop compressor. Sticky goo flying everywhere and bits of it adhering to everything it was not supposed to, the strands of fiberglass got wrapped up with the resin hose and my air hose.

At 6 p.m. I crawled out, dizzy and itching. Hugh paid me and I went home to soak in the tub, trying to get the fibers out of my skin.

At the local bar that night, I nursed a beer and studied a photo hanging on the wall: a picture of a guy aboard an ice-draped boat, holding a giant crab.

"Where's that?" I asked the barmaid.

"Alaska," she said. "That's a king crab. I had a boyfriend who went up there. Those guys make a hundred grand a year, but he quit. He said the odds of surviving a tour in Vietnam were better than surviving a year of king crabbing."

1981, STINSON FISHERIES PROCESSING PLANT, ROCKLAND, MAINE

In February of 1981, I walked into the office at Stinson Fisheries in Rockland, Maine. The foreman, Sharky, had my application in hand.

"Have you cut fish?" he asked.

"I cut weakfish and bluefish in Cape May."

"Cutting cod is a little different than cutting weakfish. Come on."

He laid my application on his desk and I followed him out the door. We went down the steel stairs, crossed the wet concrete floor, and passed through a wide door hung with long plastic strips to keep in the cold.

The temperature dropped ten degrees in the processing room. I looked around at the hoses, tanks, forklifts, and conveyor belts all hissing and rattling. We walked across the cavernous room to a row of fish cutters near an open door. Sharky leaned over to one of them and said something I couldn't hear. The man stepped down off the steel grate and Sharky took his place.

He grabbed a cod and a knife, slit across the gills up into the back of the fish's head, then down one side of its back, poking the knife all the way through once he cleared the ribs and sliding it down till it slipped out at the tail. He peeled back the meat as he cut it away from the ribs, and sliced the fillet free. He tossed it into another cutter's pan, then flipped the fish over and cut a fillet off the other side.

He looked at me and held up the carcass, a skeleton with head and tail, thinly hung with meat. "I want to be able to read a newspaper through that," he shouted above the racket. "Do you think you can do that?"

I nodded.

Upstairs again, I signed the paperwork: W-2 form, rules of conduct, etc.

"We start at 6:30 tomorrow," said Sharky. "You'll need boots and a pair of gloves. We'll give you an apron, a knife, and a steel. You pay for the knife and steel out of your first check." As an afterthought he added. "And you'll need to wear a hat, or a hairnet."

"I have a hat."

Down at Economy Clothes on Main Street I bought a pair of black, knee-high rubber boots with white soles. "That's what all the fish cutters use," the salesman told me. I wore them home.

Next morning Sharky showed me how to sharpen my knife. When he finished sharpening he swiped the knife on a steel several times then took it and shaved the hair off the back of his arm. He turned his head to me. "When you can do that, you know it's sharp enough."

I followed Sharky along the cutting tables again, this time in my boots and apron, carrying a knife and steel in gloved hands. For a hat I wore a black beret. The old cutters cast glances at me. Some nodded, none smiled. I looked them over; most had rubber door mats on the steel grate they stood on for eight hours a day, and many had knives different from company issue.

Sharky showed me my spot; I stepped up onto the bare grate and looked out the open door that kept the room cold. A conveyor belt full of fish and ice ran between two rows of cutting stations. An aluminum table with a plastic cutting board stood in front of me. To my left, near the belt, an empty hopper waited for me to fill it with the fish I would cut, to my right a plastic tray waited for me to fill it with fillets. A bucket of warm water sat near the cutting board for me to dip my hands into when they got too cold.

I looked around at the other cutters slicing quickly through their piles of cod. I slid several cold stiff fish into my hopper, and one onto my board. Sharky watched me from a distance. After I had hacked up a few he came over and gave me another lesson.

"Remember," he said. "Get it right then go for your speed. Don't worry about getting the bonus today."

Or the next day or the day after that, I found out. I had been living on one meal a day in Maine and was down to 115 pounds; some of the cod that came down the belt weighed close to that and were covered with ice. I could barely manage them. I struggled through my days wrestling with the big cod, pollock, and hake. Haddock, and the flatfish: blackbacks, dab, yellow-tail, and graysole proved a little easier to handle. I spent a lot of time looking at the various northern fish: the cod with its white stripe along the lateral line, its small barbel hanging under its chin like a goatee; the haddock, with its black racing strip and big eyes; the pollock with its long underbite. Most of the flatfish were right-handed, the side the eyes migrated to as they developed. The yellowtail had indistinct orange spots on its brown back, and yellow on the base of the tail on its eyeless white side. The graysole were so thin we only cut fillets off the top side. Fish came down the belt relentlessly, amazing quantities, and I got to know them all well.

One morning I walked down to the plant early and looked around back. A huge green boat lay there with a gantry, a towering steel framework, rising above the square stern. I had never seen anything like it. *Calvin Stinson* it said across the stern, Prospect Harbor, Maine. Baskets of fish were already flying out of her.

"How much has she got aboard?" I asked one of the lumpers.

"Over a hundred thousand," he said.

"How long was she out?"

"Less than ten days."

I cannot remember how long it took us to process that trip, but it kept us busy; one hundred thousand pounds of fish per boat seemed about average in those days and they came steady: the *Calvin Stinson, High Chaparral, Western Sea, Western Wave, Atlantic Mariner, Atlantic Harvester, Sea Bring, Irene's Way.* The fishery was still under quota management at the time, but enforcement was nonexistent and almost everyone cheated on the quotas.

The economically efficient fleet imagined by the Stratton Commission finally existed. Effort in the New England groundfish fishery had doubled since 1976, and while it might have been appropriate for the imagined abundance, in reality the stocks could not sustain the new boats that relied on them. In addition, the mesh size on the nets still caught millions of small fish that went over the side dead.

Regulators used estimates of maximum sustainable yield, MSY, the maximum amount of fish that could be taken from an individual stock of fish on an annual basis, to set target quotas. But when stocks suffered from natural declines, the often overestimated MSY stayed the same and target quotas were usually exceeded, serving to amplify natural dips in fish populations, and deplete stocks.

New money still poured into the industry; banks and other powerful investors did not favor restrictions. In spite of the intense effort, and decreasing landings, NMFS believed that while haddock stocks had reached record lows, other fish stocks had reached high biomass levels, and with a few regulatory adjustments for conservation, could withstand the existing fishing pressure. Some people may have suspected how bad things would get, but their voices went unheard.

After work I walked around the docks looking at the boats. I still wanted to get aboard one, but I had nowhere near the skills needed for the North Atlantic fishery. After a year in Rockland I took off for Alaska, where robust fisheries and a shortage of deckhands created plenty of room for greenhorns.

AUGUST 1982, THE *LAURINDA ANNE*, SELDOVIA, ALASKA

A white Ford pickup drove down the Homer spit, a windblown finger of sand extending two miles out into Kachemak Bay. I watched it brake hard and skid to a stop in the gravel alongside the road. "What the hell are you doing here?" the driver said smiling.

I looked at him too long.

"I know you from Cape May," he said. "You worked for Joe Musgrove."

"Wow, what the hell are you doing here?"

He'd brought a scallop boat around from New Jersey and they needed crew. "We could use you if you want a site," he told me.

"Thanks, but I got my own boat now."

"No shit! Well come on over and have a beer then."

"Sorry, I don't drink anymore."

"Yeah, me neither. Alright, well, come on over for a mug up when you get a chance. We're way on the outside berth."

My crewman Baruch Erez and I lay across the thwarts of my twenty-one-foot dory dreaming of baskets of Pacific cod while our longline soaked.

We rocked on the short waves, surrounded by the Kenai Mountains. Our two hundred hooks baited with herring lay anchored in the cold depths below us.

"I fished with those guys in New Jersey, there was one had some amazing stories about swordfishing. He said they cut him loose in a dory to gather the fish. They harpoon them and throw a buoy over, then he had to go fight the fish and collect them all together."

"They shoot the fish with a harpoon?"

"I don't think so. From what he said they throw it from the end of the bowsprit. He said they put him out in a dory one time and he got hold of the fish, and the line goes slack, and he knows what's coming so he jumps into the stern of the dory and *kabamm*, the sword comes right up through the bottom."

"The fish comes through the boat?"

"That's what he said, drove its sword right through the bottom. Not unusual he said. He got hold of the tail and lashed it to the gun'll then put up an oar—that's the signal of distress—and started bailing. He said he was getting pretty tired and there were sharks around by the time they came back to get him."

"Where do they do that?"

"It's a New England thing. I never tried it." I sat up and looked around. "How do they fish in Israel?"

"With bombs."

I started laughing. "With bombs?"

"Yes, they throw the bomb in the water and then the fish come up and they get them."

I laughed while he told it. "Come on, let's haul this thing."

Baruch rebaited the hooks as I hauled the line in through a fairleads, a grooved roller made from a shopping cart wheel. A tug came on the line. I looked over the side and saw a white form twisting in the water below. "Shit. It's a halibut." I pulled it up closer; Baruch leaned over to look at it. It was out of season and we had no permit. "Ten-thousand-dollar fine if we get caught with it," I said.

"What will we do, cut it loose or bring it in?"

"I'll pull it up and you cut it right at the hook."

I pulled the fish gently to the surface, Baruch cut it loose, and we watched the forty-pound fish drop out of sight.

"Shit, there goes fifty bucks. I got to get a permit before they go limited entry."

Alaska had become the proving ground for scientific management schemes the federal government wanted to impose on fisheries nationwide. Systems that would strictly control effort and total catch started with freezing of the number of licenses, and by 1982, "limited entry" had become an integral part of every fisherman's vocabulary. Although limited entry did not reduce the number of participants in heavily capitalized fisheries, as the Stratton Report had recommended, it did stop new entrants to the fishery, and provided the first step in what resource economists called the "rationalization" of fisheries.

In a nutshell, rationalization meant economic efficiency achieved through privatization of harvest rights. The theory held that this would allow market forces to govern allocation issues, and that a sense of ownership would lead harvesters to conserve fish stocks.

Regulators, struggling with the tough issue of how to control effort and limit access to finite resources, wanted to let the market do the allocation job. Privatization would enable the most economically efficient fishermen, or anyone with deep pockets, to amass and consolidate as property the harvest rights to the nation's wild fish.

Initial allocations of those rights became a controversial issue. Through a scary twist of logic, limited entry and privatization rewarded those who put the most pressure on resources, and punished those who conserved them. In the years before a fishery went limited entry for instance, effort often increased as fishermen bought permits to establish a "presence." Those who did not add effort to a fishery lost access to it. When harvest rights became privatized through individual transferable quotas, the initial allocations were based on past catch history; they rewarded those who had caught the most fish.

The salmon fishery had already gone limited entry, but anyone could buy a permit from an existing holder. Prices for permits might be as high as $200,000.

The herring fishery, too, had gone limited entry. I'd had a taste of that fishery in April as I worked my way up the coast aboard the *M/V Cape St. Elias,* a floating herring processor. In Prince William Sound we waited three weeks for the season to open; Alaska did not regulate its herring seasons by the calendar, but by the condition of the fish. When roe content reached 8 percent or more, and the eggs looked ripe, they opened the fishery for the amount of time needed to catch what they estimated to be the surplus yield of the stock. The decision often rested on the opinion of one or two biologists from the Alaska Department of Fish and Game, who continuously tested herring samples for roe content. As rumors of the imminent opening increased, seaplanes buzzed all over the sky and fifty-foot purse seiners jockeyed for position around massing schools of roe herring.

When the opening came it lasted less than two hours. The boats ran their long purse nets around what fish they could find, pursed the bottom closed and waited for a tender, a larger boat that carried the fish to processors, to pump the fish out. The purse seiners often only made one set, but we heard some fishermen had made as much as $100,000 in one opening. Other harvesters experienced equipment failures or simply missed the fish, and made nothing.

Halibut offered one of the last high value open entry fisheries in Alaska. Permits cost forty dollars in 1982, they looked like credit cards, and had to be swiped by machine every time the holder sold a fish. A fish sales slip without the appropriate card information meant trouble, and in Alaska where the fish business employed more people than any other industry, violators often went to jail.

After we cut the halibut loose, Baruch and I steamed back to Seldovia. In the harbor we came alongside the *Laurinda Ann.* Half a dozen codfish sloshed around in the bottom of our dory. Our friend Dave and his first mate, Mike, leaned over the rail and looked down at our catch. Smiles broke out on their bearded faces.

"Into the big money there."

"We need bombs."

Baruch squinted up at the hydraulic reel and the steel frames hung with hooks on the stern of the forty-two-foot fiberglass longliner. Our hands were cramped into permanent claws from hauling our lines.

Dave raised his head. "There's one more opening in 3B if you guys want to go down there with us."

One more halibut opening. I thought, I could fork out the forty dollars for a permit and maybe make some real money, but my dory could never make it to the Aleutians. "Do you want to tow us?"

"No, you come with us as crew. It's five days. I figure on fishing non-stop."

"Oh."

Baruch looked at me and shrugged. "We can only do better."

"You want this Israeli tourist, too?"

"Sure, the more the merrier."

A few days later we lay at anchor in Puale Bay, far down the Alaskan Peninsula. Alaska brown bears walked the grassy hills, a mother and three cubs. Later two more of the big bruins, a blond and a black pair, looked over the cliff edge at a caribou on the beach. An eagle flew along the cliff face, passing between the predators and their prey.

"I feel like I'm on Walt Disney," I said. That night I dreamed the bears had swum out to us and climbed aboard. I looked up and one stood in the door of the wheelhouse, breathing heavily.

At first light on opening day we set our gear. As the boat slid through the long boreal dawn, Mike set a steel tub of hooks against the aft rail. He ran the end of the groundline off the reel, a 3-by-6-foot drum, and passed it through a block overhead. "Hand me that buoy."

Baruch handed him the big orange ball; Mike clipped it to the line, and tossed it overboard. He spooled off sixty fathoms of the quarter inch nylon line, three times the twenty-fathom depth. Baruch had the anchor ready. As soon as it dropped Dave put the boat in gear, and we started snapping on hooks. Each hook hung from a fathom-long ganglion—pronounced "gangion"—or leader, the other end had a snap that fastened it to the groundline. We squeezed the snap open and quickly clipped it to the groundline.

Dave had the boat going eight knots and we had to be fast with the snaps or the line would drag the ganglion through our hands and the hook would catch us—our greatest fear. We all carried sharp knives strapped to our chests for easy access, just in case.

Before we started hauling back the gear, Dave gave us our jobs. He would steer and run the hydraulics; Mike would unclip the hooks and small fish; I would gaff the bigger fish; and Baruch would help gaff the still bigger fish. I looked at my long-handled gaff hook and the sharp point on the end.

"Try to hit'm in the cheek," said Dave. "And then get'm in fast 'cuz they go nuts."

I nodded and waited, stripping baits and bending pieces of herring or octopus onto the first few hooks as we retrieved them. Then the halibut came—like nothing we'd ever seen. For three days straight we worked the gear. "You can have a string sandwich," said Dave. "You know what that is? You hang a sandwich from a string and take a bite out of it every time you run by." By the second day of nonstop action, the joke had lost its zing. But Pat Benatar never tired. Mike had put a tape of her into the auto reverse cassette player and she just went on and on, singing, "Hit me with your best shot. . ." I still smell the distinctive odor of halibut whenever I hear her.

"Fish!" Mike hollered from the rail as the line came aboard. "Big one."

The big green fish slowly flipped its tail as it neared the boat. When it touched the hull it thrashed. The sharp point of my gaff hook sunk into its cheek. Baruch's followed and together we slid the two-hundred-pound fish aboard. Baruch slipped a loop of rope around its tail. We flipped the halibut upside down and tied its tail to the portside railing, already crowded with fish, some as much as 400 pounds, their white sides exposed.

"Soon we will have no place to tie them," said Baruch.

The procession continued without end: the day through the night. We stood at the hatch cover gutting halibut, baiting hooks. We set the hooks; we hauled the fish.

"Fish!"

We began to dread that call.

Time turned gray. Dave got strange. We all did. In the foggy dawn we searched for the end of our string, looking for the red poly ball.

"See anything?"

"Lots of things," I said, staring bleary eyed into paisley hallucinations and gray shadows that could have been horses. "No poly balls."

As our thoughts drifted away from fish towards sleep, Dave drove harder. He had three days to fill his boat, and he would not miss a set.

"How about a little nap, Dave?"

"How about a picnic? Let's go, put the skiff over, we'll go ashore for a picnic."

We three on deck looked at each other.

"Come on, let's go. It's picnic time."

He went into the cabin and lay down. We followed into the dank fo'c'sle for a fitful hour, listening to the waves slap the fiberglass hull, too wired to sleep.

"Fuck this, come on, girls."

Dave steered. Mike snagged the buoy, pulled it aboard and ran the groundline through a block slung out over the rail. He passed me the end and I ran it back and hooked it on to the spool. Dave put the winch and boat in gear and the line wound aboard. First came the anchor, followed by the hooks. Baruch took the hooks from Mike and stripped the old baits. We landed a few fish; then came a gap in the hooks. Mike held his hand on the groundline.

"Big one."

A long section of line came up shorn of hooks, ganglions, and clips. The huge halibut had stripped twenty fathoms of the groundline, and as the line lifted mighty fish to the surface the accumulated gear tangled around it.

"Get the gun," we all hollered. The fish looked to be in the four-hundred-pound-plus category.

Dave, bleary-eyed, stood in the door of the wheelhouse with a .357 Magnum. Other times he had come aft to dispatch the bigger fish before we brought them aboard, but now he just stood there.

"Get out of the way."

He pointed the gun at the fish and fired. He banged away, the fish jolting whenever he hit it. Mike leaned back as far as he could. Baruch and I stumbled over each other trying to get behind the longline reel. I looked over at Mike as the bullets passed between us. His mouth pinched, he looked hard at Dave.

But Dave ignored us; stalking across the deck he reloaded and blasted the fish at point blank range. The reports of the gunshots slammed through the air and made my eyes blink. My ears rang. In a daze I moved around the reel to look over the side. The bullets chewed up the halibut's head until the hook tore free. The fish's broad barnacled back began to sink. It turned its belly up and we watched that white spot disappear beneath us.

"Shit! There goes four or five hundred dollars."

Nobody answered him. He tucked the pistol into his belt and went back to hauling. We worked woodenly—silent except for Mike's intermittent cries of "Fish!"

We tried to put the color back in the day, but it never happened; it stayed like a black-and-white nightmare till the last haul came aboard at dusk. Like zombies we gutted and iced the fish, then set the anchor in Puale Bay, and slept—not even keeping watch.

In the morning we crawled out of the fo'c'sle and smoked while Mike made breakfast. Out of nowhere a roller came in and sent a bowl of pancake batter sailing across the galley. It went everywhere. I laughed and scooped some batter off the counter and wiped it on Mike. Mike threw some at Baruch, next thing we had it flying everywhere and even Dave laughed.

The weather turned nasty on us. It blew for a day and a night. On the VHF the Coast Guard said two dories were lost on the west side of Kodiak. Their crews gone.

"Good thing you didn't bring your dory down here."

With our fish well iced, we played four hand cribbage, and smoked cigarettes—biding our time.

The wind died down on the third morning, and Dave fired up the little Deutz; she wound over slow and barely caught. He looked at the gauges; the needle on the ammeter lay flat.

Down in the engine compartment we fussed with the alternator—poked wires into it; tested it.

"She's pooched," Dave shouted over the hammering engine.

"What do we do?"

"Don't need electricity to run a diesel. Let s run for it."

One hundred and fifty miles up Shelikof Straight and across the mouth of Cook Inlet without the radar, depth sounder, or loran—we steamed on. When the sun went down the boat ran dark. Somehow, with Dave and me pooling our limited navigation skills, we made our buoys.

I pointed a flashlight beam on the chart. "Look, this says 'Red fl 6 sec.' That means it flashes every six seconds right?"

"I think so."

"I thought you were in the Navy?"

"Yeah, on a submarine."

"Is that what made you so fucking nuts?"

We watched the buoy, counting together.

"Six?"

"Six."

"Okay we must be here. So if we run 30 degrees we should see this buoy here."

"I can get us home from there," said Dave. "I fished all around there."

By the time the *Laurinda Anne* passed the breakwater of Seldovia, she was running completely dark. Not a volt or an amp to be found aboard.

No one greeted us at the wharf. Baruch and I stumbled out to the camp where our girlfriends slept, and as the sun rose we crawled into our respective tents.

Karen rolled over. In the growing cold of early September I could see her breath. "I want to go back to the States," she said.

"Sure, babe." I lay there still vibrating from the engine—rolling with the seas. "There's a guy in Homer who offered me fifteen hundred dollars for my dory." I thought about the reality of going back and added a condition. "I'd be willing if we could live in Maine."

I walked away from a lot in Alaska. I might have bought a halibut permit and gotten a valuable quota when Alaska became one of the first states to manage a fishery through the use of Individual Transferable Quotas (ITQs), before Congress banned them.

ITQs addressed many problems. The rationale held that when fishermen know they can catch a certain amount of fish, they will fish when they want to. The system was intended to eliminate the need for fishermen to go dangerously long without sleep, or for small boats to fish in weather they could not survive. ITQs ended the "derby fishing" where all the boats chased the available fish in a rush and flooded the market, leading to depressed prices and low quality fish. Again, however, the system gave the highest quotas to the fishermen who caught the most fish, which served to consolidate fisheries by enabling the highliners—called "winners" by regulators—to leverage more quota from less aggressive fishermen—"losers." ITQs also lead to high grading, as fishermen limited in how much they could bring in threw back small fish in favor of bigger, higher priced fish.

By leaving Alaska I lost an opportunity to get in on the ground floor of that sort of "rationalized" fishery, and the management system of the future. But I felt that until I fished New England, I could not call myself a fisherman, and so I headed back east.

In five years of traveling around the US coasts, I had seen the early signs of where the goal of maximizing net profit, recommended by Stratton, would take the fishing business. The old ways crumbled before the juggernaut of the unquestioned maxim, which called for the highest net economic return. As the Stratton Report predicted, many legislators attempted in vain to protect small boat fishermen, a few of whom hung on in places like Owls Head, Maine, five miles south of Rockland.

Part Two

HOME ON THE OCEAN

ALTON'S SHOES

The smell of fish hit me in the face as soon as I stepped off the bus in Rockland. I breathed in the sweet aroma; the smell of money we called it. I was back. My girlfriend and I found a cheap room to rent and I started hunting for a site.

Feeling more confident than I had when I left Stinson's the year before, I ventured down to Owls Head on a crisp September morning. Gulls shrieked above Reed's Wharf, waiting for an opportunity. The smell of herring, salt, and rancid brine hung low in the cool air.

A fellow about my age bent over a wooden crate at the end of the wharf, weighing out lobsters. I walked down and looked in the crate, the lobsters moved slowly, feelers searching the air, their black shells trimmed with an orange red; their claws plugged with little wooden pegs, and unable to open.

I asked the dockworker about sites, but he just shrugged.

"Where you from?" he asked after a while.

"Alaska."

"No shit. I always wanted to go there."

"Well, it's still there."

He laughed and treated me different, like I might almost belong.

While we talked, an old man pulled a small lobster boat in at the head of the wharf and gaffed a line. Small black letters on the bow read *Osprey*. He had a load of traps aboard, the old-fashioned half-round wooden ones, and I wandered over to talk to him.

"How ya doin'?"

He looked up from under owlish white brows, and his eyes squinted. "Oh, not too bad, and you?"

"Good, thanks."

"I don't believe I've seen you around here before," he said.

"I just got down here, from Alaska."

"Oh, Alaska, I see." He stopped briefly, and then reached for another trap.

"And what was you fishing for up there?"

"Halibut."

"Were ya getting any?"

"Every tenth hook, sixty pound average."

"I see. That sounds pretty good."

He asked more questions, seeking details, the rise and fall of the tides in Alaska, prices for the fish, how far apart we set our hooks on the ground-line and how long we made the leaders.

The full tide brought the rail of his boat almost level with the dock and while we talked the old man continued to drag traps to the side and heave them across. They landed at my feet and I began to stack them. He needed to get the traps off before the tide dropped much further, but he worked calmly.

"Where did you get those shoes?" He asked, nodding toward my Red Wing dock slippers, smooth leather on the toe and heel, with a bit of stretch fabric between, and heavy soles.

"In Alaska, most fishermen wear them up there."

"I have the same kind. They're a good shoe aren't they?"

"They're about all I wear if I don't have my boots on." I liked him, he was around the same age my grandfather would have been, and although I could see he was no highliner, I thought it would be comfortable to work with him. "I'm looking for a site around here. Do you need any help?"

"Oh no, I've only got about fifty more traps out and I'm takin' up."

"Do you know of anybody who needs crew?"

"You could ask my son."

"Where's his boat?"

"It's the gray one furthest out."

Out beyond the lobster boats, most of them painted white, many of them fiberglass, I saw a wooden eastern rig, about sixty feet long, wheelhouse aft like the old boats in Cape May, painted gray with white trim along the rail.

"What's he fishin' for?"

"He's been fish dragging, but I think he's getting ready to rig up for shrimping soon."

"Where's he now?"

"I seen'm around. He may be over alongside the wharf there, where they keep their gear."

"And what's his name?"

"Bernard." He began to untie his lines. "Now, I didn't get yours." I told him my name, and he asked me to spell it.

"Like Molyneaux Road up in Camden?"

"Exactly."

"Is that a French name?"

"Yep, my ancestors came down from Canada. How 'bout you?"[2]

"My name's Alton Raynes," he said. Too far apart for a handshake, we nodded to each other across the gap between the wharf and his boat.

The bait shed and office that spanned the wharf had grown there over many years and showed various methods of construction and materials. Cedar shingles covered one side, clapboards on another. A big sliding door on one end had a coat of gray paint, but around its handle, gloved hands covered with herring pickle had left a halo of brown grease.

A sheltered catwalk along the outside of the wharf gave access to a row of doors that ran the length of the building. A paunchy bespeckled man with a cap askew on his tussled head stood in the open doorway

---

[2] They actually came from Canada after they got off the boat from Ireland, but I did not know it at the time.

of a gear locker, shifting around coils of rope, seeming intent on finding something.

"How you doin'?"

"Oh, not too bad." He reached into the locker and sifted through a bucket of rusty shackles. I stood there a minute. "Can I help you with something?" he asked.

"Are you Bernard?"

"That's who I am. Sometimes it snows, and sometimes it rains, and that's me Bernard Raynes. And who are you?"

I told him my name and I started to put my hand out, but noticed he had no such intention, and so let it go.

"I was talking to your father. I'm looking for a site, and he thought I might ask you."

Bernard leaned his head back so he could see me through his glasses, which had slipped down to the end of his nose, then looked back at the bucket of shackles. "Well I'd like to help you out, but we're getting ready to go shrimping now and we usually have to let a man go. Besides," he said, "we have a pretty steady bunch and don't usually need anybody."

Bernard focused back on his chore. I looked out at the boat.

"Okay, well if you do need anybody can I give you my number?"

"Well, like I said, we have a pretty steady crew thanks just the same."

"Okay, I'll see you later."

"Alright, good luck to you. Sorry we can't help you."

I was the new man in town, the unknown quantity with no credentials except that he showed up on the dock every day until finally he got a site— with somebody marginal: somebody who none of the locals wanted to go fishing with for whatever reason, usually lack of profit, no product, or sometimes the guy was just a psychopath with a boat.

I finally got aboard a lobster boat; making fifty dollars a day filling bait bags and emptying traps for Ivan Stone. I had met his father in Rockland and he said that his son needed a sternman.

When I showed up on the wharf at dawn, a dory floated near the mouth of the harbor tied to Bernard's mooring ball. The big boat was gone.

After my first day lobstering I saw Alton on the wharf, wearing his Red Wing shoes. The right one had the sole and heel built up an extra inch to compensate for one leg being shorter than the other.

He looked at me. "How did you make out?"

"I got a site with Ivan Stone."

"That's good. Ivan's a good boy."

Every morning I scooped greasy herring from the barrels on the wharf into buckets for Ivan, and we went out to haul his traps around the nearby islands. "There used to be big kelp beds out here," he told me. "Then these urchins showed up and ate'm all." He threw one of the round, spine covered urchins on deck and smashed it under his heel. When he found crabs in the traps he smashed them too.

"We may need them someday," I said. But he still smashed them.

All day as we worked, seagulls followed us and dove at the old bait. One day after emptying a bait bag over the side, Ivan grabbed the gaff quick as lightning and snagged a seagull with it. He laughed and I watched the bird receding behind us, bleeding and flopping in the water. I turned back to filling bait bags. Ivan had reverence for nothing that I could see, but I had few choices, and stayed with him until he got his traps all up in November.

The groundfish fleet, the boats that chased cod, haddock, and flounders, still dominated Rockland's economy. The New England Fishery Management Council had abandoned quotas on total catch, which could lead to shutting down the fishery after all the allotted fish were caught. The council succeeded in convincing the National Marine Fisheries Service that landings could be controlled through indirect methods; primarily mesh size on the nets. NMFS scientists expressed some concern, but the agency declined to push for continued quota management. The political firewall protecting the industry from conservation efforts seemed impregnable, and the myth of untapped vast resources led to ongoing expansion of the fleet.

Like a force field, however, the insular nature of the New England fishing community held me out. I might be accepted enough to get on a low end lobster boat when fishing boomed in the fall, but having caught a few halibut in Alaska would not get me aboard a Rockland shrimper or fish dragger. Besides, I could not mend twine. Instead I watched envious from the dock as crewmen on the big draggers plied their plastic needles, knitting together the torn meshes of their nets.

The winter months went hard. I pounded the docks from Port Clyde to Rockland and everywhere I heard the same song. "We have a pretty steady crew; I don't know of any sites; I don't think you're going to find much around here this time of year."

In the harsh environment of a Maine winter, most anyone with a job clung to it. People stuck with who and what they knew and did not take risks during the perilous season—less perilous in the twentieth century, but old habits died hard, especially in New England. My girlfriend took off to grad school, but some friends from Alaska came to visit and brought a case of canned salmon; between that and some winter lobstering I picked up, I managed to survive. But I could not find a site.

Stumped by the lack of prospects, I enrolled in the University of Rhode Island's fisheries and marine technology program. URI had instituted the program in the late 1970s, in order to train crew for the expanding high-tech fleet, but by 1983, landings began to slide and then dive—my class would be the last before the University canceled the program. Nonetheless, I looked over the brochures with anticipation. The courses included twine mending, and net design; resource economics; fish processing and fishing vessel safety, among others. Not having come from a fishing family, it seemed like the best way for me to learn the skills I needed. But classes did not begin until the fall.

On a bright morning in June, I walked the docks of Rockland at low tide, looking for a site to tide me over until school started. Beached along McClellan's wharf, I saw the gray and white eastern rig from Owls Head, the *Irene & Alton*. A crew swarmed over and under her, painting and repairing: an annual ritual.

Steel boats and fiberglass boats are low maintenance tools—inanimate objects. But when people form wood into the shapes of their dreams, the wood takes on an exalted life. Like an organ of the body it requires constant maintenance in order to function.

Every year on a big tide in late spring, Bernard moored his boat alongside a wharf, for painting and repairs—sometimes at Reed's in

Owls Head, occasionally at McClellan's in Rockland. He hung a truck tire between the hull and the wharf and piled lead ingots on the starboard side for ballast, so she'd lean in. He let her settle into the gravel and after the tide drained away his crew would scrape the barnacles off her bottom, sand it, patch any scars, and roll on a fresh coat of copper paint. They worked like bees painting and sanding the top work, oiling the decks, tarring the rigging, and lastly, re-painting the letters of the *Irene & Alton*s name.

A tall guy paused on deck. "How you doing?" I called down to him.

"Alright," he said. "How 'bout you?"

"Can't complain, wouldn't do any good if I did. What are you guys up to?"

"We're rigging up to go swordfishing."

"Swordfishing?"

"Yeah."

"Do you need any help?"

"I think so, have you ever been swordfishing?"

"No."

"You'll have to talk to that fellow back there," he said pointing aft.

The man I'd spoken to months before was scraping paint back by the wheelhouse. I walked down the dock a little ways until I stood above him.

"Hello."

From the deck ten feet below me he looked up squinting. With the sun behind me he saw only a silhouette. "Who's that?" I told him my name for the second time.

"Well, what can I do for you?"

"I was wondering if you needed any help?"

"Didn't I meet you before?"

"Yep."

"And what did I tell you?"

I said the first thing that popped into my mind. "You said, sometimes it snows and sometimes it rains, and that's you, Bernard Raynes."

Bernard looked at me for a long minute. "Come on down here," he said.

More than any crew I had ever been around, Bernard's gang worked like a team. They moved steadily from one chore to the next. Being the new guy, however, they put me on the most gruesome task: crawling under the boat to sand and scrape the bottom paint. I worked fiercely at it in the cool dark shadow of the boat, scrambling around on the wet rocks scraping paint until the red dust caked my hair and clothes.

The tall guy introduced himself as Georg. "You want to get that cleaned off of you," he said. "It's very toxic stuff. You could get blood poisoning."

The next day Bernard handed me a bucket of bottom paint and a roller and sent me under the boat again. He came down and showed me a brass fitting near the stern.

"Don't paint around this plank here." He outlined the plank with his finger.

"Okay." As the tide rose, I came out from under the boat coated in copper paint.

Brad, the mate, came down. He looked at my work, and shook his head. "That's expensive paint you know," he said, pointing at the red-splattered rocks all around us.

The next high tide Bernard took the boat back to Owls Head and ran her in alongside Reed's wharf. As the tide dropped she settled into the sand, and we felt an unfamiliar absence of motion. Certain that she'd lay well, we rode in the back of Bernard's truck to a local restaurant for "dinner," the noontime meal.

In the afternoon they hoisted me up into the rigging. Pat Wilson, whom everyone called "Spic," wrapped one end of a line around the turning bronze winch head. He pulled the line through a block aloft and lifted me in the bosun's chair, a wooden seat slung from the other end.

"Careful you don't get a riding turn and run me through that block."

"I gotcha, Cap."

I hung above the deck with my bucket of pine tar and a cotton glove on one hand. I reached into the warm black tar, scooped out a handful, and rubbed it into the steel wire rigging.

"Don't be dripping that shit on the deck," Brad hollered up to me.

But with every other handful a little bit dripped.

Spic hoisted me up and down the rigging: first the stays that ran from the tops of the masts to the bow and stern; then the shrouds, the steel wires that ran from main mast to the sides of the boat; and the spring stay, the high wire that ran from the top of the main mast to the top of the mizzen. When we finished they all shone under a coat of black tar.

"What's next?" I asked as I cleaned my hands with diesel fuel.

"A cigarette," said Spic.

After the cigarette, I climbed down under the boat to see what Bernard wanted next.

He and Brad had taken out the plank he had told me not to paint, and a hole gaped below the water line. "What are you doing?"

"Getting rid of this seacock," he said, tapping the end of a pipe that once poked through the hull.

"Why?"

"Well, why not? Don't need it anymore."

"What if you don't get her plugged before the tide comes back?"

"Somebody'll have to get in there to start bailing." He put the old plank into the back of his truck, and disappeared up the hill.

"Here, you can put these zincs on," Brad said and handed me a bag of zinc anodes, flat gray pieces of metal with screw holes in them. "Just replace the ones that are gone."

The zincs, as I understood it, protected the propeller, shaft, rudder, and other metals below the waterline from oxidation. When different types of metal are placed close together in salt water, they create an electric current that deteriorates the softer metal in a process called electrolysis. The sacrificial zincs, as the softest metal on the boat, deteriorated first, and needed replacing before the others started to oxidize.

I climbed back aboard and down into the engine room to fetch wrenches. Daylight reflected up through the hole where the plank had been, and I could see the first wavelets of the incoming tide.

By the time I got down under the boat again, Bernard had returned with a piece of wood. He fit it carefully in place. A bucket of tools sat in the gravel at his feet. The tide trickled in around it, and while I unbolted the old zincs on the rudder I watched him take a block plane and trim the new plank edge.

"What kind of wood is that?"

"White pine. Should be cedar, but I didn't have any."

The zincs bolted on easily. I tightened down the nuts and watched Bernard. The water covered his feet, but he worked as if it did not exist, methodically fitting the plank and then hammering a nail through to hold it in place. From the bucket he took a hand drill and wound a couple of holes in the plank. He fumbled in his pocket and came out with two screws, which he ran in with a bit brace.

The water started to float the bucket.

"Here you better get this out of here."

I took the bucket up to the edge of the tide. Bernard drilled the rest of the holes.

"Bring me that bit brace."

Standing ankle deep, I handed him the brace. He pulled a screw out of his pocket, but dropped it. He stared down into the water after it; then pulled out another.

Bernard screwed the long bronze screws in, and I carried the bucket to him. "Stay here a minute," he said.

"I'll stay while I can. My boots aren't as tall as yours."

"Well, you could take'm off."

He pulled a roll of caulking out of the bucket and jammed a wad of it into the new seam. With a blunt chisel, a caulking iron, and an iron-bound wooden mallet he hammered the caulking in, continuously folding it back on itself until he made the circuit of the new plank.

"I think I got to leave you soon, Bernard."

"Hand me that seam compound before you go."

I handed him the caulking gun. He ran a bead around the seam, and put a dab in every screw hole before scraping them all smooth with a putty knife.

"Have you got your paint bucket there?"

I handed him the bottom paint he'd brought, leaning out with it to reach him.

As he stepped back I saw the water about to crest his boot top. But he very carefully dipped the brush, wiping off the excess paint on the rim of the can. He must be on tiptoes I figured, as he smoothly brushed on the paint, dabbing it into the cracks. He finished and sloshed out of the water.

"I guess that's enough for the day. You boys close her up." He kicked off his boots and dumped the water out, then put his tools back in the truck, and drove away without looking back.

"Every time I've ever seen anybody else try something like that it turns into a major panic." I said to Georg as we cleaned up and put tools away. "In fact, I don't think I ever saw anybody try anything like that."

"Bernard knows his stuff. Alton too, he designed the boat and Bernard built her."

"He built her?"

"Oh yeah, you didn't know that? He took a year off from fishing and built her in his back yard."

I looked at the boat, the smooth shape of her hull, the tide rising toward the new plank, visible now only by a swath of bright paint. "Wow."

"So, you going fishing with us?" he asked.

"I don't know. He said if the regular guy doesn't go, I can go."

"That's Glenn, I don't think he's going."

A few days later we steamed back to Rockland and tied up at Knight's Marine. We needed their crane in order to finish rigging up. Thirty feet above deck, Spic and I leaned relaxed from the cross trees of the main mast, watching as the crane swung the aluminum topmast toward us. He reached out with his long arms and snagged it. Together we guided it into steel rings on top of the main, and signaled the crane to let it down; it slid down into place scraping up the new white paint as it went.

"You go up and untie the stays."

Being the lightest, I climbed the unsecured topmast towering over the harbor, cut loose the coiled stays, and lowered the turnbuckle ends to Spic. He fed them through the other rigging to Brad, who shackled the backstays to chainplates, steel plates bolted to the stern. The forestays we dropped down to deck, awaiting the pulpit, and climbed down.

The crane lifted the pulpit, the twenty-foot extension we would bolt to the bow. Fashioned from two long four-by-fours painted the same gray as the boat, it was decked with aluminum grate and had a rail of thin pipe around the end, where Bernard would stand to harpoon the fish. As the pulpit swung toward us, Brad and Spic grabbed it and wrestled it into place, calling directions to the crane and each other, while I stood by with the bolts.

"Up! Up!"

"Bring it to me."

"That's all you got."

"I can't see the hole. Take it forward some. There."

I slid the bolts into place and we screwed on the nuts.

The sweat dripped off us all.

"Regular heat wave, ain't it, Cap."

"Ah, Jesus." In the commotion Brad had leaned against the fresh tarred forestay. He looked with disgust at the black spiral tar print across the shoulder of his blue T-shirt, and turned back to the work as we ran out the topmast stays and shackled them to the pulpit. We then uncoiled the shrouds from the pulpit and ran them back to the rails, sorted out the confusion of wires, and tightened all the turnbuckles until everything felt stiff.

Bernard went aft to check the angle of the mast, now taller than the boat was long. "That looks alright."

Bernard drove home with the trailer he had brought mast and pulpit on, and we pulled out from Knights with Brad at the helm of the *Irene & Alton*. Back in Owls Head, Brad brought the boat, now bristling with lengthy appendages, gently up against the wharf. Bernard met us and we piled into his truck to fetch the last pieces of gear that would go aboard: the harpoons, lines, and buoys.

Before stacking the boxes of harpoon line and bronze darts, the long shafts of the harpoons, and radar reflectors into the back of the truck, we filed into Bernard's kitchen for dinner. His wife Eleanor had a pile of sandwiches ready, and we sat down around the table. I watched the other guys taking off their hats and followed suit, jamming my cap under my leg. Pictures of Bernard's four daughters hung on the walls, and we saw the girls around off and on, but they were rare participants in the fishing work. Eleanor's mother lived in the house, too, and she shuffled through the kitchen smiling at us.

After years of living mostly alone or aboard boats I felt an aversion to such a level of domesticity. I ate self-consciously, and finished quickly. With something like relief I followed everyone out of the crowded kitchen and went back to work.

That afternoon, as we tied the last buoys to the winch, Bernard called me back to the wheelhouse.

"We have a site for you if you want it," he said. "It'd be half-share. That's only fair till we find out if you can spot fish."

Georg came back after the 4th of July and slept aboard the boat. In the morning I went with him to buy grub and we filled three carts: box after box of bread, meat, cakes, cookies, a carton of cigarettes per man, vegetables, soda—$1,000 worth of food for five men for two weeks. Georg pointed to a sunglasses display. "You want to get a couple pairs of them for up in the mast," he said. "Make sure they're polarized. And be sure to bring warm clothes; it gets cold up there."

At O'Hara's dock we took on ten tons of ice and twelve hundred gallons of diesel fuel. Once we were ready though, the weather turned foul. Regardless, Bernard called us down to the boat every day. We'd stand around under the gray sky, looking out at white caps, as the east wind blew in our faces. He'd tell us to go home and come back tomorrow—drills, we called them.

Early in the morning of July 8th we set out. Marshall Island sheltered the harbor, and as soon as we cleared it Brad untied the gaskets that bound the stays, the triangle of canvas spread between the main mast and the smaller mizzen mast aft. Spic and I hauled together on the halyard and watched the sail run up the mast. The middle of the white canvas carried a blue scallop shell, blazoned with a capital "R." It snapped in the breeze as we tightened down the halyard and tied it off. We set the smaller sail from the mizzen, and went forward to hoist the big jib, a tall triangular sail that tapered from the bow all the way to the top of the mainmast. While the staysails reduced the boat's roll, the jib helped drive us, conserving precious fuel. "She adds another knot," said Georg.

With all the sails flying we passed Vinalhaven; a half hour later, Seal Island and the Wooden Ball slipped by on our starboard side. In the aftermath of the past storm the boat rode up the long swells and dropped down into the troughs as we headed out into the open ocean.

Georg explained the watches to me. "We stand two-hour watches on the way out and when we lay to at night."

"No fishing at night?"

"No, we usually shut everything down and lay to, drifting all night. Anyway, you're on first, then you wake Bernard if he's asleep."

In the wheelhouse, with nothing but open water between Georges Bank and us, Bernard stepped away from the wheel and I took over.

"South by a quarter east," he said.

I looked at the compass. It had no numbers on it; instead, a series of diamonds and triangles laid out like petals of a flower—the "compass rose."

"Do you know how to box the compass?" he asked.

"Box the compass?"

He stepped back next to me. "These are your cardinal points," he said, pointing to North, South, East, and West marked on the compass. "These are your intercardinal points, northeast, southeast, nor'west, sou'west, south southeast, and all them."

The progression began with north, then north by a quarter east, north by a half east, until you got to north by east, then the reference point doubled back, and it went north northeast by north. The reference points flipped back and forth like that all around the compass.[3] The quarter points seemed complicated, but I saw the pattern and picked it up quickly. After fifteen minutes I boxed the compass perfectly. The next time I stood watch, he quizzed me, pointing to different diamonds and triangles, and I named every little petal of the rose.

"What would it be if you was goin' that way?"

"South by a quarter east."

"Well, ain't that the course I told you to steer?"

"Yeah." I spun the wheel to put us back on course. It took practice to keep the boat going straight, but I passed the compass test.

---

[3] "There ain't no such thing as north by nor'west," Bernard said to me later. "Somebody gave you that direction you'd be standin' there scratching your head while the boat ran ashore. But they say it anyway, name books and all after it."

There is northwest by north, but the direction north by northwest, does not exist.

After my watch I climbed out to ride on the end of the pulpit. At the crest of each wave it hung thirty feet or more above the trough. As we topped the waves my hands gripped the rail and the pulpit would drop out from under me, stopping with the water only inches beneath my feet. Finally the boat came off a big one and dipped the pulpit into the sea. The water surged powerfully around my knees, and I realized it would not take much more to tear me overboard. I climbed back into the boat and we steamed on for Georges.

Seven

SWORDFISH! 1983

In the darkness, 200 miles offshore, long ocean swells gently rock the *Irene & Alton* as she drifts with the current. The silhouette of her sixty-foot mast sweeps across the night sky.

In the fo'c'sle a cone of aluminum foil wrapped around a lightbulb focuses its beam on a man reading at the galley table. Three sleepers in their bunks breathe in rhythm with the creaking hull and the lap of waves against wood. Two inches of cedar separate them from the sea. Dolphins swim by and their shrill whistles carry through the planks. The only discordant sound is the tearing of pages from a book.

Moby-Dick. I had come to the chapter where Melville admonishes captains and ship owners not to send young dreamers into the mast, for their ships will sail past shoals of whales and never sight a one. "'Why thou monkey,' said a harpooneer to one of these lads. 'We've been cruising now hard upon three years and thou hast not raised a whale yet.'" How simple it would be for Bernard to open the book and be awakened to the fact that I am that monkey—everyone has seen a fish but me.

I drop the pages into the stove, and watch them curl into black balls, feel the warmth. Up the ladder the doghouse doors open into the night, and the empty deck lit only by the masthead and running lights that confuse the storm petrels, small black seabirds that live far out of sight of the land. One lands on deck and I hear it flapping around clumsily, unable to take off. I go up to toss the stranded bird overboard, and look around. Scanning the darkness for the lights of other boats, I see nothing but stars and a black edge of the horizon where they disappear. All seems well, and I slip back down into the fo'c'sle.

As I settle down in the quiet, the engine roars to life. The boat slams into gear and surges ahead. I jump up the ladder and run aft to the wheelhouse. "What's going on, Bernard?"

"Supertanker."

"I was just up here. I didn't see anything."

"When they're coming right at you, you can't see the lights."

"How did you know?"

"I heard its engines." Bernard waves me up into the wheelhouse. "Have a look here."

I watch the phosphorescent bar of the radar make its circuit around the screen. A massive blip flashes inside the one mile marker ring off our starboard quarter. Outside, the dark silhouette passes astern of us. Running and masthead lights are now clearly visible.

Bernard stays at the wheel and runs for an hour back toward our cruising grounds. The watch changes and I am back in my bunk when he shuts the engine down. We drift again, over the one-hundred-fathom edge of Georges Bank.

Ten thousand years ago glaciers scoured New England and left the wealth of the region deposited out here, covered by the sea. The Labrador Current brings cold arctic water sweeping around Nova Scotia, where it mixes with tropical eddies spun off from the Gulf Stream, causing seasonal upwelling that boils with nutrients, the foundation of the marine food chain. We drift through the turmoil. In alternating wafts of cold and warm air we can smell icebergs and coconuts.

At dawn the smells in the fo'c'sle overpower everything: bacon, diesel fumes, tobacco smoke, and the farts of four unwashed men just waking. Georg the cook reaches his long arm up into my bunk and taps my foot. "Breakfast. You wanna go get Bernard?"

On deck I light a cigarette. Bernard stands in the door of the wheel-house, bathed in an orange glow as the first tangent of sunlight slices across the water. I stay by the doghouse, the sheltered entry to the fo'c'sle, and take a look around, watch the light turn to gold. Bernard disappears. A moment later the engine fires up and I feel a familiar jolt as he slips her into gear. We steam into the light breeze, back toward the edge.

I swing up next to Bernard. "Morning."

"Well, good morning, Mr. Paul."

"Breakfast is ready."

"Good. Keep her going west by north, a quarter north."

I watch him waddle up the slanted deck and disappear below. In the wheelhouse the chill of the night still lingers.

Below us, somewhere in the depths, swim swordfish, warm water travelers who cross into the cold water to feed on the abundance of boreal forage fish: squid, herring, and sandlance. They have charged slashing through the schools of herring, turned back and swallowed up the dozens of injured fish. Now they must warm themselves in the sun to jumpstart their metabolisms and digest their feed.

Out here near the edge—where ice-age rivers once cut deep canyons in the continental shelf: Oceanographer, Hydrographer, Corsair—the big fish, two hundred pounds and up, rise toward the light.

We want to meet them, to drive our sharp bronze darts through the fabric of each fish's tough skin, through the lean muscles of its back and into its guts. There the dart turns like a toggle firmly anchoring the fish to one hundred fathoms of three-eighths-inch line. Ten fathoms from the dart we hook a fifteen-pound steel weight that distracts the fish and keeps it from charging the boat. Halfway along the line we hook a small float; at the end, a large orange polyurethane ball, still anachronistically known as a keg, and a radar reflector, or "highflyer," marks the fish. The fish pulls all this through the water until it tires and dies.

Brad comes on deck and lights a smoke; he saunters aft. Out of the corner of my eye I see him with his back to me, knees braced against the lee rail as he pisses over the side. Bernard comes across the deck and steps up into the wheelhouse. He checks my course and the loran. I hear the chart table drop open behind me.

After a few moments: "Steer north by west."

I ease the spokes around, until the needle begins to drift and then counter back. Bernard watches me steady the new course. "Alright, you can go get your breakfast."

As I reach the doghouse, Brad cuts past and dives into the fo'c'sle ahead of me.

"The *Ocean Clipper* got a fish," he says to Spic.

"This early?"

"I just heard Bernard talking to Dickey Stinson."

Brad begins suiting up to climb aloft. He pulls insulated coveralls over his jeans and sweatshirt, puts on oilskin pants over that, grabs his hat, sunglasses, and cigarettes, and heads up the mast. Spic cranes his neck up to look out the doghouse. "What's Bernard doing?"

"Nothin."

He lights a one hit pipe and takes a long drag, holding the smoke in tight, before he relaxes. "You sure you don't want some."

"Nah."

"Might help ya spot a fish, Cap."

I shake my head. He springs up the ladder and follows Brad aloft.

"It's only seven o'clock," I say, looking up through the doghouse.

"You can't predict these fish," says Georg. "Sit down and eat. The *Ocean Clipper* keeps a man in the mast whenever it's light enough to see."

I bolt my eggs, and at an unheard of hour head up into the swaying rigging. I climb the tarred ratlines. Up the aluminum topmast, around the radio box, I keep looking up, conscious of every move.

"Where the hell you been anyway?" Brad looks away at the water, not wanting an answer, as I climb past and up onto my little perch at the top of the mast. By the time I reach it the roll of the boat is accentuated to the point that I am flying in twenty-foot arcs through the air as I hop over the aluminum ring and into my seat. Alone, I roll within a sphere of ocean and sky, supposedly looking for swordfish to kill. Below me Brad and Spic talk, and laugh. I watch the sea, mesmerized by the swirling blues and greens of the Northeast Peak, where warm waters of the south collide with the cold waters of the north.

"The edges are where you find the fish," Georg tells me. Though he did the cooking, and spent more time on deck than any of us, he also spotted the most fish. "You can't stick'm if you don't see'm."

I try to scan the ocean Georg's way, let my mind empty and see the whole picture. "You're looking for two crescent fins or a purple torpedo," he says. Everyone else has raised a few fish, but I am still dragging myself out of a reverie every few minutes and remembering to look. Exposed to the chill air and constant breeze, my sunglasses fog up; I clean them with a tissue, rubbing the lenses between numb fingers.

Sixty feet below us, the pulpit protrudes from the bow; the harpoon lashed alongside it. Bernard comes out and unties it. He repositions the eighteen-foot-long shaft across the safety rail, which runs around the end of the pulpit, and lashes it there, ready. And so *Irene* cruises, with her harpoon held out foremost, as if she carried it across the palm of her outstretched hand, offering it to a fish.

In the wheelhouse Bernard watches the temperature gauge. Most fish bask in water between sixty-one and sixty-three degrees. He listens to the VHF, scanning the channels to pick up the talk of other boats, such as the *Ocean Clipper.*

Dickey Stinson, captain of the *Ocean Clipper,* first went swordfishing with his grandfather out of Block Island, Rhode Island, when he was eight years old. His grandfather had moved from Maine to Block Island as a young man in the late 1800s, and helped start the swordfish fishery. Stinson knows as much as anyone about swordfish. He believes there are two groups of fish, the southern group that used to show up around Long Island, and is now virtually wiped out, and the northern group that shows up later in the summer on the northeast peak of Georges Bank. Bernard only started swordfishing in 1980, so he talks to Dickey, and reads books about the biology of the fish and the history of the fishery.

Georg trades books with Bernard. He gives me the highlights as we sit in the mast. "They used to harpoon the fish from a schooner; they'd go from fish to fish there were so many, and then set a man over in a dory to gather up the kegs; that made it easier for a boat under sail to keep going." According to Georg, the season used to start as early as June off Long Island. "But since the longliners have been fishing down south every year there's fewer and fewer fish," he says. The longline boats, promoted by NMFS in the 1960s, set out miles of line strung with baited hooks that catch fish of all sizes. The fleet follows the fish from the Gulf of Mexico to the Grand Banks. "They've been working the spawning grounds off Florida," says Georg, "killing the pups."

"I know," I say, glad for the chance to bring up the one swordfish I have spotted that summer. "I saw one in a fish market in Philadelphia when I was down there visiting. It was about two feet long without the sword. I said to the guy, 'that's a damn small swordfish,' and he says, 'that's a big one.' I told my brother we never stick anything under a hundred pounds, and most are a shitload bigger."

We cruise toward the northeast peak, headed for a small canyon known to fishermen as Fiddler's Cove. On the radio we can hear people talking in a strange language.

"What the hell is that?" I ask. "Chinese?"

"They're speaking Acadian French," says Georg.

Among the chatter one deep gravelly voice stands out, switching back and forth from Acadian to English. "That's Franklin d'Entremont," says Georg. "Everybody knows Franklin," he adds. "He used to fish on our side then he went home and taught all those guys."

The Canadian boats amaze us; we pass a forty-foot lobster boat with plywood nailed along the rails to keep the waves from swamping her, and a pulpit made out of nothing but a plank. A boy about twelve looks up at us from her deck. We wave and go our separate ways, searching for fish in the expansive waters of what we call the "gray zone," the northeastern area of Georges Bank where US and Canadian claims of jurisdiction overlap and both countries' fleets fish side by side.

"I'm waitin' to see a canoe," I say after passing a few more small boats.

"Those guys are closer to home than we are," Georg says of the Acadians. "They come out here in anything."

"Where do they fish out of?"

"Pubnico, down below Yarmouth."

If we get blown into Yarmouth, Nova Scotia, Georg tells me, there will be a big softball game. All the US fishermen play the Canadians for a trophy: a swordfish sword mounted on a plaque.

As Georg tells me about past games a streak of white and red screams out of the sky, shattering our conversation. Fred Brooks buzzes the Piper Cub two-seater around the boat a couple of times.

"Morning boys," he says over the VHF.

We watch the plane and wonder about his night ashore.

Brad grabs the mike out of the radio box. "Did you bring cigarettes?"

"I'll drop'm on the next pass."

The plane comes in low, a garbage bag drops out from under the wing, and splashes down ahead of the boat. Bernard, listening to the radio in the wheelhouse, comes out and gaffs the bag. On deck he opens it, shakes out a wet newspaper, and tosses the cigarettes in front of the doghouse. Fred heads out to fly his lazy circles around our perimeter.

"Now maybe we'll see some action," says Spic.

Days of no fish come often enough in swordfishing. We had seen a week of them already this trip, but with calm seas, good water temperatures, and the plane on hand, they particularly frustrate us. A few false alarms cut the tension in the mast. "Swordfish!" I holler.

"That's a shark," says Georg.

"So you want to be a flatlander but you don't know how to wear sandals eh by?" Brad mocks me with a parody of a National Sea Products commercial, done in a Newfoundland accent.

"Swor—!"

"Where?"

"It's gone."

"Got one over here Bernard. Two o'clock, thirty boat lengths." Fred's voice crackles over the VHF.

He's got a fish. Brad hauls down on the throttle and steering ropes, making a hard turn to starboard. The boat surges forward and Bernard comes out of the wheelhouse.

"Eleven o'clock, twenty-five boat lengths, she's pretty deep."

I drop down the ratlines onto deck and take my station along the starboard rail just forward of the mainmast shrouds. Twelve feet out on the end of the pulpit Bernard stands with his harpoon resting on the narrow railing that keeps him from falling overboard when he throws.

"Twelve o'clock, six boat lengths. She's deep," Fred's voice comes from a speaker lashed to the forestay behind Bernard.

We bear down. Standing on deck, I can see nothing until the last moment. Bernard swings his harpoon around, poised to throw, one hand on the very end, with two fingers capping the butt of the long shaft, his other arm stretches out as far as he can reach toward the point. He rests that forward hand, and the weight of the harpoon, on the rail. Two loops of line hang down from the harpoon and swing with the roll of the boat: one ties the shaft to the boat, the other runs from the dart, fitted on the end of the shaft, back through a series of clips along the pulpit to a milk crate holding one hundred fathoms of line.

"Twelve o'clock, three boat lengths."

By now Brad has visual contact and he lines Bernard up on the fish. "One boat length."

Bernard sees his target, a swordfish about eight feet long lolling beneath the surface. His whole body turns toward it as the harpoon comes up and he lets fly. He drives the dart deep into the fish just behind the dorsal fin. As the line snaps out of its clips toward me, I throw the fifteen-pound weight I have ready. The big fish dives toward it, attacking its perceived enemy, and not our boat. The line sings out over the side. I throw half the coils over and in the resulting slack moment, snap on a small poly ball; Fred's voice comes over the radio again: "I can see three fish right now Bernard. Ten o'clock, three boat lengths." I toss the rest of the coils overboard, followed by a large poly ball and a high flyer already tied to the line.

"Swordfish! Four o'clock!" Georg has one.

Out of the corner of my eye I see Spic land on deck. I run a new dart, trailing its line along the length of the pulpit, out to where Bernard stands, straightening his iron. Quickly I hook up another weight and check that the lines are running clear. Spic brings more poly balls and high flyers forward. Bernard swings the long harpoon around and readies for another throw. He hits the fish hard, and before the iron leaves his hand I can see the shock move up through his arm. The fish breaks the surface, spraying blood. I toss the weight, and heave the coils overboard.

"The fish chase the weight straight to bottom," Georg once told me. "We hauled one back once and its mouth and gills were full of mud. If they get out beyond the one-hundred-fathom edge you can kiss your gear good-bye. They'll take the whole works down."

The fish keep coming; Fred spots them from the plane, Brad and Georg from the mast. Spic and I race around on deck passing Bernard fresh darts, and rigging up the lines. Bernard stays cool, seeming to move in slow motion in comparison to us.

"I don't know what we're going to do about kegs if this keeps goin'," says Spic.

I pass him a line and he ties it to an old high-flyer with a chewed up Styrofoam float on it.

Bernard strikes another fish and I throw the weight. Spic tosses the poly ball and high flyer over while I carry another dart out to Bernard. The VHF speaker is quiet. Aloft, Brad and Georg are silent.

"Look at that." Spic points aft. The sea behind the boat is littered with bright orange balls and high flyers: fourteen fish in less than an hour. We finish the massacre with three rigs to spare.

In the aftermath, as I stow gear I hear people talking about fuel, and Nova Scotia. Brad comes down out of the mast.

"What's going on?"

"Fred's low on fuel, he's talking about going to Nova Scotia."

"How much closer is it?"

"He could trim about fifty miles off, but the wind's swingin' 'round to the east'ard. Counterclockwise too. You know what they say when the wind backs around counterclockwise."

In the end Fred chooses the tailwind for home.

The breeze picks up; choppy seas make the high flyers hard to spot as we start to haul the fish in. Only Georg stays in the mast. He continues to look for fish, and keeps an eye on our gear, now spreading in all directions under a darkening sky.

Bernard gaffs the first high flyer and passes me the line. He usually insists we haul by hand—less chance of pulling the dart out and losing the fish. I begin hauling; taking long pulls and gathering in the slack.

"Go ahead and use the hauler," says Bernard.

I bend the line into the groove of a hydraulic hauler set against the port side rail, and open the valve.

"Easy, we don't want to lose him."

The line flakes in loops into a milk crate.

"There it is."

I bring the fish thrashing alongside, and Spic slings a heavy rope around its tail and hooks it to the jilson. The line runs aloft through a single block and back down to Bernard. He takes the line a few turns around the winch head and hoists the sleek giant up out of the water. It swings above us and in over the rail. As soon as the fish lands, I grab the sword and cut it off with a saw. Spic drives an ax into its throat and blood spurts across the deck. I saw down across the back of the fish's head while Spic chops off the fins and tail. Together we roll the big fish belly up and I begin to open it. Spic goes for another fish Brad and Bernard have hoisted aboard. I straddle the fish and with a sharp knife I begin a slit at the throat. As soon as I cut enough down toward the anal vent I reach in under the knife to hold the lining of the guts out of the way, carefully opening the belly. I make a cut around the anal vent, so as not to nick the intestines and have that mess to clean up. I run my hands down around the guts, loosening them from the body; feeling for the dart, which I pull out and retie to the line. I then twist the head off with the innards trailing it.

"Open his stomach up and see what he had for dinner," says Bernard, watching me from the winch head. I cut open the guts and long thin fish spill onto the deck, exuding a tangy smell of bile.

"What are these?" I ask, looking at them.

"Sandlance."

In the pile of guts I see the heart, still beating. I pick it up and hold it in my hand, feeling its ebbing pulse the life of the fish.

"If you want to be a swordfisherman, you've gotta eat the heart of the beast," says Brad, noticing me.

I hand it to him and he takes it down forward.

Bits of guts spill out the scuppers, and fulmars, larger cousins of the petrels, float close alongside, gobbling them up, paddling hard to stay near the bounty. Spic and I offer slivers of fish to the silent white and gray birds, and they take them from our hands. This close, we look at their strange beaks, their tubular nostrils.

"Why do you suppose they're like that?"

"Beats me."

The roll of the boat continues to increase throughout the late afternoon; the fish on deck have to be slid aft and jammed between the rail and the wheelhouse. Brad opens the hatch and climbs down into the hold. One by one we lower the carcasses to him, weighing them as we do and calling the weights to Bernard who writes them down. By evening Brad has the fish all entombed in ice.

With the decks cleared we pound into a head sea from the northeast, hunting down the last two high flyers lost in the deepening night. The staysail, stretched between the main mast and the wheelhouse, snaps loudly back and forth.

After an hour the boat slows and the decklights come on. Bernard appears from out of the wheelhouse. He scoops up the gaff, stretches it out into the darkness, and snags a high flyer. Spic lifts the rig out of the water. Bernard hauls on the line. I get behind him and together we lean back hauling on the wet rope. Seawater dripping from our knuckles, we gather in the slack, and haul back again, until the fish comes to the surface. Spic lassoes the tail and I hook up the sling. The fish comes out of the water heavy. Its smooth skin scraped from the bottom.

"What'd you think of that, Cap?" asks Spic.

"Man."

Spic and I dress the fish quickly and lower it into the hold. Brad jumps down, shoves some ice into its belly, kicks a little more around it, and that's it. He climbs out and goes aft to talk to Bernard while we fit the hatch covers.

With everything tight, Spic and I dig out our cigarettes. He has his lighter out first and lights mine. We stand there savoring the moment, looking out into the darkness for the last high flyer.

Brad comes forward with a heavy tarp and drops it on the hatch. Spic and I get the message and lash it down.

"Bernard wants to get the parachute ready," Brad tells us.

That and the growing waves give us our weather report. Bernard has brought a new parachute in case we have to lay to in heavy seas. The open parachute dragging heavily through the water will act as a sea anchor, holding our bow into the wind and oncoming waves.

We continue searching for our last high flyer: out there somewhere, marking a big fish, dead by now, dragging blindly along bottom. I think of a man in his dory, with the fish lashed alongside, an oar up, waiting in the dark for us to come find him; the growing black seas lift him with humble certainty.

We go below. "I heard the Canadian forecast," says Spic. "They're calling for fifty- to sixty-knot winds with higher gusts."

"Surf's up, Moondog."

Georg comes down into the fo'c'sle. "Braddy, Bernard wants to set the parachute, and set up a lifeline."

"What ails him, that fucking parachute ain't going to hold this boat." Brad and Spic go on deck and we hear them thumping over our heads as they set out the sea anchor and make it fast to the bow cleat. They then run a line from the doghouse to the wheelhouse, so we can go back and forth with something to hang on to.

The boat swings around and comes tight on the anchor, the rolling stops, and we ride over the waves smooth and steady. The six hundred feet of nylon line to the parachute acts as a shock absorber. Bernard kills the engine, and we can hear the wind.

Spic's watch starts at ten; the rest of us turn in. "Somebody put the aluminum foil on the light."

Spic wraps a piece of foil around the bare bulb, and in the darkened fo'c'sle we lie listening to the wind picking up in the rigging. Brad comes below and Spic goes up the ladder to stand watch.

I wake up a little while later to the sound of voices. Someone strips the aluminum foil off the light. The boat rolls violently and I wedge myself into the bunk to keep from sliding out. *Irene* lays down hard to port on every roll and never comes all the way back. Bernard has the engine running and we can feel him bringing the bow up into the waves.

I crawl out of my bunk.

"The parachute broke."

"No shit."

"I told him that piece of shit wouldn't hold us. For Christ's sake, Bernard."

"What time is it?"

"Almost midnight," says Spic. "I was about to wake you up."

"Is the water hot?"

"No, the stove's off."

"Is the Lister on?"

"No."

"Shit."

"Forget your fuckin' coffee. Come on, get the parachute in."

On deck Spic and Brad start to haul in the parachute line as Bernard jogs forward. I coil the sodden hauser into a box lashed along the starboard rail. Cold spray blasts in over the rail and slaps the pillow warmth off my face.

The parachute comes aboard in silky shreds, literally blown to pieces from the strain of the boat. We stow the remains in a box lashed to the portside rail and go below as the boat climbs steadily over the mounting seas.

The auxiliary engine starts—I brew my coffee in the electric kettle, but spill most of it trying to make my way aft across the canting deck. In the wheelhouse, Bernard hunches over the chart table, plotting a run somewhere. Spic stands at the wheel, trying to keep the bow into the seas, occasionally getting blindsided and rolled.

"Okay, Spic."

"She's all yours," he says, and slides out the lee door as I step into the wheelhouse.

I check the radar. Blips and storm scatter flash all over the screen, but no lights show around us. Outside the rails of the boat, uniform darkness surrounds us. The sea and sky, rain and wave form one black roiling mass.

Bernard reaches up and adjusts the throttle. He takes the wheel and in a lull turns the boat around. He puts us on a course running ahead of the storm.

"West-southwest," he says, stepping away from the wheel.

I glance at the chart: we are heading for Cape Cod and it looks like a tight squeeze. In order to get around Nantucket shoals, Bernard quarters the waves rolling in out of the east as close as he dares. The waves roll into our port quarter, some hitting us a little closer to broadside. "If you see a big one coming turn away from it," he says.

If I see a big one? I can't see shit. I can only feel a big sea lift us from behind and turn us sickeningly as if it will roll us, our great high mast now acting as a lever to heel us even further over and hold us there indefinitely.

Heeled over like that in a cross sea, the green water pours across the deck driving the lee rail out of sight. The boat spends more time under water than out. Bernard sleeps: *Irene* will find her way.

Later in the night, I see Brad come up out of the doghouse. He stands there with a cigarette hanging out of his mouth watching for his chance. In a lull he weaves his way down the deck to the lee rail and starts to piss over the side.

A big one picks us up, I can feel the boat accelerate as the wave gets a hold of her and drives us into a cross sea that crests the bow and sweeps the deck with a three-foot wall of water. I hold the wheel until it passes and then look out the door for Brad. Gone. I turn to holler, "Ber—" but stop short. In the open porthole at the back of the wheelhouse, above Bernard's bunk, eight white fingers show.

Brad lets go and comes around next to me.

"I thought you were gone."

"Nah." He looks at the compass. "Where you going?"

"Who knows?"

Brad waits his chance again and runs forward, vanishing into the dimly lit fo'c'sle.

I stand alone at the helm, glancing at the clock, and out across the deck. Whips of windblown spray stream out of the black, through the meager light on deck, and back into the rich darkness—glimpses of nocturnal waves.

Another big one starts to lift us, I spin the wheel down hard to starboard, but the stern rises and twists sickeningly broadside again, burying the starboard rail; the great mast heels us down.

I hear Bernard shift in his bunk behind me as the big sea loses its grip and rolls past.

"It's almost your watch, Bernard, do you want me to get you anything?"

It is our custom for the man who stands watch before Bernard to bring him a soda or coffee. Tonight I only want to get forward into my snug bunk and let the storm rage on.

Bernard gets up, checks the gauges and compass, and takes the wheel. "You could get us a better place to be," he says.

"Maybe." I stand back and look at the chart. "So where we going?"

"Same way we been going, only further."

"Looks like we're headed around the Cape."

"Well, maybe that's a good idea, better than staying here."

In spite of Bernard's ambiguous answers, I am reluctant to leave. I light a cigarette and jam myself in the leeside door, feeling the occasional warm blasts of tropical air waft over us. Bernard stands at the wheel and squints out past the bow, in concentration.

"You can learn a lot by watching," says the little plaque above him, but I have been watching him all summer and still don't know much about him. "So did you grow up in Owls Head?" I ask as a wave lifts us and Bernard rolls the wheel hard down to leeward.

"No, I grew up on Matinicus."

"Were you born out there?"

"No. I was born on Vinalhaven," he pauses, glances at the rocking compass, and to my surprise adds, "on the Fourth of July, but I never heard a sound." Holding the frame of the door, I cough and laugh as he, in rare form, continues. "I can't remember much about the time I was born, but a couple of years later I realized I was on the island."

A wave slams into the side of the boat and spray smacks across the windows. Water streams down the panes, reflecting the red light of the compass in its binnacle.

"Your mother must've been there—when you were born."

"Well, I think so, but I can't remember. It might've been her, could've been somebody else. I don't know."

I laugh again, wondering why he still lets me come fishing with him when I have not spotted a fish all season. The boat lays over hard to starboard, and I grab the doorjamb quickly to keep from falling.

"Did you go fishing with your father?" I ask.

"Some, mostly I fished with my grandfather, Dalton," he says as *Irene* pulls herself back up.

"Did he build his own boat?"

"Most everyone did."

Waves continue to pound us. We can hear the wind-driven spray hit the staysail like buckshot, but we hang on, dry and safe in the dimly lit wheelhouse.

"Was it a dory?"

"No, my great-grandfather Horace was the last to go dory fishing. There were three boats started taking dories to the Grand Banks out of Belfast. Horace got on with them and stayed with them for years. Grandfather had an open boat with a rounded hull."

"Like they use on the south coast of Newfoundland."

"Something like that."

I flick my cigarette out into the black; its little red spark vanishes in the turmoil. At four in the morning Bernard's watch ends, but I take the wheel rather than leave him while he's in the mood to talk.

Foaming green waves continue to roll in over the bow, washing the length of the boat. I imagine a boat of my own—something very much like *Irene,* maybe a little bigger.

"I think about getting a boat," I say. "But I don't know. Things don't look good. It seems like when I first started there were a few fish around, now it seems like things get worse every year. I don't know, but it don't look too good for the future."

"You were Catholic weren't you?" Bernard asks.

"I don't think I became un-Catholic just 'cuz I stopped going to Church."

"You must have heard of Our Lady of Fatima?"

"Yeah."

In the wheelhouse, now lit only by the red light of the compass binnacle and the green glow of the radar and loran, Bernard talked about the prophecies of Our Lady of Fatima. The Virgin Mary had appeared several times to three children in Fatima, a small village in central Portugal, and spoken with them. Catholic clergy interviewed the children, and the message Mary left remains a church secret, but Bernard offers what he knows.

"They don't say exactly what she said, but in the next five years there are going to be some changes. They've already begun. What they are we don't know," says Bernard. "But they're not going to be good."

In the end of the night we stop talking. No seas have washed the deck in the last half hour. I roll the spokes back and forth delicately, holding our course, thinking, I don't need the Lady of Fatima to tell me things are getting worse. But it's nice to be in good company in that prediction.

At dawn Bernard takes the wheel and turns back northeast into the rising sun. To the west we see the thin line of Nantucket on the horizon. In the fo'c'sle Georg cooks the swordfish heart for breakfast and I sit down to eat it.

Sitting there chewing relentlessly on the tough swordfish heart, I look up at the staysail and its blue emblem. "What's with the scallop shell on the sail Georg?"

"Eleanor and the girls had that made for Bernard after we hit the scallops out on Cashes."

"Oh, yeah? When was that?"

"Nineteen seventy-eight. Bernard went down there looking around and started finding a few, next thing you know he had her deckloaded. My friend Donald Pelrine—you know Donald—he was with him and he brought me aboard to cook. It was amazing," Georg says. His eyes sparkle with the memory as he pours a coffee and sits down across from me. "We had the boat packed. There were guys without bunks sleeping in the engine room or taking turns in one bunk. Not that we did much sleeping. We used to come in shell stocked, scallops piled between the rails, and the shuckers would be lined up on the dock waiting for us. That's how Brad started with us; he came on as a shucker. They'd come aboard and start helping us cut, we'd have the music going; it was great. We had'm all to ourselves for two years. We were all makin' money, till the big boats found us."

Eight

THE *SEA TREK*

In early May of 1978, the *Irene & Alton* floated over deep ocean swells, anchored by her dredge above Cashes Ledge as the crew shucked a deck load of scallops. A rising wind blew out of the east and patchy rain reduced visibility to less than a mile. Bernard, in the wheelhouse, watched two small blips on his radar. He could tell that they were fishing boats by their erratic movements. Gradually they drew nearer, and Bernard kept his eye on the obscured horizon. After a few hours two lobster boats hove into sight.

Bernard pulled down the mike from the VHF mounted above the wheelhouse windows and tried to make contact on a working channel. "This is the *Irene & Alton* to the two lobster boats there. You fellas lost? Over."

A minute later a voice came over the speaker. "No, we come down to set some trawls."

"It was some fellas from Friendship come all the way down there in their lobster boats to set halibut trawl," Bernard recalled later, filling in the blanks of a story Georg had told. "One was about forty feet, and the other was a bit smaller, and they had extra fuel barrels on deck.

"The wind come northeast, and it started to blow that night. By the next morning, there was a pretty good sea on. I told'm we was going to head in to Provincetown, and they didn't even know where that was. They said they was going to head for home, but it was blowing about forty, and they was pounding right into it."

As the crew lashed down the dredges and Bernard headed the *Irene & Alton* south, they watched the two lobster boats recede: the smaller one struggling in the lee of the bigger one as they climbed over fifteen-foot seas.

An hour after the boats parted company, Bernard looked at his loran and radar. He had traveled almost ten miles from where he last saw the lobster boats, but on his radar the blips showed inside his ten mile ring. The small boats had lost ground to the wind and waves. He called them again.

"How you fellas makin' out? Over."

"Not too good. A big one took out our windows."

"Well, I can tell you, you ain't gettin' anywhere. I been watching you. I got a loran on board and you've lost ground by what I can see. Over."

After a long silence they called back.

"Where the hell you say you was goin'?"

"Provincetown, over."

"I guess we better follow you then."

"We'll lay to until you get here."

An hour later the two boats appeared on top of a distant wave and surfed down the front of it out of sight, appearing again on the crest of the next one. Gradually they made their way toward the *Irene & Alton* and the three boats steamed on together, running ahead of the wind. By suppertime they reached the shelter of Provincetown Harbor, and the smaller boats rafted outside Bernard. Georg had cooked them a big dinner, figuring they'd be tired and hungry, but they walked straight across the *Irene & Alton* s deck and up the wharf to the bar.

"I guess they needed a drink more," Bernard said to Georg.

Back on Cashes after that spring storm, Bernard hunted for a productive bed of scallops. Using his sounding machine for reference, Bernard formed a mental image of the bottom. He worked to stay along the thirty-fathom contour he visualized, and the crew noticed the dredges producing more as Bernard homed in on the scallops.

Glenn Lawrence put the winch in gear and began to wind in the wire. He looked at Donald Pelrine, standing by the gallows ready to hook the dredge. Water snapped out of the tight wire as it passed through the bollard, and the boat leaned over with the load. Both raised their eyebrows in a signal of anticipation.

When the dredge rose above the rail, the bag bulged with orange and white scallop shells. They dumped it and ten bushels of big scallops spilled across the deck, some still snapping their shells together in a vain effort to escape. The port side dredge yielded another big pile.

They put the dredges back on the rail. At the ring of the bell Donald and Bernard's Uncle Deke knocked them loose. "Stay on that tow," they hollered toward the wheelhouse, as they grabbed baskets and waded into the pile of clean scallops.

"We found we was getting them in a certain temperature of water at about the twenty-eight to thirty fathoms," Bernard said as we rehashed the old days one evening in his kitchen. "Scallops float around awhile after they hatch, then settle to bottom, some was higher, some was lower, but most of them were where the bottom met that layer of water. No matter where we went, Fippenies, Jeffries, we was gettin'm in that layer. The gillnetters put us on to'm down on Cashes, 'cuz they were gettin'm in their nets there was so many. They didn't say nothin' to nobody else and we didn't say nothing. We had that all to ourselves for two seasons.

"But then late in the second year one of them southern boats come by on their way to Canada to buy swordfish or something, and they come over to us 'cuz they needed cigarettes, or our boys needed cigarettes. Anyway, they come right alongside and saw what was going on.

"We finished up that season alright, but when we went back the next year those Portland boats had heard about it and fished there all winter, and there wasn't much left."

Bernard made a couple of average trips before he found another little hot spot: a thirty-fathom hole only a couple of miles long, packed with scallops.

"We filled the hold and deckloaded her in a day, and came in. It took about three days to get that mess cleaned up—all cut and sold—and then we headed right back out there. On the third time out the fog had come in."

Working fogbound, Bernard kept glancing from the loran to the depth sounder; trying to stay on the tow, the path he had established along the narrow contour the scallops seemed to prefer. He checked the radar, and noticed a blip, but ignored it; figuring it must be a gillnetter or another lobster boat chasing halibut. As the boat plowed along, Bernard listened to the familiar clatter of shells above the hammering of his engine, and concentrated on staying in the thirty-fathom hole. He looked at the radar again, the blip had grown much larger than anything made by a lobster boat, and was moving directly towards him. "Shit."

Bernard slowed the engine and rang the bell to signal a haul back. In a minute Glenn had the winch in gear and the drums rolling, winding in the dredges. Even with the abbreviated tow, when they raised the dredges, the full bags of scallops hung in the air like billboard advertisements, just as a one-hundred-foot black scallop boat burst out of the fog.

"I shoulda got out of that hole as soon as I saw that blip, but I didn't," said Bernard. Pretty soon here comes Dougie Anderson with Pete Kelly's boat—the *Sea Trek*. She's one scallop killer, that *Sea Trek*—big fifteen-foot drags on both sides. He come out of the fog and saw what we had. He followed our wake back to that hole, and set out his drags."

Bernard made his log entry for Wednesday, May 28, 1980: "Wed . . . Doug Anderson set on us and ruined the tow." The following day: "Thurs . . . moved to the NW a little." And the next day, after his catch dropped from around 1,500 pounds a day to 400: "Fri 30 . . . Hunted around Breeze at sundown—inbound."

Doug Anderson, and the more aggressive fishermen of the day, thought they could do better running company boats, than they could fishing on their own. But guys like Doug had to accept a tradeoff. The company boats offered more in terms of size and technological advances, but the absentee owners demanded a high return on their investments.

By the time Doug set his dredges in Bernard's last little honey hole, both knew the score. Doug had to fill his hold; if he didn't, the *Sea Trek*'s owner would find someone who would. With his larger, heavier boat, Doug muscled Bernard off the tow and took the scallops.

"Word had got around that Bernard had a couple good trips out there. We went out looking for him, and found him," Doug recalled twenty-three years later. "I probably shouldn't have done it, but I had a boat to fill, and a crew breathing down my neck; the guys were saying, 'Get over there, they're gettin'm over there.'"

A game that had always been competitive gradually became more cutthroat.

"We took our load in and came back as fast as we could, but there wasn't a scallop left there," said Bernard. "We could have got two or three more trips out of that hole, but he cleaned it in one day."

The Stratton Commission only re-articulated what had been the goal of post–World War II fisheries development: economic efficiency. In 1960 Congress had established the Fishing Vessel Construction Differential Program, a subsidy program that compensated for the fact that US fishermen must use US-built boats, when they could probably buy them cheaper abroad. In 1967 the Bureau of Commercial Fisheries (BCF) approved $4.2 million in subsidies, which covered 40 to 50 percent of the construction costs for qualified vessels. The *Sea Trek* qualified for the program and was built that year at the Fuller boatyard in Boothbay Harbor, Maine. Although the exact figure is not available, her original owner, Norm Lapire of Lakewood, MA, would have received somewhere between $60,000 and $100,000 from the program.

The program criteria stipulated that an approved vessel "must be of advance design, which will enable it to operate in an expanded area, and be equipped with newly developed gear, and that it will not operate in a fishery if such operations would cause economic hardship to efficient vessel operators already operating in that fishery." Although made of wood, the *Sea Trek* contained what in her day were advances in design, including watertight bulkheads, AC power, split fish holds, and an advanced pumping system.

Norm Lapire originally set the *Sea Trek* up as a fish dragger, but the foreign boats had hammered the northeast groundfish stocks and he could not make it pay. In 1968, when Georges Bank groundfish landings dropped to seventy-four thousand tons—half of what they were in 1930—he sold the boat to Roy Enoksen of New Bedford, who rigged her over for scallops.

"She cost me two hundred thousand, and I put twenty thousand into her," said Enoksen. "I'll never forget it." It was Enoksen's first boat.

Norm Lapire went on to captain a New Bedford scalloper, the *Navigator,* and was lost with his twelve crewmen in December 1977. The *New Bedford Standard Times* reported the story on Monday, December 12, 1977:

The vessel was last heard from last Wednesday when she was in radio contact with the scalloper Oceanic . . . *The* Navigator *was expected to return to port on Friday after a ten-day fishing trip. She was reported overdue by her owner on Saturday afternoon . . . The Coast Guard official said the weather in the search area this morning included snow flurries, winds up to twenty-five knots and five-foot seas. The weather conditions Thursday through Sunday had been much rougher, with twenty-five to forty knot winds, seas up of fifteen feet, snow and snow flurries . . .*

The Coast Guard official, Dale Gardner, refused to call the vessel presumed lost. "We don't know," he told the *Standard Times*. "We haven't found any debris. It's hard to say what if anything has happened."

Two days later the Coast Guard called off the search after finding no trace of the *Navigator*.

"I was running the *Pocahontas* at the time," said Doug Anderson. "Norm was fighting for his job in them days."

According to Doug, the *Navigator* was one of six boats owned by Myron Marder. "When you worked in the Marder fleet it was pretty competitive, and Norm was getting beat by three or four thousand pounds every trip.

"We were shell stocking at the time," said Doug—the crew shucked what they could but brought most of the scallops in whole. Boatloads came in to New Bedford daily. They loaded un-shucked scallops onto tractor-trailers that trucked them to places like Lund's in Cape May. I might have been shucking some of Doug's scallops. Boatloads came in almost daily.

"We were rounding'm up on deck from rail to rail," said Doug. "Every tow we'd send the boys up to throw rocks over, it was awful rocky in the channel in those days." The rocks made the boat top-heavy, and Doug recalled that he had to pay close attention to the amount of weight on deck.

"The trip before, about five guys had left the *Navigator*, and come with me. They said Norm wouldn't let them go forward to throw rocks. He thought it took too much time away from the cutting box. He said the boys could throw rocks when they went up to pick the pile, until then, leave'm there. They told him he couldn't keep doing that, and they got done.

"I saw Norm the day before he disappeared. He was fishing sou'west of us near round shoal channel. It blew around thirty to forty that night, Norm steamed to the south'ard; we went up to the north'ard. When morning came, they were gone. I think he rolled her over in the night."

"We were down there, too," said Bernard, when I asked him about it later. "Fishing what they called 'The Channel.' I seen the *Navigator* just before dark."

Norm Lapire died, but the *Sea Trek* went on, and continued to attract the best fishermen on the coast.

For Doug Anderson, his own evolution within the industry could be expressed in one concept. "It was the money," he said that persuaded him to give up his own small boat and head for the scallop beds off Cape Cod.

Doug came from a background similar to Bernard's. "My grandfather and his people were all dory fishermen," he said. "My grandfather had two tubs of trawl like the rest, but he was one of the first to go dragging. He started around the same time Alton did. He had a twenty-eight-foot boat with a Model A engine in it. It held exactly twenty-eight hundred pounds of fish. He'd head out and fish all morning till he got that, then he'd come in. He'd take off the doors and net to lighten her up, gas up and put an extra can aboard, and then steam ten hours to Portland to sell at Burnham and Morrill. He'd steam all night, he told me, and he'd hold a five-pound dory anchor in his hand. If he started to fall asleep, he'd drop the anchor and that would wake him up."

Doug could have stayed home and fished the local waters his family knew, but he walked away from that for a chance to be on the cutting edge of the nation's technologically advanced fleet. "I had big dreams back then. I'd heard about Georges Bank and there was this mystique about it and I wanted to go. I was twenty-five and Georges Bank was like a magnet drawing me down there. And there was the ego; I'd hear about these big shot captains and I wanted to be one.

"I took Alton's old boat, the *Ethel B.*, down there in 1976. We were shell stocking, running into Provincetown. We were living crazy down there for six months. I brought her back in December, and a couple months later I got a call that Jimmy Downey was looking for a mate aboard the *Blue Sea*. I said sure, I'll go mate. Next trip he asked me if I wanted her. I said, sure. She was seventy-five feet, an old sled built in Waldoboro, Maine in 1933."

Doug fished the old boat successfully and rose to better ones: the *Pocahontas,* and the renowned *Sea Trek.* He got his wish and became a big shot captain. I wish I could say I saved some of the money from those days," he said. "But they say the harder you work the harder you play, and it's all gone."

Men like Doug, Norm Lapire, and Roy Enoksen, who built a substantial fleet, fit the mold formed by the drive for economic efficiency. What happened between Bernard and Doug on Cashes Ledge fulfilled the intention of the policies that subsidized boats like the *Sea Trek*. The resource was being re-allocated to the more efficient fishermen, efficiency meaning those who could harvest it the fastest.

If Bernard had been a businessman first and a fisherman second he would have sold his boat the minute the weather got to be too much for her, and bought a bigger one so he could fish all winter. By utilizing the Capital Construction Fund, another subsidy designed to upgrade the fleet, he would have avoided paying any capital gains taxes.

"Maybe we were foolish," he said in retrospect. "I thought about getting a bigger boat so I could fish winters on Cashes. But I liked the way this was working and we didn't want to be out there in the middle of winter."

With his choices, Bernard identified himself as one of the Stratton Commission's fishermen who "may be perfectly aware that a half a dozen modern, efficient ships could harvest the permissible crop with high monetary return, but they still may prefer a system under which a number of families can eke out what, to them, is an adequate living of the kind they prefer."

Bernard trusted that there would always be something to turn to in the sea. When scalloping slumped in the early 1980s, he took the surplus from his bonanza years and rigged over for swordfishing.

In spite of a push by the NMFS to open up and expand the longlining sector of the swordfish fleet, Bernard set his operation up for harpooning; a hundred-year-old New England tradition. He traveled to Point Judith, Rhode Island and talked with the experts, Dickey Stinson and Chet Westcott.

"I got the design for the mast and the pulpit from the Westcotts," said Bernard. "And they showed me how to rig the rest of the gear up."

After I joined Bernard in 1983 I seldom missed a trip swordfishing. I spent the winters going to school at the University of Rhode Island, and fishing aboard groundfish draggers out of Point Judith. I learned how to write a business plan from an old Norwegian economist at URI, Andreas

Holmsen, and during shrimp season, from December to late March, I would drive up to Maine every week, load up Bernard's shrimp, and sell them all around Rhode Island. I made more than the crew, but I didn't tell them that. Every June I'd be back in Owls Head, tarring the rigging of the *Irene & Alton*, and hoping to spot a fish.

Nine

SWORDFISH! (REPRISE) 1985

The *Irene & Alton* steams ahead through choppy seas and patchy fog. Every surface of the boat shines slick from what might be called a heavy mist or a light drizzle. As Bernard comes up from breakfast and makes his way back to the wheelhouse, the droplets collect on him, coating his clothes and hat in silver gray beads before soaking in.

At the helm I continue to steer while he checks the chart and the loran. He looks at the radar, a few blips show in the outer rings; they have been there all morning. "Probably scallopers, fishing up against the Canadian line," he says and stands in the door surveying the day's prospects. Not good—on days like this we often shut the engine down and drift, periodically steaming to maintain our position. We usually make a big pot of coffee, turn on some music, and play cards in the fo'c'sle all day.

Bernard looks up at the mast; my empty seat at the top is visible through the haze.

"Ain't going to see much from up there today," I suggest.

"Well, I suppose you fellas ought to go on up and try it."

After three days we have yet to see a fin, and after three years in the mast I am still searching for my first fish. I spotted a bluefin tuna the trip before, and Bernard harpooned it, but the swordfish continue to elude me.

In early August 1985 fewer big fish bask near the surface on Georges, and we have fewer places to look for them. The "gray zone" where we fished together with Franklin d'Entremont and the other Canadians has disappeared. The US and Canada had taken their boundary dispute to the World Court at The Hague in 1984. Predictably, the World Court split the difference, establishing a new boundary that gave Canada the Northeast Peak of Georges Bank—and Fiddlers Cove, where Bernard once struck fourteen fish in an hour.

The big fish that used to fin on Georges Bank have grown scarce. Most have crossed the new Hague Line into Canada. On their circuit of the North Atlantic, they migrate across the Grand Banks, farther east to Spain and then back to the Caribbean and Gulf of Mexico, where the long-line fishery has expanded over the last two decades, subsidized by federal research. Scientists from the Bureau of Commercial Fisheries (BCF), and later NMFS, prospected around the Gulf and Caribbean, discovered concentrations of swordfish, and encouraged fishermen to rig up for longlining. (But longlining takes the big and the small. Landings peaked in 1982, and the number and average size of the fish have been declining for several years.) We will have to work for every fish.

Down forward, I put on an extra sweater and my raingear. "Going to be shitty up there today," I say to Buddy Ripley, who has come aboard since Brad decided to take the rest of the summer off. Georg and Spic have gone too: Spic figured he could make more money clamming, and Georg has taken a job as an observer for the National Marine Fisheries Service; he works aboard Japanese tuna boats fishing in US waters.

Looking up toward my seat, I slowly climb the wet ratlines, maneuvering around the crosstree in my bulky clothes. The higher I go, the windier it gets, and the mast snaps back from every roll on the steep waves. Halfway up the topmast I reach for the next rope. In the moment I take hold of the wet line, the boat heels over. Before I can get my other hand up, a gust of wind grabs me and I lose my footing. For a moment I hang there one-handed, looking down between my feet at the dark ocean. When the boat rolls back I catch the mast and hug it, waiting for my heart to slow down before I resume my ascent. Once in my seat I strap on the often ignored safety line and hunker down to light a cigarette.

One by one the rest of the crew make their way up the mast. In their orange slickers and oil pants, I only recognize them by where they sit in the mast. Buddy comes up after me, and takes Brad's spot at the steering station. Joe Bray, a lobsterman from Owls Head, follows and takes Spic's spot on the port side, and the new cook, an old merchant mariner named John, comes up last. All of us silent, the radio crackles intermittently, as we look out into the fog.

"Gonna have to run right over'm," Buddy finally says, but no one replies.

After three hours the drizzle turns to rain, and when we go down for lunch Bernard tells us not to go up again. We start watches and Bernard stays down forward and plays a few hands of spades with us.

The sky clears that night, and late in my watch John comes up and points out dozens of constellations: Orion has come more into view; it is late in the season.

In the morning, sunlight shows through the skylight. I lay in my bunk looking up at it. The boat rolls quietly on a calm sea, and I look around the vacant fo'c'sle. Whoever has the watch must be on deck. I roll out fully dressed and pull my socks from the foot of my bunk. John lays silent in the bunk above mine, and I shake him awake. "Breakfast," I say, and climb up on deck as Buddy comes back down.

The first rays of the sun cut across the flat sea. I can see Bernard moving around in the wheelhouse and I walk back aft.

"Good morning, Mr. Paul."

"Mornin'."

"I was talking to Georg last night," he says. "He's on one a them Japanese boats working out in the deep water off here."

"No kidding. What'd he say?"

"I guess they was doing okay, he said he's been aboard her for almost a month and they was gonna put him ashore in Halifax."

I miss Georg, and I smile at the thought that he is still out here with us, in a way.

After breakfast we all climb the mast and look out over the sparkling sea.

"Freddy ought to be here today," said Buddy, hoping for the spotter plane.

"No," I tell him. "Bernard says it's still foggy ashore."

"Shit. What the hell's he got a plane for if we can't use it?" Fred gets a full share, no matter how many days he flies.

The sea around us looks tropical blue. Bernard has found a warm core eddy, spun off from the Gulf Stream, and it teems with life. First thing in the morning we watch a turtle swim by.

"Probably a loggerhead," I say, having taken Georg's place as species identifier.

Simultaneously Joe and I spot fins in the distance. "What's that?" he asks.

"Looks like a shark," I say. "But we got market for it, only sixty-five cents a pound but it's better than nothing. Head over there, Buddy."

"Shark! Bernard!"

Bernard comes forward from the wheelhouse and climbs out onto the pulpit. He unlashes his iron and holds it there on the rail.

"Hammerhead. Four boat lengths, dead ahead." I drop down out of the rigging and land on deck ready to toss the weight. Bernard is right-handed, and at the last minute Buddy turns the boat a bit to port to give him a clear throw on the starboard side.

I watch Bernard drive the harpoon down into the water, and the line tears out of its clips along the pulpit, snapping its way toward me. I see the shark thrashing powerfully next to the boat as I throw the weight. The line sizzles out over the rail; I toss the coils over, snap on the buoy, toss the rest of the rig, and watch it go.

Bernard puts a new dart on his harpoon and lashes her to the rail. He has a little swing seat that he clips in place when he wants to stay in the pulpit. He sets it up and sits down. Leaning on his harpoon he looks like he's praying.

We haul the shark back quickly so that it does not foul the gear. On deck it thrashes between the rail and the hatch cover until Buddy gets hold of the rope around its tail and lifts it while I beat its hammerhead with a hammer. Bernard has market for mako sharks, but without its head and fins the hammerhead and most other sharks look like makos.

Over the next three days searching that core we harpoon a variety of sharks—and we see more sea life in one place than I have in three years. An ocean sunfish, *Mola mola,* a tailless fish the size of a barn door, flaps clumsily on its side near the surface. They say the apparently helpless sunfish have such a foul taste that the sharks leave them alone.

We continue on in our search; sea turtles—loggerheads—swim in the current. And whales. At one point we find a fifty-foot fin whale swimming alongside us. Lashed to the pulpit, the long point of the harpoon sticks out into the air above its rising back. Bernard stands looking down as the blowhole breaks the surface beneath him. Hot vapor bursts from the nostrils and salt water sprays over the pulpit as the whale baptizes Bernard with its spout.

He shakes his head and turns. "That fella's got bad breath," he calls to us. High above him in the mast, we are all laughing.

From my seat above everyone else I see a cloud of pink trailing behind the whale. "Look," I called down. "What's that?"

Bernard looks at me from the pulpit. "They gotta poop, you know."

On another occasion we spot a pair of humpbacks, a mother and calf breaching; their black bodies and white fins bursting from the water and crashing down again in a shower of spray.

"When we were down to Block Island last trip we saw basking sharks doing that," I say. "I think they were spawning 'cuz one of them started chasing the boat. I don't know if he was horny for us or pissed off 'cuz we got in his way."

As we get closer to the humpbacks I watch from above as the mother opens her huge mouth, like a big balloon, around a mass of krill near the surface.

Later we see some unusual looking whales in the distance; when they blow, their spouts angle forward. I have read *Moby-Dick* enough to make a guess. "I think those are sperm whales."

From the mast, Buddy steers us over for a look, and as we approach Bernard runs aft to take the boat out of gear. We drift toward the whales and they float tail down with their heads up out of the water, their jaws facing us.

"Spy-hoppers," I say. "That's the only way they can get binocular vision is when they look at us past their jaws like that."

After we appraise each other for several minutes, the whales begin to sink slowly out of sight. From the mast we watch their forms growing fainter and fainter in the depths.

After supper the sea lies calm. I go out to the end of the pulpit, hook the seat up, and sit in it. A whale blows in the distance. I look for its spout or long black back rolling out of the water, but can see neither.

I hear Bernard moving around in the wheelhouse and the sound of sporadic chatter on the VHF. Somebody relays a message that Freddy will be out tomorrow. Bernard comes on deck with a hook and some heavy line; he baits it with squid saved from a shark's belly, and tosses it over the rail.

"What are you trying to catch?"

"You never know," he says.

Sitting in the fo'c'sle that night, reading *Shogun* under a cone of light, I hear a racket on deck, the line snapping and sliding on the rail. I jump up the ladder and reach for the line. A powerful animal pulls it out of my hands, but I grab it again and start to haul it in toward the boat. It breaks the surface in a flash of sparkling green lights—phosphorescence.

"Got a fish here!" I holler, and Bernard comes out to help boat it. Together we lift it over the rail and a five-foot long blue shark lands on deck, banging and thumping as it arcs and writhes, trying to escape. We let it tire itself out and when it quiets down I give it a slam on the head with the hammer. Buddy gets a shark on his watch too, and the shark fishing contest becomes our night job.

Off and on during the day, schools of common dolphins chase after us to ride in our bow wake. As they approach we see them leaping and spinning in the air.

"I think if I got reincarnated I'd want to come back as a dolphin," I say, and hear a couple of grunts in assent.

Shearwaters, fulmars, and petrels glide across the tops of the waves. We approach a line of cooler green water mixing with the blue, and Joe calls, "Look! Look!"

Buddy turns the boat toward a pod of at least fifty pilot whales. "Holy shit, look at that little one," says Joe. A newborn pilot whale, still wrinkled and gray, swims close beside a full grown one.

I watch them as we cruise past. "That thing is hardly a day old." Bernard runs along the warm/cold edge toward the line. Freddy makes it out to us in the plane and flies wide circles southwest of us. On the radio we hear Franklin's familiar voice: the Canadian boats are getting fish. But in the distance we can see a 125-foot Canadian Coast Guard cutter, the *Chebucto,* recognizable by its distinctive red hull and white top.

"It's the *Chabute,*" says Bernard when we go down for supper. "The shitty boot." We are six days without a fish; Bernard wants to get to Fiddler's Cove, the only place he can put a trip together. But the Canadians value their fisheries too much to let us in.

Ernie Kavanaugh, an old friend of Bernard's, has already been hauled into Halifax for fishing across the line. The scallopers, too, lost their best grounds on the Northeast Peak. Several have had their boats and gear confiscated for poaching in Canadian waters, and it is primarily the scallop boats that the *Chebucto* is watching. Off and on we see black smoke belch out her stacks as she moves in toward the more aggressive New Bedford boats. "There she goes," says Joe.

"I was all around the Maritimes in between trips last summer and none of those guys wanted the line," I tell Joe and Buddy. "We went in and played softball one time, us against the Canadians. We played for a trophy, a swordfish sword mounted on a plaque, and I never met one fisherman who wanted the line. It was the goddamn oil companies. They were the ones that pushed this into the World Court."

"Who won the softball game?"

"They did."

Near the cold water the fog returns, and on the seventh day we climb aloft to search a small circle of gray ocean with no help from the plane. Midafternoon, sitting in the mast, my hands numb from the damp cold, I look out at the blank water ahead. Scanning the gray green waves to my left my eye hooks onto something, a dark spot. In slow motion an image of two crescent fins resolves itself in my mind and the word sticks in my throat.

"Swordfish," I finally spit out. Basking, it makes a gentle flip with its tail; I can see the sword. "Swordfish!"

Buddy turns the boat, and I drop past him to throw the weight. Bernard hustles out into the pulpit and handily harpoons the fish.

After an hour without any more action we bring it aboard, not wanting to lose it in the fog. The fish comes aboard lively, and Bernard keeps its tail in the air with the jilson while I grab the ax.

I stand looking at the sharp sword, the smooth gray blue body, and the big saucer-like eye, staring, distracted-like, up into the rigging. This is the fish that finally makes me a swordfisherman. "Thank you," I say before driving an axe into its throat and watching its blood flood the deck.

"Don't cut his sword," Bernard says after the fish settles down.

"Why not?"

"There's a fellow up home says he can mount the head."

That night the fog thickens. The loran has been acting up, losing the signals that give us our position, and when I come on watch I find the radar has failed. Bernard steers for home by dead reckoning, and he gives me the course: due North by the compass.

"Where's the tide going to set us?" I ask, knowing enough about navigation by now to realize that we have to compensate for the effects of the tide and wind on such a long run.

"Goin' to set us nowhere, it's movin' all the time," says Bernard.

I smile, and try again. "Which way's it moving and how fast?"

"It runs two ways on Georges," he says. "Out here it's more east west. When we get in a ways it's more northeast sou'west. Kinda splits round Nova Scotia."

"So how'd you calculate for that?"

"Well, it's a twenty-four-hour run so we don't have too much, whichever way it sets us it'll set us back the same way. Out here it sets us a little more to the east'ard, when we get in it'll set us more to the west'ard. If we miss Matinicus light we'll hit Monhegan. One or the other."

"Matinicus is a steady light right?"

"That's right."

"What about freighters?"

"Well, we'll have to hope for the best. Maybe they'll see us."

We steam through the fog all the next day and make the buoy off Matinicus Rock that night. Bernard threads his way up around Seal Island and the Wooden Ball, and plots a course for White Head on the mainland.

Toward the end of his watch Buddy comes down into the fo'c'sle.

"Bernard wants everyone in the bow," he says

"What are we doing?"

"Listen for the horn at White Head."

Bernard slows the engine and we hear the horn dead ahead, a little to port. Buddy points. Bernard closes with the land. We can barely see from one end of the boat to the other but we can make out the dim light through the fog. Bernard turns for the home stretch.

He is running the courses and speeds Alton wrote down years before. He runs for so many minutes on a certain heading at a certain speed until he reaches the buoy he's aiming for, a new point of reference. As we head up Muscle Ridge Channel, he has to run at three-quarter throttle because that's the way Alton timed it.

"Father wrote all the numbers down between the lights and the buoys," Bernard told me later. "He knew how long you had to run on what course to get from one to the next. Thing was he wrote'm all down for three quarter throttle, so's you're going quite fast."

In the old days everyone ran courses and speeds; that was all they had. "That's how O'Hara's lost their schooner, running in the fog like that and a freighter cut her bow right off," said Bernard. The *Atlantic Mariner,* which I had fished aboard, met a similar fate. Renamed the *Starbound,* and equipped with advance electronics, she nonetheless disappeared under the bow of a Russian freighter in 2000. Of her three-man crew, only the captain survived.

Regardless, we must barrel ahead through the fog, knowing any deviation will drive us onto the rocks on either side of the narrow channel. Bernard stands at the wheel, glancing from his compass to his watch. He concentrates; everything hangs on maintaining continuity, each buoy leads to the next. We make the buoys right on the money. After a tense hour, Bernard cuts the engine back, and we crawl ahead. Joe mans the spotlight. We see nothing until our dory, tied to the mooring ball, appears in the misty beam of light.

When we tied to the mooring we completed the final trip made by any Maine boat strictly to harpoon swordfish. My first swordfish was Bernard's last.

We knew it, and as we took the gear off I felt a sense of loss, like being stripped of a treasure the moment I'd found it. But during the years I carried his shrimp to Rhode Island, I plied Bernard with a thousand questions about his and his family's past, and gathered a bit of understanding about how they had survived. Like most fishermen he was generous with his stories, and I soaked them up until, in a way, I was living another man's memories.

Part Three

THE WAY OF THE FISHERMAN

Ten

ROCKLAND, MAINE, 1926

The artist set his easel aft of the hatch cover and began to sketch the forward deck. The sweeping lines of the bow drew his eye; the weave of rope and wire; the textures of wood and steel, all framed by the slim dark shadows of a summer afternoon. But the smells of the place, the aromas of an alien environment, are what defined it. The millions of fish that had slid across the deck left a scent no amount of washing could remove; an effusion of pine came from the tarred rigging as it warmed in the sun; the salt rot odor of pilings and seaweed wafted across the deck in cool drafts from under the wharf. A gull screamed and flew from the masthead, trailing a stream of white that splattered into the harbor.

Edward Hopper finished his rough sketch, opened his paint box, and wetted a palette of soft earth tones. Within the borders of his canvas he painted a picture of the deck of the beam trawler *Osprey;* vacant, but alive with signs of recent activity: a chain with a fresh patina of rust lay crumpled near the mast; the forward trawl door, five hundred pounds of steel-bound wood, balanced lightly against the rail, emanating power. The 120-foot beam trawler represented the future, where industrial technology would replace human skill and knowledge on the fishing grounds.

As Hopper chronicled the arrival of modern trawlers and the imminent end of the hook fisheries, another chapter of an older drama unfolded just beyond the horizon.

By 1926, Bernard's ancestors, the Acadian French LeBlancs on his mother's side, and the English Rayneses on his father's, had lived in the area surrounding the Gulf of Maine for at least 280 years. They spent a century of that time in almost continuous warfare for control of the rich fisheries in the Gulf and on Georges Bank.

After years of contention between descendants of French and English colonists in the region once known as Acadia—now, Maine and the Canadian provinces of New Brunswick and Nova Scotia—Sam LeBlanc and two of his sons were following their own desperate trajectory. Steering their leaky sloop toward Boston, where they hoped to find work, Bernard's maternal grandfather and uncles arrived accidentally at Criehaven on Ragged Island, just south of Matinicus, and twenty miles outside the margins of Hopper's canvas.

Rather than join the burgeoning fleet of beam trawlers, the LeBlancs joined the Rayneses, and together they continued a centuries-old mode of fishing, and held the door open for one more generation.

Eleven

THE LEBLANCS' JOURNEY

On March 10, 1924, in Petit de Grat, Nova Scotia, they had lowered Minnie LeBlanc, Bernard's maternal grandmother, into her grave, dead at forty-one of breast cancer. Simon "Sam" LeBlanc stood beside his eleven children in the cemetery of St. Joseph's Church. His daughter Irene held Marc, the seventeen-month-old baby. At sixteen years old, she became surrogate mother for the infant and the four youngest ones burying their heads in her skirt. While the priest prayed, a warm wind blew in off the Atlantic, promising rain. Irene looked out at the patterns of gray cloud over the choppy sea. Her right arm tired, and she switched the baby over to her left.

Two years later Irene lived alone with the little ones. Fish had grown scarce near Petit de Grat, and three of the older boys went away to fish off Louisburg. Her father had headed for Boston with the two eldest.

In spring of 1926, Sam and the boys sailed their thirty-foot sloop across Jordan Basin, the deep water between German Bank, off Nova Scotia, and Jeffrey's Bank, off the coast of Maine. Frothy waves washed along the sides of the vessel Sam had built of spruce and larch, and he and his son George looked pensively out at the sparkling expanse of blue and silver, the long swells rolling toward them out of the southwest.

The cold water pressed against the old boat's wooden hull, pushed around a loose plank and seeped into the bilge. Sam steered due west by the compass, but gradually shifted to the north as the water in the bilge rose.

George stood in the companionway, pumping steadily. Sam regarded his son. "We'll put in at Matinicus," he said in Acadian French. "Wake your brother."

Joseph heard, and rolled out of his bunk before George could call him. He nodded to his brother and took over the pump. As he worked the long handle back and forth, spurts of seawater gushed out the hose and over the side.

In the late afternoon, as they approached Matinicus and Ragged Island, the wind increased out of the west, and they tacked slowly toward the harbor, anxious to get in before dark.

"There, look." George pointed to a white building that had come into view on nearby Ragged Island. Sailing on the port tack, they bore away for it: Criehaven.

Sam stood in the cockpit gauging his approach as they reached the outer harbor. "George, look out for rocks. Joseph, drop sail."

The heavy boat bore on without sails, gradually slowing, until Sam cut the tiller hard and rounded in close to a wharf that stood high and dry at low tide. George tossed the anchor, and when the breeze stretched them out, they lay within easy hailing distance of a man standing above them.

Mike McClure had seen them coming in and walked down to the harbor in the last light of the day. He looked out at the little Novi boat, and waved. He could not make out the faded paint of her name, but saw her homeport: Petit de Grat, N. S.

"Hallo," Sam called in English. "Do you have a place for us to haul out?"

"You can kedge her right over to the other side of the wharf here when the tide comes in. You see where it's good and flat there?"

Sam had already noticed the gravel beach exposed by the tide, and nodded. "Okay."

He and the boys took turns pumping until high tide. After midnight Sam spoke in Acadian to the boys. "George, the anchor. Joseph, take a trawl anchor and kedge us in." Joseph tossed the light anchor toward the wharf and when it gripped the bottom, he pulled the boat slowly toward it. "Should have thrown that fellow a line when he was here," he said.

They moved quietly through the moonlit stillness. As soon as they came close, George jumped up the ladder and Joseph threw him the spring line. George took a turn with it around a piling while Sam and Joseph grabbed at the dock. Together they stopped the boat.

Joseph tossed the lines, and by the light of the full moon, George caught the looped ends of the ropes and slipped them over the pilings. Aboard the boat Sam and Joseph adjusted the strain on the cleats.

"Go down below and shift some ballast to port."

Joseph jumped below, pried up a floorboard, and one at a time lifted a dozen rocks up onto the floor on the port side. He tried to set them down easy but he was tired and the heavy stones thudded onto the spruce boards. He looked at the hatch, waiting for a harsh word from his father, but none came.

"See if there is an old tire or coil of rotten rope, George."

George found a fat coil of old rope in the muck behind a bait shed and brought it over to lay between their hull and the wharf. "You couldn't find something that smelled worse?" asked Sam shaking his head.

Joseph came on deck, and cursed. "Sacre Tabernac! Get away with that, we'll get your blanket and use that." George went back to the head of the wharf and managed to find a tire. They lashed it alongside as a bumper and waited for the tide to drop away. When the boat settled down onto the beach, they all turned in, and slept their first easy sleep since the leak had started a hundred miles to the east.

At daybreak Mike McClure's footsteps crunched in the cool gravel as he walked down to meet the visitors. Sam stood by the boat. Joseph and George squatted under the bilge, examining the garboard plank. As the first plank it took the most strain of the flexing hull, and a seam had opened where it met the keel.

Mike noticed bare wood showing through the peeling paint in several places "Morning," he smiled. "Where you folks hail from?"

The lean dark boys stood up and looked at their father. Sam stood there as lean as his sons, but taller, and balding. "Nova Scotia," he answered in English. "You know Petit de Grat, on Isle Madame?"

"I do now. Where you headed?"

"Boston."

McClure nodded. "What's wrong?"

"She leaks, along the garboard?" He said it as a question, watching to see if McClure understood.

"Well, you're welcome to lay right here and fix her."

"*Merci.*"

"Sam told him about having a lot of little mouths to feed, and how fishin' had dried up around Petit de Grat," said Bernard, as I looked through a family photo album he had been putting together. "They was headed for Boston to get aboard the beam trawlers. But Mike offered to grubstake them. He told'm the fishing was good around the islands, he had a house they could live in and he'd buy their fish.

"So Sam settled down there, and by and by he brought the rest of the family over."

One of the first of the family to come over in the summer of 1926 was Bernard's namesake, sixteen-year-old Bernard LeBlanc. He drowned in Criehaven Harbor not long after his arrival. "It was a strange thing," said Bernard. "They was swimmin' in the harbor and I guess he got cramped up."

Among the pictures I found one of Bernard's mother standing on a dirt road with a bicycle. She looked strong and content. "She come over with the last of the little ones in 1929," said Bernard.

The LeBlancs had endured generations of emigration, either forced by economic circumstances or compelled at the end of a bayonet. Their family history, which includes the Acadian deportation made famous in Henry Wadsworth Longfellow's epic poem "Evangeline," reads like a saga across oceans, landscapes, and governments.

Daniel LeBlanc, a farmer from the village of Martaize, just outside of Loudun, France, had found his way to the port city of La Rochelle, in the year 1645, and became the first LeBlanc to immigrate to Acadia.

In La Rochelle, the principal port of French ships sailing to the waters off North America to catch and dry cod, the smell of fish would have been hard to escape. LeBlanc would have been assaulted by the odors of low tide and dried fish as he arrived at the docks where bluff-bowed sailing ships and a forest of masts stretched out into the harbor. The ships were built of wooden planks, fastened to oak frames with wooden pegs; their linen canvas sails had been woven by hand, and their hempen ropes laid in long alleys called rope-walks. Thousands of human hands contributed to the construction of the ships, which exemplified the cutting edge of technology at the time.

Daniel LeBlanc could have found a site aboard one of the small fishing boats leaving for the Grand Banks, but he was a farmer; handpicked by agents of Charles D'Aulnay, the Lieutenant-General of Acadia. A merchant vessel, perhaps D'Aulnay's 250-ton *Saint Jehan*, would bear him and others like him across the Atlantic, along with a cargo of livestock and farming implements.

Daniel LeBlanc went aboard and spent the next two months cramped below deck as the vessel labored against the prevailing wind and currents of the North Atlantic in its effort to reach Acadia. On arrival he received land from D'Aulnay.

Rather than fell trees and dig stumps to open the land, the first Acadians diked the salt marshes around the Bay of Fundy, drained them, and turned them into fertile fields.[4] They built thatch-roofed cabins and several forts, including one at Port Royal. In 1650 Daniel married Francoise Gaudet, also from France, and began his long line of descendants. Most Acadian LeBlancs can trace their roots to Daniel; he is to them what Abraham is to the Jews and Muslims.

---

[4] Modern excavators still turn up the remains of the Acadian *aboiteaux*—sluice gates—along the Bay of Fundy and Minas Basin.

The French claimed Newfoundland and all lands south as far as the Kennebec River in what is now Maine, and D'Aulnay hoped to plant the seeds of a new empire. But a lack of support from the French government, a shortage of supplies, and internal feuds between D'Aulnay and other Acadian leaders combined to stymie the colony's growth. What help LeBlanc and other early arrivals received came from the Natives: the Mi'kmaq and Malecite taught the French how to hunt and fish, and cope with the frigid, snow-laden winters. Many Acadians intermarried with the Native population and though the colony remained fragile, the roots of the Acadian people grew deeper into soil and sea.

But the English also coveted the land once held by the Mi'kmaq. John Cabot (Giovanni Caboto) had sailed an English ship, the *Matthew*, to North America in 1497. He staked an English claim to the area around the Bay of Fundy and as far north as Newfoundland, and the Acadians lived a tenuous existence under the rapidly expanding shadow of the Plymouth and Virginia colonies to the southwest.

English colonists who arrived in Virginia in 1607 resented what they perceived as French encroachment; they wanted the French out, and in 1613, made their first attempts to destroy Acadia. Captain Samuel Argall (Argyle), known as a tyrant even among his own, first raided a French settlement on what is now Mount Desert Island, and then sacked Port Royal, now Annapolis Royal, on the southwest shore of Nova Scotia. In both raids Argall managed to land when the Acadian men had gone hunting. He and his men then landed, took the Acadian women and livestock aboard, and burned the settlements.

One hundred years of on-again, off-again warfare followed, along with constant depredations by pirates of both flags, until October 1710, when the English launched a grand assault on the Acadian capital of Port Royal. English troops and militia from Massachusetts, which included Maine at the time, blasted the clay and wood fort with cannon and captured it after a nineteen-day siege.

The Treaty of Utrecht in 1713 gave the English control of Acadia, which they had already renamed Nova Scotia. The LeBlancs and several thousand other Acadians chose to stay on their farms. Their farms' produce fed the occupying garrisons, and so the Acadians were tolerated, even

The mailboat to Matinicus in the 1940s. It served as the island's primary link with the mainland.

Mike McClure, the fish buyer on Crie Haven who welcomed the LeBlanc family to the USA.

Del in in his stocking feet, standing at the helm of a Friendship sloop, possibly the *Narwhale*.

Del and Ethel's houseboat. Alton is squatting by his father's feet. Note the sail and cod-drying on the roof. Circa 1915.

Out on Crie Haven, one of Irene's sisters playing the accordion, a mainstay of the Acadian music Alton always listened to.

Irene Leblanc, 1929, on Crie Haven/ Matinicus.

LLIE. MARC. BETTY. WILBERT.

After her mother died, Irene (center, rear) became the mother to her younger siblings. The sea would claim four of her seven brothers.

Irene and Alton in a studio portrait with their first child, Bernard, 1932. It was normal to put baby boys in dresses.

Left to Right: Back Row—Irene, Linwood Hooper, Lamond, Bernard, Wilbert, Marc. Front Row—Victor, Sylvia Ranyes, Patricia Ranyes (holding son, Barry White), Valma. Circa 1944-46.

One of Alton's early boats, the *Ruth*, used for lobstering and fishing with hooks. "Every boat he built had a sail on it," Bernard said.

The *Blanche R.*, one of Alton's first draggers at the dock in Vinalhaven. The aft "door" hangs near the stern, and rollers of the sweep lie on the rail. Circa late 1930s.

Showing off a wolf eel, also known as an ocean catfish. When fishermen step into a pile of fish dumped on deck from a net, they have to be careful of the wolf eel's strong jaws and teeth, which can bite through a person's boot.

Bernard's Uncles Lamond "Snookie" LeBlanc (standing), and George talking at the dock, spinning yarns, as they say. Lamond was lost in 1950 aboard the trawler *Theresa A.*

Alton and George playing music on the steps of Alton and
Irene's house in Owls Head.

Bernard and his aunt Loretta at Owls Head in the late 1940s.

Irene sitting among the meshes of Alton's net, knitting while Sylvia
and Patricia look on. Circa late 1940s.

Alton posing with a sloop in the 1960s. Alton often worked running yachts like this for summer visitors.

Left to Right: Sylvia, Patricia, and Alton give Del's new boat a shakedown cruise.
Circa late 1940s.

One of Alton's boats, the *Al & M*, with a load of lobster traps.

Loading fuel for the islands. The *Dora & Peter*, a Newbert and Wallace built eastern rig trawler, in the background.

The *Irene & Alton* at Reed's Wharf in Owls Head around 1999. Her home port is now in Spruce Head, but as of this writing, she can still be seen carrying supplies to the islands of Penobscot Bay and bringing lobsters back to the mainland.

encouraged to remain, in Nova Scotia. Referred to as the "Neutral French," they took oaths of allegiance to the British Crown, with the qualification that they not be required to fight the French of Quebec. But having a suspect Catholic culture in their midst riled many of the English. Between 1744 and 1750 the French from Quebec and their Mi'kmaq allies made several attempts to reconquer Acadia and pirates from Louisbourg, Cape Breton Island continuously harassed English shipping, eroding English tolerance of the neutrals.[5]

In July 1755, Rene LeBlanc, the fourth generation from Daniel, lived in Mines (Minas), where he was the notary public. After more than a decade of increasing violence between French and English colonists, and with all-out war imminent, Governor Charles Lawrence summoned Rene the notary and several other Acadian delegates to a meeting in Halifax.

At the meeting, conducted in English, Lawrence demanded that LeBlanc and the other delegates take a new oath that would make them unconditional subjects of England, liable to be called upon to bear arms against their fellow Frenchmen in Quebec. When the fourteen delegates refused, Lawrence imprisoned them aboard a ship in Halifax Harbor, and ordered the deportation of all Acadians from Nova Scotia. On September 10 that same year, the mass expulsion of a population of over ten thousand people began with Colonel John Winslow's embarkation of 230 Acadians from Grand Pre. Winslow targeted the most volatile group first: the young men.

On a cool afternoon, as smoke from the houses drifted into the clear blue sky, Colonel Winslow addressed the people of Grand Pre. He ordered them to separate into three files. The families parted slowly: women with children, married men, and the young men who would be the first to embark. When ordered to march, however, the Acadian boys refused to cooperate. They called to their fathers and attempted to reunite with

---

[5] Members of the Raynes family joined the ranks of those who fought the French. Francis Raynes had arrived in North America around the same time as Daniel LeBlanc, and settled in York, Maine, near the border of Acadia, and several Raynes men from York, Bernard's ancestors, joined the force that took Louisbourg in 1745.

them. Winslow's soldiers stood between the sons and their families. They grabbed at the boys to drag them along, but the young men shook free and interceded for each other. Winslow ran out of patience. "Fix bayonets!" he ordered. The soldiers reached to their sides and for a moment the only sound was the rattling of cold steel on the musket barrels, punctuated by screams and shouts.

"You, you, you . . ." Winslow pointed at each young Acadian. "March." Under the protection of his troops' bayonets Winslow manhandled one lad, whom the others appeared to look up to, and pushed him down the road toward the harbor. The rest followed. Most of the 141 young men, some bleeding from the prick of the sharp bayonets, others bruised by musket butts, would never see their families again.

Winslow returned for a second group, and speaking in French, ordered the townsfolk to choose 109 married men for the next lot. A group assembled, but on the mile-and-a-half march to the ship, wives and daughters clung to their men. Many screamed hysterically and beat at the English soldiers, who succeeded in putting only eighty-nine men aboard the transport ship. Winslow reported the oversight in his journal: "And thus the number of prisoners put on board that day was but 230."

The deportations continued all fall and into the winter. All told, Governor Lawrence managed to ship 7,100 Acadians out of Nova Scotia, and scatter them among the English colonies from Massachusetts to Georgia. The English appropriated the rich farmlands, and burned the Acadians' homes. "The flames roared for six days," wrote historian Thomas C. Haliburton, noting that in the aftermath, cattle gathered where the barns had stood, lowing for their feed, "while all night long the faithful watch-dogs of the Neutrals howled over the scene of desolation."

Thousands of Acadians, several of Rene LeBlanc's children among them, managed to escape into the woods, living with their longtime allies the Mi'kmaq. The natives took care of the refugees and helped them reach French settlements in Quebec, Ile St. Jean (Prince Edward Island), and Ile Royale (Cape Breton).

Governor Lawrence put Rene LeBlanc, the notary, and the other Acadian delegates aboard the transport ships. LeBlanc and two of his children landed in Philadelphia, where he died in 1758, at the age of seventy-six.[6]

Rene's grandson Mathurin, the sixth generation from Daniel, was born around the year of the expulsion. His parents had escaped to Quebec, but were captured in 1760, along with about three hundred other Acadians who had sought refuge in Restigouche, at the southern end of Gaspe.

The young Mathurin went to prison in Halifax with the rest. After the LeBlancs' release in 1763, they established themselves around Arichat on Isle Madame, where Mathurin married in 1775.

While legally allowed to return to Nova Scotia after the Treaty of Paris in 1763, the Catholic Acadians lived under penal laws similar to those enacted against the Irish: Mathurin LeBlanc could not legally teach or attend school, vote, hold public office, or own land.

The English had confiscated the Acadian farms. With few options left to them, many returning refugees such as the LeBlancs and the ancestors of Franklyn d'Entremont of Pubnico, Nova Scotia, turned to the sea and became fishermen.

Mathurin lived like his fellow Acadians, in indebted servitude to fish traders such as Charles Robin and other French-speaking Protestants from the Channel Isles between France and England. In the late 1700s, Robin owned the only store in Arichat and bought all the fish: his operation, the Robin Company, survived in Petit de Grat until 1910.

Although England lifted the penal laws in 1784 and the Robin Company eventually lost its monopoly, prejudice against the Acadians

---

[6] Henry Wadsworth Longfellow included Bernard's ancestor in the poem "Evangeline":

> "Bent like a labouring oar, that toils the surf of the ocean,
> Bent but not broken, by age was the form of the notary public;
> Shocks of yellow hair, like the silken floss of the maize, hung
> Over his shoulders; his forehead was high; and glasses with horn bows
> Sat astride on his nose, with a look of wisdom supernal.
> Father of twenty children was he, and more than a hundred
> children's children rode on his knee,
> and heard his great watch tick."
>
> (Years later I found that Rene LeBlanc was also one of my ancestors.)

remained strong even into the early twentieth century. Undaunted by what would now be called ethnic cleansing, the LeBlancs held tightly to their religion, and kept their family and culture intact.

"They had it hard in them days," said Bernard. "There was still a lot of prejudice against them in Nova Scotia. They fished for one company and always owed the company store."

Bernard seldom stood still when we talked, and I followed him out to his barn, where he worked surrounded by relics of his father and grandfather's lives: boat models Alton had carved; hand tools almost one hundred years old, a serving mallet for instance, used to wrap line around spliced wire. Bernard inherited most of his skills as a fisherman and boatbuilder from his father's family; from his mother's, he got the tenacity of survival.

Bernard found a short piece of white pine, and taking up a block plane, began to carve a model for a new skiff. The old dory we'd used in the 1980s had sprung too many leaks.

"Father's people were new to the islands, too. They sold over to McClure's and the two families got together that way. They say father was sweet on Mike McClure's daughter, Etta, but when mother come over that all changed."

Irene had got word from her father and brothers a few weeks after their arrival on the island. Her sixteen-year old brother Bernard left right away for a place that was only a name, Criehaven, and not long afterwards word came back about his drowning.

She may have felt a sense of foreboding, but after taking care to make sure her mother's grave would be cared for Irene gathered her siblings, who had become her children, and in 1929, headed overland for Maine. When she met her father at the border in Calais she was twenty-one years old.

The two families, the Rayneses and LeBlancs, kept to their old ways on the islands, handlining from open boats. Together they dried their fish and helped Mike McClure fill his markets. Bernard's father kept a daily log and in his own cryptic style left a record of one his best days fishing during those high times: "June 21, 1930. Come out here today anchored at 3:30 p.m. got about 700 dressed before supper. Buddie is with us. He's six years old. . . . June 22, Come in tonite at 9 p.m. from Haddock Nubble, fished 20 HR got $70. 00 Buddie was with us. All big cod."

Alton met his crewman Wesley Laird that morning at the dock in Matinicus Harbor. They had meant to set out early in the morning, but couldn't get any herring for bait. So they dug some clams at low tide and motored across to Ragged Island. At Criehaven, Mike McClure's six-year-old son Buddie begged to go, and Alton took him aboard.

Alton had arranged to head out in company with two of the LeBlanc boys, George and Lamond. But it took a while for everyone to get ready, and it was midmorning before they headed offshore: George and Lamond in their boat, Wesley, Buddie, and Alton in theirs. Five miles out, a wall of fog marked the deep water, and one after the other the two boats disappeared into it.

Alton felt the cool on his face as they entered the close and confined world of fog. The horizon vanished, beyond the rails of the open boat the view remained as constant as the chug of the engine—shifting patterns in shades of gray. The smell of exhaust wafted around them in the occasional downdraft. Mist beaded along the wooden rails and dripped from the buff-painted oars lashed along the riser. An easy swell slipped in from the southwest and rolled through their circle of diffuse light. The wooden boat rode up the gentle slopes and slid down across the troughs.

Alton stared ahead into the fog, occasionally glancing down at the compass, or off to the sides. After four hours, he stopped the engine. He took the lead line out and leaned over the side. He touched his thumb to the bottom of the dense gray weight in his hand, feeling the tallow in the hollow there, and wiping it clean. He watched the gray sea slide by the painted wood, reflecting the gray hull, and the gray sky, and then tossed the weight ahead. The line rattled off the spool until the lead hit bottom: sixty-three fathoms.

He handed Buddy the spool to wind in. When the weight came up Alton checked the tallow plug—mud. He wiped it clean again, wiped his thumb on his pants, and looked around. "Tide musta set us some," he said. Buddy looked around, too. The nearest land, Matinicus Rock, lay twenty miles to the northwest.

"Start the engine," Alton said, and Wesley cranked the Palmer P. A. L. to life. Alton veered a couple of points to port and checked his watch. After a few minutes he nodded to Wesley to cut the engine again.

The boat fell off broadside to the swell and rocked side to side as it spent the last of its momentum. Alton heaved the lead; when he hauled the lead back from fifty-three fathoms bits of gravel and sponge clung to the tallow. He nodded and Buddy heaved the heavy anchor over the side.

The boy watched the line snake out, hissing excitedly over the rail, until it stopped, limp as death. He tossed out a couple of loose coils and they drifted downwind until the anchor dug in. Alton nodded with approval. It was 3:30 in the afternoon.

Sound moves in peculiar ways over the water on a foggy afternoon. An engine in the distance slowed down, voices carried so that a conversation could be heard from a quarter mile as if it were taking place three feet away. "*Sacre Tabernac*," George swore. Laughter came across the water. Like wraiths, the LeBlanc brothers materialized out of the fog thirty yards away.

"You on bottom?" asked George, hardly raising his voice.

"We're just setting out," Alton said as he and Wesley rigged their hand-lines baited with clam, and let the hooks drop out of sight, pulled by half-pound lead weights into the dark water.

"Now we'll see." Alton sat on the thwart and Wesley stood forward of the engine, braced against the rail and they jigged off opposite sides of the boat; hauling the tarred cotton line up and letting it sink back again in time with the waves, so that the rocking of the boat accentuated their movements.

Alton pulled a pair of gloves out of his pocket and put them on. Moments later, he felt the pull of what he knew immediately was a big cod. "Get your gaff," he called.

As Alton hauled, the line gathered at his feet and the big fish drew closer to the boat, Buddy jumped across the engine box, and handed him the short handled hook.

The cod appeared on the surface and Alton grunted as he sunk the gaff into the fish's head and slid the big cod in over the rail.

The green speckled fish arched and writhed in the bottom of the boat, but to no avail.

"Must weigh a hundred pounds," said Buddy.

"Close," said Alton.

The fish lay shivering in the hazy late afternoon light; Wesley had landed another next to it before its tail stopped flapping.

Out in the fog the men heard the heavy hammering of a big engine. "Beam trawler," said Wesley. "Listen."

They marked the direction of the sound. If it changed they were safe. If it kept from the same direction it meant they would have to haul anchor and move. The bearing of the distant boat changed.

"He's off for deeper water," said Alton. "They haven't found this spot yet."

By 7 p.m. they had seven hundred pounds of big cod dressed in the "hold," little more than a partitioned area amidships. George and Lamond motored over, their white-hulled boat bathed in the ethereal light of a foggy sunset, and the two boats anchored together for the night. George and Lamond came aboard for supper. Alton had made a chowder from some of the clams, and the LeBlancs brought a jar of cheeks and tongues they had cut from the cod. "If you have a little oil we can fry these too," said Lamond.

After their meal they sat around the cramped cuddy cabin forward and smoked and drank tea. Lamond winked at George. "Alton, you coming over for the dance Saturday night?"

"If we get home in time."

"You'll be home in time," Lamond teased. "You never miss a dance since my sister come over."

They hauled anchor at four the following afternoon and headed back toward the island with over 1,400 pounds of fish dressed in the hold, now covered with a tarp. The boats lumbered home, steering north-northwest through the dark and the fog. They made Matinicus Rock by eight and tied up in Criehaven, before nine. Next morning they sold to Mike McClure.

"Seventy dollars for twenty hours fishing—not bad," said Alton, and he wore a satisfied smile when he met Irene at the dance that night.

"They used to have dances every week in them days," Bernard said, as he marked the stations along the model; each one represented a full-sized form he would build.

Alton's logbook tells the story of his shifting affections in the simplest terms: The logbook was inscribed as a Christmas gift from McClure's daughter, Etta, in 1929, and Alton made the last entry in November 1930: "Went to visit Irene."

In 1931, as New England fisheries peaked and began to decline, Irene LeBlanc married Alton Raynes. They had a son, Bernard, the first of the LeBlanc line born in the new country, named after his uncle, the first to die there.

"Mother wouldn't never speak French with us," said Bernard. "She spoke it with her sisters, but for us she said we was in a new country, and had a new life."

Twelve

HADDOCK NUBBLE, 1930

*B*elow, *in the world of the unseen, every sound and motion, amplified through water, touches every inch of every creature living there. Under the weight of sea and sky, a loose school of fat codfish swims along bottom, moving toward the lead weight bouncing in the muddy gravel. A flick of its tail, and a thirty-year-old female, six feet long and weighing over one hundred pounds, surges forward through the green murk. She smells a clam. Her lateral lines vibrate with the crashing of the lead on bottom, and the pulses of other fish moving in the same direction—competition fierce for every morsel.*

The fish passes the pale, slightly glowing form of the clam, then turns back quickly and snatches it up. As soon as the fish bites it feels the hard steel, and tries to spit it out, but the hook tears into her mouth, and she feels herself suddenly yanked off bottom, drawn upward by a steady heaving. The big cod rises toward the increasing light. She makes one mighty lurch, gains back some depth, but is snubbed up short. The hook tears deeper into the bones of her mouth, but holds. With the taste of clam on her lips and tongue, the powerful fish rises upward again. Relentless tugs draw her toward a slim shadow in the silver light above.

"I never could find it," said Bernard, and he set the model upside down on the handsaw. "They said it was nothing to catch one-hundred-pound codfish out there."

"Where was it?"

"Twenty-one and a half miles south southeast of Ragged Island. I went out there looking, but the beam trawlers got in there after the war and drug it all away."

For what it was worth, Bernard remembered the exact coordinates of a place he could not be sure he had ever been to, because it no longer existed. Haddock Nubble had become a myth.

"It wasn't much of a rise really, no nubble, just a different kind of gravel bottom. Father found it, or Mother's people, the LeBlancs—I don't know, they all fished it.

"They used to go out and look for it with a lead line. The weight had a little hole in the bottom, and they'd put some grease in there and when they got onto the right spot, it would come up with bits of that gravel and the coral that grew there stuck to it. By the time I went out with Grandfather, it was all gone."

"When was that?"

"Oh, all the time I was a kid. I spent every summer on Matinicus, fishing with Grandfather."

Bernard's mother Irene had insisted they move to the mainland; she wanted him to have better schooling, and looking back at the way Bernard tells the story, it seems she hoped he would find other work besides fishing. Irene knew the fishing life, and she knew the price of it, but she did not know a way out.

"It was all any of us ever did," said Bernard. "Her father was a fisherman, her brothers were all fishermen, she married a fisherman; I don't see why she would have thought I'd do anything different," he said.

"When I was fifteen, she gave me a beating every day," he added in a moment of reflection. That was 1947.

In post-war New England the fisheries still seemed infinite, and at 4 a.m. in the darkness of an August morning, fifteen-year-old Bernard heard the stairs creak under his father's weight. The screen door from the kitchen squeaked open, and a few moments later he heard Alton's truck start. The wheels crunched through the gravel of the driveway and Bernard drifted back to sleep.

The staccato revving of a boat engine woke him again and he stayed awake, listening to the sound of the boat recede as his father headed off-shore. In the quiet of the closed doors—his, his mother's, his sisters'—he imagined his own boat: a silhouette rolling a white bow wake over the swells, its engine hammering in the predawn gray, and while his father and uncle Deke steamed for the fishing grounds, Bernard plotted his own escape.

At ten minutes to eight that morning, cars and trucks rolled down Main Street in Rockland. The smell of cooked fish from the rendering plant choked the air, but no one complained. It was the smell of money.

Bernard ran down Tilson Street to the docks. A crew of lumpers in their black boots and oilskin aprons unloaded one of the big beam trawlers at National Sea, a Canadian fish company that had moved to Rockland during World War II. A dripping basket of redfish and ice rose out of the hatch; it hung from a boom angled out over the boat. A man on deck swung the basket toward the dock, where another man caught it, dumped the fish into a hopper, and swung the basket back. Bernard ran on, dodging puddles where ice had spilled and melted. Proud steamships bound for Boston and Bar Harbor lay at the wharves. Bernard passed them with hardly a glance.

Black smoke erupted from the exhaust of the mail boat to Matinicus. Bernard ran to the edge of the wharf and looked down at it, the sixty-foot *Mary A.*, rocking against the pilings.

He begged for a ride to the island.

Stuart Ames, in his grease-stained khakis, looked up from under thick eyebrows and nodded. "Let the lines go."

Bernard raced from piling to piling, slipping the spliced loops off and dropping them to Ames's crewman. He slid down the ladder and sprang onto the *Mary A.*'s deck. Ames's crewman pushed off from a piling, and Bernard went to work coiling the mooring lines.

The boat steamed out of the harbor, past Owls Head, and Ames pointed her bow offshore. After an hour running, a small island gradually rose above the horizon: Matinicus, with Ragged Island hidden behind it. The *Mary A.* barely slowed an hour later as Ames ran straight through the Matinicus harbor to the stone wharf. At the last minute Ames threw the engines into reverse and gunned them hard. As he maneuvered into the dock, his wake rocked a muttering lobsterman on his mooring. Bernard jumped onto a ladder bolted to the great granite blocks, climbed up onto the wharf, and turned to catch the lines.

An old one-cylinder, make-and-break engine drove a winch on the *Mary A.;* it chugged along, banging slowly until Ames's crewman hoisted the bags of mail, boxes of fishing gear, and engine parts. Under a load the banging sped up: *bang, bang, bang* until Bernard grappled the boxes onto the dock. As soon as the load came off it, the engine slowed again: *bang . . . bang . . . bang . . .* They worked swiftly to those alternating rhythms. Ames kept to a tight schedule, he had more cargo to drop at Criehaven over a mile away, and he planned to get back to Rockland by 12:30.

On the backside of Matinicus, Del Raynes, Bernard's grandfather, watched the boy come up the lane toward the house. "Company, Mother," he said to his wife Ethel.

She put a handful of grated cabbage into a bowl of shredded carrots and leaned over to look out the window. She turned back to her work, spooned mayonnaise into the bowl and mixed it in with the vegetables. Moving over to the stove, she lifted the cover from a pot; the smell of hake and potatoes wafted out in a cloud of steam. Del breathed deep.

Bernard bounded up the stairs and across a porch they referred to as the piazza. In the kitchen he gave his grandparents the latest gossip from on shore and watched eagerly as Ethel made coleslaw. "You musta known I was making ragbag," she said without looking at him. "Course he did," quipped Del. "That's the only reason he swum over."

After "dinner," the midday meal, Bernard and the old man worked away the afternoon. In the heat of August they sat down by the cellar door below the kitchen. Bernard's grandfather told stories and teased him while they sharpened hooks for their handlines, and tarred cotton line for their lobster traps. But the old man worked with meticulous care. He took a hook from Bernard, touched his thumb to the point, and shook his head. "You need to do more than get the rust off," he said, and handed it back.

Next morning Del limped across the kitchen and lit a fire in the stove. He winked at Ethel as she passed by on her way to the barn. He walked back into the dining room and banged on the rafter with his cane. Bernard rolled out of his low bed in the gable end. He pulled on blue jeans and a plaid flannel shirt, and padded downstairs in his stocking feet. In the kitchen Ethel poured fresh milk through a strainer. Del stood before the stove with his suspenders hanging down around his knees as he cooked and sang.

"I'd head over there every chance I got," said Bernard. "I'd always get word home. Somebody would call Mother and tell her where I'd got to." He pushed a green button on the handsaw and the teeth disappeared as the blade sped up.

"One morning Grandfather asked, 'Well, boy, do you think we ought to rig up and see if we can catch some of them pollock they're getting down to the Gully?'" Bernard said, and he raised his voice as he moved the model toward the whirring blade of the band saw. "I said, yes, and we started off for the harbor. He walked with a crutch and a cane, and it took him an hour and a half to walk across the island."

"How far was it?"

"A mile."

After a hasty breakfast Bernard went down under the kitchen and gathered up their handlines. Ethel took out an ash-splint basket and put a bottle of milk, some fishcakes and a jar of coleslaw into it. Del hitched up his suspenders and put on his cap and a canvas jacket. Outside, Bernard wedged three frames wrapped with their handlines into the basket and slung it over his shoulder. Del picked up his crutch and cane and they set off. The old man moved slowly, his hips stiff with the pain of rheumatism.

Approaching the crossroads in the middle of the island, he stopped to rest. He pointed south past the cemetery. "Down the road there's the Ameses' place we was gonna have."

Bernard nodded.

"Ames told us he'd sell it to us," Del said, turning to the boy. "In them days a man's word was what you went by." He shook his head. "So out we sailed in the old *Narwhale*." Del said the name with affection. "She was a fast little sloop, thirty-eight foot, drew nine. The wind flunked out so Grandmother and I rowed her into the harbor, towing two dories astern, and a skiff. Had your father, Aunt Margaret, and everything we owned aboard. Dropped anchor right in the harbor, didn't even have a mooring. Then old Ames come down and said he'd changed his mind. Seems his boys had got talking to him and the mother took their side and they wouldn't let'm sell."

Del shifted his crutch forward and started to walk again. "There was a fellow on the back side of the island though, had the farm we got now. It was about the size of Ames's and he was looking to get out of it. He sent a boy over to us and I went out there and talked to him. We bought the whole thing right there, oxen, sheep, everything. I said to the folks on the island, 'we're moving in, anybody wants to help us is more than welcome.'"

"And only two did."

"That's right."

In 1898, Del had kept a journal that now sits on Bernard's bookshelf; it details how nineteen-year-old Del spent the year fishing around Eagle Island and upper Penobscot Bay, an area where his mother's people had settled after the Natives were displaced, and the Acadians driven out of nearby Castine. At the end of the nineteenth century Del worked from a thirty-foot sloop, the *Remora,* and fished much the same way his ancestors had since Sir Francis Raynes arrived in Maine sometime in the 1640s.

Del tells of building herring weirs—traps made of posts and brush—in the coves where the small fish massed in the summer; he set hooks for cod and hake, and fished a few lobster pots in the fall. Del's family farmed too, and he probably milked cows, but he didn't write about it.

As the number of inshore fishermen increased, Del had moved successively farther down Penobscot Bay. At one point after he married Ethel, they built a houseboat and lived aboard it, moving around the islands off Owls Head and Port Clyde. Matinicus and Criehaven marked the end of the line, and he got there in 1924.

"They didn't want him," said Bernard, as the saw bit into the soft wood. Repeatedly he sliced the model like a loaf of bread, each cut showed the shape of a mold he would build.

"They made it hard for him, set his boat adrift, and things like that. But he fished his traps on the back side of the island and sold over to Criehaven. By the time I went out there they were used to him."

"Did he still have the *Narwhale?*"

"No, he had an open boat, a double ender about twenty-six feet long with a Knox engine, one of them old make and breaks they made up in Camden," said Bernard as he set the slices of the model aside and continued cutting. "She was decked over fore and aft, like this skiff's going to be, except she had an engine set almost in the middle. He had to shut the engine down to stop and he couldn't do it so fast so he took me as 'engineer,' he said, and I'd stop and start the engine for him."

"Did he have a sail?"

"Course he did. He had a sail on just about everything he built." Bernard finished and shut off the saw.

Del's boat sat peacefully on its mooring when Bernard and his grandfather arrived at Matinicus Harbor. Bernard set the basket near a piling, climbed down to a ring driven into the granite and untied the haul-off, a long loop of rope that disappeared under water. Pulling the rope loop through another ring on Del's mooring, Bernard brought the boat toward the wharf.

Del's boat slid the last few yards toward them. Bernard stopped pulling and put his foot out to keep the bow from crashing into the rough stone. Del passed the basket to him and Bernard dropped it into the bow.

"Go on over to Philbrook's, boy, and get us a handful of herring." Bernard took a greasy bucket out of the boat and walked quickly down the wharf to Philbrook's bait shed. Flies buzzed around him as he grabbed a short handled scoop. He dipped a single scoopful of herring cuttings into the bucket and hurried back to where Del waited.

Bernard untied the painter, jumped aboard, and held the boat steady as Del eased himself down into the stern. Together they turned the boat until the bow pointed away from the wharf.

"Alright, Mr. Engineer, start your engine."

Bernard cranked the single cylinder Knox over. It coughed to life immediately, and the boat surged forward. "Open your throttle up a bit."

At the tiller, Del steered the little boat toward Seal Island and a bald rock called the Wooden Ball. Bernard put on his oil pants and boots, passing his leather boots to Del, who stowed them with his own in a dry space under the afterdeck. The old man put on his boots and slipped a "barvil" around his waist. It was made of oiled canvas like Bernard's oil pants, and with the same sort of bib in front, but instead of legs it had a skirt. Del stood by the tiller in his rubber boots and skirt, and looked around, ready for action.

To the south, two miles away on Ragged Island, a shingled white house marked the entrance to the harbor village of Criehaven—where the LeBlancs had landed in 1926. A generation later they had all left, and Bernard and Del motored at four knots across the wind riffled waters.

Five miles to the east, the sun stood above Seal Island, and Del squinted into the glare off the water. After a half hour run they could see other boats ahead, haloed shadows on the dappled sea.

"You might as well bait us up, boy."

Bernard bent a herring head onto the single hook at the end of each handline. The steel hooks had no eye for the line to slip through, instead the end was hammered flat and the line was seized to the hook with thin thread. Bernard examined the lashings to make sure they were tight; he had lost fish that way before. In preparation for setting out he unwound several fathoms of the tarred line from each of the two-foot long wooden frames. While the boy worked, Del primed him. "Your great-grandfather Horace went to sea in the dory schooners out of Belfast, did you know?"

"You don't say," said Bernard, playing his role in a well-rehearsed skit.

"It's true, didn't I tell you about him?"

"Not me."

"He made a little song about his first trip."

"How'd it go?"

Del cleared his throat. "I'll see if I can't remember." Tapping his foot he timed his tune to the beat of the engine.

> *As I got tired of being on shore, my health was leaving me*
> *So I thought the best thing I could do is take a trip to sea,*
> *So I went to Belfast City on the Sanford it was true*
> *And then what followed after that I should like to tell to you.*
> *I went around to Puddle Dock, a place you all know well*
> *And there was a schooner laying there, her name was the City Belle.*
> *She was a dandy little craft, I heard the captain say*
> *And all she needed was a breeze, to carry her away.*
> *I quickly shipped onboard of her, she needed one more man*
> *Sixteen there was the crew all told, you see she was well-manned.*
> *With plenty of barrels of salt pork, junk, and provisions, too*
> *And all she needed was a breeze to plow the ocean through . . .*

"That's good Bernard, slow your engine and pass two aft here." Bernard passed two lines back to Del. The old man let one pay out astern and tied it to a ring on the short afterdeck. He lined up their course with the other small boats trolling through the gully and tossed his other baited hook over the starboard rail. "Alright Bernard, let out about fifteen fathoms on yours." Bernard let his line out over the portside, and they settled in trolling along at about two knots as Del continued the song, accompanied by the steady popping of the engine.

> *Twas early the next morning, when the northwest winds did blow*
> *We took our parting glasses, we knew we all must go.*

We bent our canvas to the breeze, and quickly sailed away
And like a thing of life she flew, down the Penobscot Bay.
We anchored at Hog Island, and there the night did stay
Twas early the next morning, when we got underway.
Twas down by Eagle Island, Ship Channel we did steer
Adieu to Ozie Walker and all of them so dear.
Now adieu to Ozie Walker, that's where you got your rum,
Adieu to the bowling alley, that's where you had your fun,
Adieu to all those Belfast girls, they are so mighty neat
Their waists so small, so mighty and tall, their stinky little feet.

Bernard laughed, "I thought it was 'dainty little feet.'"

"Did you smell them? Pew! I think they musta walked barefoot through the bait shed."

Bernard laughed and leaned on the combing; he felt it lift, press into him, and then drop away as they passed through the wake of another boat. He saw a flash out of the corner of his eye—a man aboard the other boat lifted a writhing fish and slid it in over the rail.

A patch of small herring boiled the surface ahead of them. Del pointed to it. "Watch now, d'you see them brit?" He knew the pollack had chased the little fish to the surface. A moment later the line off the stern snapped tight.

Bernard reached quickly to close the throttle. Del grabbed up the line and hauled a slim pollack toward the boat. It dashed beneath them, but he kept it moving, up and away from the other lines. He pulled the struggling fish aboard, unhooked it, and flipped it across the engine into the bottom of the boat. "Grab him there, boy, and cut some slivers out of his belly."

Bernard shoved his gloved hand into the pollock's mouth and felt the pressure of its lower jaw bear down on his palm. He pulled a sharp knife, a ripper, from its slot at the front of the engine box, made a quick slash across the fish's pearly throat, and then slid the knife down its smooth white belly. Guts spilled loose and Bernard pulled them out and tossed them over the side as chum, a bloody meal that would attract more fish. Bernard cut strips, each about an inch wide and six inches long, from either side of the pollock's belly. "Good," said Del.

They hauled in their lines and rebaited with pollack belly. Bernard tossed his hook back over and watched his shimmering bait disappear as the boat plowed ahead. The iridescent strips drifted down into the cold green water. A school of big pollack, all twenty-pounders and up, shot through that translucent jade ten feet beneath Del and Bernard. The glint of the sun caught on the spinning strips of pollack belly and a hungry fish snapped one up on the fly.

The shock nearly took Bernard's arms out of their sockets. He felt the heat as the line slipped through his gloved hands. Wordlessly he bent the tarred cotton down over the rail to slow the fish, then started to haul it back in, bending the line back down whenever the fish surged.

Del hauled in another one on his own line, but the one on the stern line broke loose. Bernard pulled his pollack into the boat, unhooked it. He stood by the rail, his hands shaking a bit, looking down at his fish as it arched and beat the grates in the bottom of the boat.

Del laughed, "He give you a fight did he? Go on and gut them so's we can chum that school back."

Bernard sliced the fish open and tossed their guts into the herring bucket. He cut more strips from the bellies, rebaited his line, and the stern line for Del. They tossed their hooks over again and Bernard stood by the rail with the guts.

"Alright, throw that over a little at a time."

Bernard ladled the gurry overboard with the palm of his hand. Gulls came in and dove at it, snagged some, but most of it sunk in small, dispersing clouds of blood. Again the school struck, slamming the lines taut.

Years later, in his barn, Bernard gathered up the pieces of the model and carried them over to his work bench, where light poured in the window. "We'd get a few fish, then chum the school back with the guts of the ones we caught," he said, as he reached for a small ruler. "We'd fish the end of flood tide and then head in to salt our fish."

The run that summer day in 1947 lasted for two hours and by the time it ended Del and Bernard had over two hundred pounds of pollack aboard. "We might as well go in and split these," said Del. A few other boats had already turned toward home; some headed for Matinicus, others for Criehaven. As they motored back home, Del veered away from the harbor toward the backside of the island. Bernard sat on the furled sail, and leaned comfortably against the combing as Del fell into another song. The old man could fit any tune to the rhythm of the Knox engine.

It was in the month of January, down in the southern seas
Our ship lie at anchor on a coral reef, awaiting for a breeze
The captain he was lying down below and the crew they were lying all about
When a splash was heard up off the bow, and the forward watch cried out
There's a man overboard, there's a man overboard, and forward we all hands ran
And clinging to our best bow chain, such a funny little bluff of a man
His hair was red his eyes were blue, and his mouth it would make three
And the great long tail he was sitting upon was a wiggling in the sea
Oh you dropped your anchor in front of my house and it's blocking up my only door
So my wife can't get out to roam about, nor my children two, three, and four
Oh it'd break your heart to hear their cries for the times they've had with me
Now at night I am roaming all alone at the bottom of the deep blue sea.

Bernard opened their dinner bucket and laid a cold fishcake on the engine box for his grandfather. He opened the jar of coleslaw and forked the spicy sweet mix into his mouth. Del stopped to eat his fishcake and Bernard passed him the milk. The old man took a long drink. "Save me some a that ragbag," he said, nodding toward the jar before he sang on.

Our anchor shall be weighed, the Captain said, and your wife and your
chicks will be free
But I never saw a scale from a scrod to a whale that could ever talk to me
Your face it is of a sailor boy, your voice of an English man
But where'd you get the tail you are sitting upon, pleases tell to me if you can
Three years ago on the ship I was on I was lost overboard in a gale
And there in the bottom of the deep blue sea, sits a pretty little lass with a tail

She saved my life and I made her my wife, and my legs turned instantly
And now I'm married to the pretty little ass at the bottom of the deep blue sea.

"Lass!"

"I guess she was seahorse."

Bernard took over the steering and Del prepared to split the fish. After sharpening his knife, he picked up a pollack and laid it on top of the engine box. He slid the knife down one side of the fish and laid the flesh open, brought the blade back over the ribs on the other side and broke the backbone just behind the blood line, careful not to taint the meat. He cut the ribs and most of the backbone out, tossed it over the side, and flipped the splayed fish skin side down into the bottom of the boat. Bernard watched the gulls screeching above and diving after the sinking bones.

In less than an hour Del dressed out the whole catch. As they motored along, the old man tossed a bucket with a rope tied to the handle over the side. He pulled it in, poured salt water over the split fish, and covered them with a tarp. Bernard steered around West Point and into Burgess Cove. The farm lay a quarter mile away, hidden from sight by a small knoll. Bernard killed the engine and leaped forward over the thwarts as the boat silently bore ahead toward the rocky shore. At the last minute he jumped out and caught her before she struck. Del rolled himself out of the boat and Bernard helped him over the rocks.

They had a fish shack just above the high water mark and Bernard carried the fish to it by the bucket full. The old man had pried open a cask, and using a wooden scoop, he scraped the pure white salt loose and spread it in the bottom of an empty barrel.

Bernard brought the fish, and watched as Del began laying them skin side down in the barrel. When he had the bottom covered, Del nodded and Bernard scraped more salt loose and spread it over the layer of fish. Del put the next layer skin side up, and Bernard salted each layer as they went. "Flesh to flesh; skin to skin," Del said to Bernard. When they finished Del covered the barrel with a tarp. "We'll bring them up to the piazza in a couple of days, when they get good and hard.

"Throw some coils of rope on that so it don't blow off," he added, as he picked up his crutch and cane and clambered up the hill toward the house. Bernard gathered their gear into the basket, put the boat on a haul off, and followed.

Under the piazza they washed up. Del opened the spigot at the bottom of the rain barrel, a fifty-five-gallon drum Bernard had found during the war.

Back when U-boats ranged off the coast, sinking freighters, Bernard and an older man named Charlie Durang had found the barrel and several others, floating half submerged near the beach. It had been full of lime juice, and they guessed it came from a sunken British ship. Del had them empty the barrel out, then he put a spigot on it and set it up under the piazza, under the downspout from the gutters. "He said we wouldn't have to carry buckets no more," Bernard recalled.

"Around Christmas a year later, I was home here, going to school, and Charlie was combing the beach by himself," Bernard continued as he marked and measured the cut sections of the model. He wrote down numbers—offsets, distances of certain reference points from a baseline— that would enable him to form the boat's shape in abstract space. "He found a round thing with what looked like spark plugs sticking out of it. Well he took out his jackknife and started poking at one of those things, and it blew up. It was the detonator, a mine." Luckily for Charlie the mine itself did not explode.

"He come up to the house and grandfather was lying on the couch in the kitchen and he heard this scratching at the door. He called, who is it, and Charlie says, it's me. Grandfather said, come in, but Charlie said, I can't. So grandfather got himself up and went to the door, and Charlie was standing there with one hand just hanging by a tendon, and the fingers all gone off the other.

"He used to haul lobster traps, but after that he had to come ashore. He opened up a store on the island and ran that for a long time."

The morning after they went trolling for pollack Bernard and Del set out again, Bernard carrying their dinner as Del limped along. He loaded lobster bait from his grandfather's shed, and they set off for Del's string of lobster traps.

"When I went engineer with him, he'd sell his lobsters and he'd get so many dollars and change, and I'd get whatever change there was," Bernard said as he double-checked his measurements. "Some days I worked for a nickel, other days ninety cents.

"When we come up on a buoy it was my job to cut the engine, or put her in reverse. With them old engines you had to unhook the spark and let'm wind down. Then just before it died, I'd hook the spark up again, and she'd kick herself in the face and go round the other way."

As they approached the first blue and white buoy, Del nodded. Bernard cut the engine. As they drifted by, Del gaffed the buoy. "Got her."

Streams of moss hung from the underside of the wooden buoy, and it thumped dully as Del dropped it into the boat. Bernard hauled the trap up. Del got beside him and together they slid it aboard and opened it. Del plucked out the biggest lobsters, measured them, looked for a punch hole in the tail, and checked their sex. Punch tails went back in the water. "They belong to the governor." In those years, the state of Maine bought egg-bearing female lobsters from the fishermen, punched holes in their tails, and let them loose again to contribute to the fishery.

Bernard emptied a few crabs and small lobsters out of the trap and handed Del a mesh bag of old herring. Del tied the bait in place and closed the trap.

"Engineer."

Bernard cranked the engine over. Del steered into the wind for a moment, looked around to check his position and slid the trap off the rail. Working together, they hauled along the north shore of Matinicus, making their way toward the backside of the island. Bernard watched a young girl rowing a peapod—a fifteen-foot double-ender. Approaching a buoy, she gracefully shipped her oars and snagged it barehanded. Moving smoothly, she stood up in the bow, bent the line through a wooden roller on the rail, and started to haul. They waved to her, but with her hands on the line she could only nod back.

Back in Burgess Cove they put their lobsters into a crate and left it floating, tied to their mooring. Del's own peapod lay on a mooring nearby.

Two days later they pulled the crate of lobsters aboard and prepared to haul the traps again, working their way back to Matinicus harbor to sell. "It's Friday, boy," Del said, and looked at Bernard. "We better get you aboard the mail boat today if you don't want to miss your schooling on Monday."

They could see the mail boat appear from behind the north end of the island as they hauled their last trap. They waved; Ames waved back and kept going. That suited Bernard—but ultimately there was no escape.

"One time Grandfather had to bring me over in the peapod," Bernard said as he put his tools away.

"Like the peapod down in the other barn?"

"That's the one, that's Grandfathers old boat. It was the end of summer and he brought me back home so's I could get to school on time. We had a fair wind and sailed across. Next morning I woke up and he was gone. He didn't have any wind so he rowed all the way back to the island."

"Twenty miles?"

"Afraid so, old son."

Thirteen

IRENE & ALTON

Two powerful forces shaped Bernard in his youth: tradition—the places where his family gathered up their memories and sorted through them, remembering particular humorous or terrible events that in the end held the meaning of their lives—and Irene. She continued to try to push Bernard toward a better education that might lead him away from fishing, though in the day-to-day world she and her family had nothing to offer him but the fishing life, and he was already deeply immersed in it.

After Del brought Bernard over in the peapod, Irene invited her brothers and sisters over for a Labor Day picnic. George and his wife, Loretta, brought much of the family over from Vinalhaven in George s lobster boat, with lobsters and clams enough for the whole crowd.

George and Alton covered a pit full of hot coals with a layer of seaweed. It began to steam as soon as they laid it down, and George covered it with a layer of lobsters, their dark shells gleaming. The doomed creatures flipped and protested at first, but soon went limp with the heat, and Alton covered them with more seaweed.

Loretta planted her squat frame on a rock and smiled a big toothy smile at Bernard. "Did they have much fireworks out on the island, Bernard, celebrate your birthday in style?"

Irene set her mouth and gave Bernard a warning look. "Don't be smart like your grandfather," it said, but to no effect.

"Sure we had a big party: parade, Roman candles, dancing over to Criehaven, the whole works."

"Listen to you, you're as bad as your uncle George," said Loretta, laughing. "I may forget, but I'll never forgive him for taking me out to that rock." She put her hands on her knees and looked out to the southeast, toward the islands beyond the horizon.

"Aunt Loretta loved to tell about the first time she come out to the island," Bernard said, as he pulled two sheets of plywood into the barn and laid them on the floor.

"She was a city girl, from Halifax, and she met George out in Buffalo. He was working on a dredge out there and she was working in the boarding-house where he stayed. 'Well, I thought he was awfully nice,' she said. 'He told me he lived in a big city on an island with electric lights and everything: refrigerators, movie theaters, and streetcars that came right to the front door. So we got married out there and he brought me back,' she used to tell us. She said, 'We got off the train in Rockland and he carried my bags down to the dock. Those great big steamships were coming and going, and I looked at them and thought, well this'll be fine. I wondered which one we'd get on and then George calls to me, Come on over here Dear, we're going on this one.'

"Well, back then the mail boat was just an old lobster boat barely thirty feet long, and she weren't too impressed," said Bernard. "She said, 'I thought, well, maybe this one doesn't have to go so far, that's why it's so small. So I got aboard and we headed out. We kept passing islands, and going further and further out. Well, it made me kind of nervous. Are we going back to Nova Scotia? I asked George. Oh a much nicer place than that, he told me. By and by we got to Matinicus, and it's a godforsaken place, and I thought, oh I hope we don't get off here, and I was some relieved when we pulled away, but then we got to Criehaven and it's worse. Oh no George, the last place was bad, but not this, I said.

"'And he says, Well this is it honey, we can't go no further.'

"'Well the boat left, and there I was. There were no electric lights, no theaters, and no streetcars at all. I just sat there on the wharf crying and crying. After a while it started to get dark and George comes down and says, 'Well you might as well come home.' And I said, 'Home! This is not my home!' 'Well you might as well come along,' he says. 'Supper's ready. He took the last bag I was hanging on to and finally I had to follow him.'"

Bernard chuckled. "She said, 'I was so tired. Then he got us up in the morning, and the sun wasn't even up yet! Well, I started looking around for the eggs and milk to make breakfast and I asked him where they were and he says, out in the other room in the refrigerator. I go out there and there's a lobster crate with another one set on top of it and the food in it.

"'Now I ask you,' she said. 'Is that a refrigerator, a lobster crate?'" and Bernard laughed as he remembered her saying it. "She liked to make that story sound worse every time she told it."

Alton and George dug the lobsters out of the pit and everyone ate. Afterwards they tossed the shells into the sea and went back up to the house. George strapped on his accordion and Alton tuned his fiddle. The two men sat on the front steps playing their favorite old reels, while Loretta and Irene sat in the grass and talked about the LeBlanc boys. Wilbert had headed for the big boats after he was discharged from the Navy.

"He's down in New Bedford getting into trouble with Lamond," said Irene. "Those two, when they come ashore with some money," the two women exchanged a knowing look.

"Where's Bert?"

"Bertram is down to Boston, he and the cousins have been fishing together. They claim they're making a lot of money, but they probably spend it too. Victor says he's coming home though; he says he wants to fish around here."

Prior to the early 1900s, fishing had primarily been conducted with hooks, harpoons, and traps of various sorts, such as lobster pots and herring weirs. Some fishermen dragged for scallops and Bernard recalled that Del used to drag for scallops under sail.

"When there wasn't no wind he used to sweep; they pulled the drag rowing," he said as he measured and marked the plywood sheets according to his scaled up offsets. He scribbled arithmetic on scraps of wood and paper as he worked.

"They rowed?"

"That's right."

The steam-powered trawlers changed that, and much more. The arrival of steam trawlers like the *Osprey* led to increased landings and a glut on the market. Though fishermen of the day protested.

In the 1913 Master Mariner's Association program book, Captain William H. Thomas of Gloucester wrote disparagingly of beam trawling:

You cannot say we Captains and fishermen are opposed to it merely because we are jealous, and that it is too much of a competitor for us in the race for dollars. Oh no, not on that ground, for it is an admitted fact that it is a drag and a scraper of the bottom of the fishing grounds.

It Scrapes and Tears and Scrapes and Tears the Fishing Grounds
It Kills and Kills the Small Fish—How many, man cannot tell.
This mode of fishing is like the selfish man who 'Killed the goose that laid the golden egg!

Let this method alone, and not many years hence, in my opinion, a dearth of fresh fish will be certain, and the owners of the Beam Trawlers . . . as they read the statistics . . . will wonder how they were ever induced to engage in such a murderous mode of fishing. . . .

Yet the trawler fleet grew to three hundred boats by 1930. In 1929, US haddock landings from Georges Bank reached a record 115,000 metric tons. But an estimated seventy to ninety million juvenile haddock were discarded dead that same year: caught and killed by the small mesh nets, and shoveled overboard.

As Captain Thomas predicted, the resource could not stand the abuse. In 1930, haddock landings began to decline. The increasing sophistication of trawling technology made it impossible for groundfish fishermen to continue working with hooks; a trawler could usually catch more fish in two hours than a hook fishermen could catch all day, especially as fish grew scarcer. Throughout the 1930s many fishermen switched from hooks to trawling in order to stay competitive. By the opening of World War II, the nets had caught the fishermen as well as the fish.

While overall landings rose after the war due to the development of new fisheries, the numbers masked the problem of resource depletion. In Boston and Gloucester, fishermen landed fewer and fewer haddock and redfish, but they supplemented those fisheries with increased whiting catches. On the other side of Cape Cod, the old whaling port of New Bedford gained new eminence as the center of a growing fishery for sea scallops, one of the first species to recolonize the ravaged bottom.

During World War II the beam trawlers of Rockland caught over one hundred million pounds of redfish annually from the Gulf of Maine and Georges Bank. The US government bought most of it for the armies in Europe. After the war, freshwater perch stocks in the Great Lakes declined, and the Rockland fleet owners such as National Sea and the O'Hara Brothers shipped redfish to the Midwest under the name "ocean perch."

The redfish industry grew fast, but redfish grow slowly, and reproduce at a low rate. The resource could not withstand the depredations of the beam trawlers and the redfish stocks dwindled as the company boats out of Rockland systematically extirpated redfish throughout the Gulf of Maine. Then, with help from the Bureau of Commercial Fisheries research vessel *Delaware,* which located new redfish stocks, the fleet moved continuously farther from home—until it reached the Grand Banks and beyond, to the limits of the resource. "My father, Ed Ames, captained one of the National Sea boats, the *Crest,*" said Ted Ames, whose family lived among the islands of Penobscot Bay with Bernard's. "He chased those redfish to the Flemish Cap and beyond. He chased them up to Greenland till they reached the ice and couldn't go any further."

Landings of redfish from the nearby waters of the Gulf of Maine and Georges Bank dropped over 60 percent by 1952, but boats going to distant grounds brought home 260 million pounds that same year.

"He come home from a trip one day and said, 'Well son, that's it. We can't find anymore. It's all over.' After that they just moved onto the next thing."

Serial overfishing continued, as one species of fish after another faced intense fishing pressure. Dark economic and environmental clouds began building on the horizon, but most fishermen carried on oblivious to the coming storm.

Catches remained high, and the crewmen on the big boats often earned more than the captains of small inshore boats. The lure of money and the opportunity to be a top man on a new frontier attracted fishermen from all over New England and the Maritimes. As the fleet modernized, some of Bernard's uncles found sites aboard the big boats. Going under the English translation of their name, "White," they shared up well on the beam trawlers and scallopers, one-hundred-foot boats of wood or steel. Like many men from the outports, they hoped to fish for several months, then take a trip off and return home in style, maybe driving a new car.

Although the LeBlanc family had already lost two sons—Bernard LeBlanc, drowned near Criehaven in 1926, and Joseph, dead in 1938 of lead poisoning from boat paint—the industrial fleet took a still higher toll on them. Lamond, known in New Bedford as "Snookie," disappeared with all hands aboard a scallop boat, the *Theresa A.*, in 1950.

In spite of Lamond's disappearance, Bernard's only thought when he graduated high school had been to follow his uncles to the major leagues of fishing. "We thought the big boats was all the future," he said, as he climbed onto a stool and slid long thin pieces of flexible wood, battens, down out of the barn rafters. "All I wanted was to go down to Boston or New Bedford."

But Irene would have none of it.

The porch in front of the house in Owls Head overlooked the harbor. "She stood there and looked down at me," said Bernard. "She said, 'Three is enough for one family.'"

But three was not nearly enough.

Irene's brother, Bertram, and some cousins had steady sites aboard the *Lynn,* an eighty-foot haddock boat out of Boston. That fishery seemed safer than scalloping out of New Bedford; so after a struggle Irene relented, and Bernard headed for Boston to fish with his uncle and cousins. Bertram took a trip off to get his nephew settled, and on November 28, 1951, the *Lynn* sailed without him.

In the days before radar the fishing boats had to leave Boston Harbor between seven in the morning and seven in the evening. The tankers and freighters left in the night. "You know how fishermen are," said Bernard, nailing a batten to the plywood along a set of marks, and tracing a fair curving line along its length. "A lot of them waited till the last minute."

The crew of the *Lynn* cast off her lines at 4:30 p.m. She headed out haddocking with thirteen men aboard, including Irene's cousins, Thomas and Lorenzo, the sons of Sam's brother Michael, and their brother-in-law Tommy Michaud, who had taken Bertram's place. The boat ran through the early winter darkness, and the men went down forward. In the fo'c'sle they sat around the galley table and traded stories as the cook set out cups of coffee and biscuits. Some men laid in their bunks, catching precious sleep that would be rare once the fishing started.

The captain headed the *Lynn* into North Channel. Unseen, an outward bound tanker, the *Ventura,* had caught up with and overtaken her. Hearing what he thought was a bell ahead of him, the captain of the *Lynn* turned hard to port, directly ahead of the fast-moving *Ventura.* The 10,000-ton tanker ran up onto the fishing boat and rolled the fo'c'sle under.

Slammed against the bunks in the sudden darkness, the brothers called to each other. As cold water flooded into the fo'c'sle they rushed for the ladder, but the freighter had pushed all the nets and gear against the doghouse door, the only escape.

Hours later, rescuers cleared the boat and raised the *Lynn*'s bow up. When they dragged the heavy twine away from the doghouse, they found Lorenzo's body in rigor mortis, still clawing at the door.

"They carried him to the funeral home that way," said Bernard, as he continued to nail the batten along various sets of marks and trace the long sweeping curves it created. "Mother and them came down for the funeral and that was the end of it. They took me home with them."

Bernard still wanted to see something else of the world, so after Irene held him back from joining the expanding industrial fleet he figured he would join the Merchant Marine. He went back to Boston and Bertram took him down to the hall to get him a ticket. At the seamen's hall in Boston, Bernard saw a ship on the board sailing from New York. With his dwindling purse he headed to the Bowery, but when he got there the ship had sailed. With the last of his money he took a steamship from the Bowery to Norfolk, Virginia, where he landed a berth on a tanker bound for South America.

For a year he traveled between the US and South America, visiting the major ports of Venezuela and Brazil. In 1952 he returned from Caracas and Recife, and the draft board called; war again, this time in Korea, and Uncle Sam needed him. Bernard naively told the induction officer that he knew Morse code, and the Army assigned him to the signal corp.

Irene seemed pleased when Bernard told her, it sounded safe, like an office job. He kept it to himself that signalmen had the highest casualty rate in the service.

"I should have stayed in the Merchant Marine," he said, as he rubbed a line out and re-nailed the batten on the correct marks. "But anyway, they sent me to Germany so it wasn't too bad."

Back in Owls Head in 1954, Bernard went fishing with his father and Uncle Deke, aboard the *Ethel B.*, a fifty-two-foot eastern rig Alton had built after the war. Alton had inherited the bad hip from his father, and it kept him off the beam trawlers.

"National Sea started with the B-boats during the war, the *Billows* and the *Breaker* and another one. Then they got those other ones, the *Wave*, the *Surf*, and *Crest*. They just kept getting bigger and bigger," said Bernard, as he finished drawing lines on the plywood—loftings they were called—they revealed the shape of the skiff laid down in its two-dimensional form.

"Them big boats left a lot of men behind," said Bernard. "Father couldn't go out on them. They stayed out too long, and he couldn't stand it in the bunk; the shifting around hurt his hip. So he always fished his own boat around the islands, and he come ashore at night."

They fished three handed from spring through the fall. Deke went offshore lobstering that winter, and when spring came Bernard and Alton fished the boat two handed.

Bernard put the battens back into the rafters. "We'd start in March, when the whiting started showin' up around the islands." But the work was harder without Deke, and riskier.

Near Vinalhaven, Bernard and Alton winched the doors up and started to haul the small net in over the side. They brought the heavy sweep aboard, thick chain strung through heavy rubber rollers, which held the lower jaw of the net's mouth on bottom. With the sweep on deck now anchoring the net to the boat, they started to haul in the twine. Bernard grabbed handfuls of the net and bent over the rail. He leaned against the bulwarks, pinning the twine there until his father lifted it with the tackle. Alton wrapped the line around the turning winch head and hoisted a great swath of twine into the rigging. Bernard struggled to hold the rest as Alton let off the slack. "It's heavy," he said.

Alton had felt the strain. "I don't know what we got here, son. It's early for dogfish, feels like a piece of a wreck." As Alton let the jilson down, the weight of whatever they had caught began pulling the net irresistibly back over, lifting Bernard right off the deck. He held on as the boat rolled to port.

Alton ran to the rail to try to help Bernard. He had on oil pants that buttoned through the bib, and when he laid down on the twine it caught hold of one of the buttons and started to drag him over. In one roll of the boat the twine slipped overboard and Alton went with it.

Bernard reached desperately for his father, and Alton struggled to get aboard. The swells rolled over him and when he surfaced from beneath the frigid water he bellowed. "Bernard!" But the sweep had pulled tight against the gun'll and pinned Bernard's legs; he watched helplessly as Alton broke free and crawled his way up the twine. Boots full of water, clothes heavy and wet, Alton stayed just ahead of the sinking net.

Bernard managed to slip out of his boots and oil pants, leaving them clamped between the sweep and the rail. He fell onto deck barefoot and raced to get a line to Alton. He passed the jilson, a single rope through a block aloft, with a hook on the end, down to Alton, who wrapped it round himself. Bernard took a turn around the winch head and hoisted his father aboard. Alton came over the rail and Bernard watched him swing across the deck.

"I dropped him on the hatch cover and he was clawing at the jilson trying to get it free. It had come tight around his chest and squeezed him so's he couldn't breathe. He was a while comin' round." Bernard paused as he searched through his stock of lumber. "That was a scary time," he said.

"After that we hauled the net in and tied it off bit by bit. When we finally got it up we saw we had the wheelhouse of an old sardine carrier that had gone down there a few years before. We brought her in and put her on the beach," said Bernard, and he pulled out some scrap plywood to make molds for the skiff.

Bernard and Alton had good summers fishing for whiting in the early 1950s, but the winters offered little by way of income. In 1954, Alton bought an old Novi boat, built two decades before out of green spruce. He planned to fish lobsters with it in the winter, then switch over to ground-fishing with the *Ethel B.* for the rest of the year. In those poor years for fishing, it was the best plan he could think of to maintain a steady stream of income for his son. Crew that found other work in the winter often did not return in the spring, and he wanted to keep Bernard with him. But Alton's idea backfired.

When Alton started the engine, Bernard stood on the back deck and watched blue smoke pour out the stack. Alton pulled the switch for the bilge pump and Bernard leaned over the side to see if she was pumping. A steady stream of clean seawater poured out of the hull fitting just below the rail. It ran for a long time before the oily black dregs started to come up. Alton stepped below, and Bernard shut off the pump.

He examined the stacks of traps; over 150 wooden half-rounds piled four and five high. He knew the winter lobster fishing would take them almost to Matinicus, and he wondered what Alton was thinking.

"It didn't make no sense to be going way down there in the winter time with that old slab," said Bernard, as he prepared to pick up the shape of his model in the full scale molds. "She was unsafe, not fit—then fishing the good boat around inshore in the summer. It was right backwards."

Two hours later, down below Green Island five miles west of Matinicus they started setting their gear. Bernard had hefted four traps onto the rail and he and Alton were tying buoy lines to them when a swell hit them broadside.

The boat rolled down hard and the traps slipped. Bernard grabbed for the last one and held it, straining while Alton started the hauler and through brute strength managed to get a line into it. Slowly he hauled the traps back up to the side and Bernard pulled them aboard, all except one, which they had not tied. Bernard pulled another trap from the stack, tied it on with the others and they set them over.

He looked off to the islands and thought of his grandfather. The old man was still out there. But he wasn't fishing anymore, and he'd sold the cows.

By the time Alton tossed the last buoy the wind had come on out of the northwest. Cold spray coated the deck with ice as they pounded home through growing seas. Alton pulled the switch for the pump, Bernard checked the outlet periodically and every time he did, he saw clear water pouring back into the sea, a sure sign of a steady leak.

Two more winters passed where Bernard and Alton took the old Novi boat down below Green Island whenever the weather let them. Sometimes they didn't get out for weeks in January and February. While Alton could afford to stick with what he knew—his house on the hill was paid for and the girls were grown—Bernard had a lot to think about.

In 1955 Bernard married Eleanor Daniels from nearby Tenants Harbor. She did not come from a fishing family, her father worked for the telephone company. So she watched Bernard go, oblivious to how the business worked.

Gradually Eleanor drew a mental picture of what Bernard experienced out there in the blowing snow, fingers half-frozen as he handled the traps and bait bags. She drew another picture from the accounts she kept. The money was good, when it came, but it came too seldom.

In 1957, Eleanor and Bernard lived in a twenty-foot mobile home on a plot of land they'd bought a mile in from the water. She was pregnant and the demands remained steady: mortgage, taxes, doctors, lights, telephone, car repairs, etc. By spring the young couple had bills it would take half the summer's fishing to pay off, and after that they'd be saving up for the coming winter. A crew share on a small inshore dragger barely supported them.

They needed more money, Eleanor explained. It was time to start looking for another site. Alton did not say much when Bernard told him he was not going back out on the Novi boat another winter.

In September of 1957, Eleanor gave birth to their first daughter, Deanna. Two months later they hitched the mobile home to an old station wagon and headed to Florida for the winter, where it would be easier to keep their newborn warm.

"I figured I could find some kind of site fishing down there and that we could sell the trailer before we came home," said Bernard. He laid the plywood on the loftings and traced the lines onto it. "But it didn't work out so good."

Bernard found a site with a fellow named Max Young, seining Spanish mackerel. In the balmy weather they worked from an open boat not far off the beach and circled their net around huge schools of mackerel. Although they landed plenty of fish, they got less than a penny a pound for them and Bernard and Eleanor struggled through another winter. In March they managed to sell the trailer, and headed back to Owls Head.

Bernard turned on the bandsaw again, cut a mold, and shut it off. "Coming through New Jersey it started to snow," he said, comparing the cut plywood to the lofting. "It kept comin' harder and harder till finally we had to stop. We found a hotel and figured we'd be able to set out again next morning, but we was there for three days."

The late blizzard of 1958 dumped snow all over the Mid-Atlantic states, and caused massive blackouts in New York and Philadelphia, shutting the region down for almost a week.[7]

Back in Owls Head again, broke, in spite of their ingenuity, Bernard and Eleanor borrowed money for another trailer and material for a house. Bernard made a trip on a beam trawler, the *Flo,* out of Rockland. It was a transit site, temporary; they steamed out to the Grand Banks, got a trip in eight days and came home. Bernard went back aboard with Alton, and he was working on the *Ethel B.* when word came that Del had died.

"We was fishin' down around Metinic, comin' in every night and sellin' at 40 Fathom," said Bernard, and he nailed the molds for the skiff in place on a beam, a strongback, he had set up. "We'd meet every morning around 3:00 and head out. On August 8, 1959, we didn't go out. And I found out later why. 'Cuz Grandfather was dying. When he passed away, I went out in the woods and cried and cried."

"I know what you mean," I said.

---

[7] About sixty miles from the Rayneses' hotel room, my parents had a two-week-old baby bundled by the gas stove for warmth: me. That was actually the first storm Bernard and I shared.

In 1960, with a second daughter, Dawn, six months old, Bernard met a Newfoundlander named Ernie Kavanaugh, and signed on with him to go longlining swordfish on the Grand Banks. Ernie had brought the eighty-foot *Mariano* up from Panama City, Florida. Like many southern boats, the *Mariano* had been built with long outriggers to help stabilize it, but Ernie took them off and left them down there. He knew they actually decreased a boat's stability, and wanted no part of them where he was headed.

They left Rockland in early September for a thirty-day trip. For five days they steamed across a thousand miles of ocean, Ernie joking with or hollering at his crew all the way.

On the Bank, they put over forty thousand pounds of swordfish aboard the *Mariano*. Bernard learned how to handle the new gear and dress the big fish for a growing market. Coming home in bad weather in October, Ernie took his boat up inside Sable Island, steering clear of the deep water and the Gulf Stream. "Ya never want to go near t'at deep water t'is time a year," he told Bernard. "T'at s where t'e big ones [waves] grow." (Thirty years later the crew of the swordfish longliner, *Andrea Gail,* operating without, or contrary to that advice, would meet those waves and vanish under them. An event that became the catalyst for a book and a film, *The Perfect Storm.*)

Although Bernard shared up $3,000 for a thirty-day trip, enough to carry his family through the winter, he said the trips were just too long. He did not go back with Ernie the next fall. The demands of a growing family increased in 1963 when Eleanor gave birth to fraternal twin daughters: Denise and Delisa. Bernard had to find something that would meet all their needs, and it might not be fishing. Eleanor's spirits rose that summer when Bernard and his Uncle Marc landed jobs aboard a boat used to create charts for the Navy. She envisioned life with a steady paycheck, and benefits. For a year she had it, and saw a chance it would go on indefinitely. The contracting company, Vocaline, finished its work in New England and offered Bernard a bonus if he would go south with them. Bernard shipped out to the Bahamas, but Vocaline reneged on the bonus and its promise to bring Eleanor and the girls down, and Bernard quit. When he came home he found work back aboard his father's boat while he looked for a more profitable site.

As Bernard returned to fishing, however, word came from New Bedford that the sea had taken yet another of his uncles. When Wilbert went to New Bedford in 1945, the men there all called him Snookie II, because he resembled his brother Lamond. At forty-six years old he had survived many close calls, and only a year before he had been rescued from a sinking boat. In the winter of 1967 he headed out groundfishing with Captain Woody Bowers, aboard the *Ellen Marie,* and far out on Georges they set their net in heavy weather.

The night masks the height of the waves until they hit, lifting the boat before letting her roll down into the trough. Four men on deck heave the cod end over the side and it splashes into the dark water beyond the lights. As the boat drifts to leeward, the waterlogged twine sinks, pulling the rest of the net over the rail after it. It hangs heavily from the side of the boat, and drags the rail down so that the waves sometime wash aboard. The wing ends that will herd the fish into the mouth of the net hang from the gallows frames—heavy steel arches, one forward braced to the mast, the other aft, braced to the wheelhouse.

The winch men jump to their stations. Wilbert grabs the aft quarter rope and wraps it around the starboard winch head—the bronze drum driven off the engine, turning relentlessly.

On the port side, the other winch man wraps the forward quarter rope several times around his winch head. Wilbert looks at him and nods, and together they lift the big sweep. The two hookup men push it out over the rail, and the winch men ease it into the sea. As it moves they look the gear over—everyone watches for a thousand things that can go wrong.

With the net ready to set, Wilbert loosens the brake on the winch and the ground line, thick cable strung with hundreds of "cookies," three-inch diameter rubber discs cut from old tires, rolls off. The cookies, meant to protect the groundline from chafing, slide clumsily through rings on the doors. Stoppers, fat chunks of steel, on the ground cables catch in rings on the big steel and wood doors. The drag of the net comes onto the doors, pulling them out away from the hull. They hang there suspended above the dark water, the net trailing deep behind them.

Wilbert and the other winch man let the wires out, and the doors slowly sink to the ten-fathom mark while Woody turns the boat in a wide circle, keeping the gear away from the propeller. As the boat runs side-to in the swell, the deep hull snaps back and forth with the seas, tossing the men against their stations.

Sharp-eyed Wilbert must be the most watchful, not to let his door get back into the propeller and rudder. He's good; hands on the winch brake, he feels the pressure on the door. Together the two doors will catch in the water like kites, spreading and opening the net. Wilbert nods to the other winch man. Together they loosen the brakes, and wire rolls off the drums of the big Hathaway winch. They count their marks, calling them off to each other, until they reach 250 fathoms. They slow the drums and then snub the wires up tight. The engine hammers louder as the net digs in.

After two hours they haul back. The whole process in reverse, except the men must haul the twine in with the tackles. One man pulls the folds of the net together while another cinches a rope sling around the bunched twine and hooks a tackle to it for Wilbert to draw up on. As the net rises they get ready to strap it again for the other winch man.

Like everyone else in those days Wilbert throws the rope over his shoulder to keep it from kinking up as he hauls it around the winch head. Together the two winch men raise the net in long pulls: the dripping twine ascends into the rigging silhouetted by the light from above, and then drops down to deck as the next length goes aloft. The winches work like two hands, pulling one after the other until the cod end bumps against the hull.

In the foul weather the men exchange nods and glances loaded with meaning: pull, stop, let go, you ready? One man hooks the tackle to the splitting strap on the full bag, and gives the nod. Wilbert wraps the line around the winch head and braces himself against the wheelhouse as the boat leans over with the weight of the cod end. A black wave laced with foam rolls in over the rail, and the water turns frosty green under the decklights. It washes around the legs of the men on deck, and gushes out the scuppers. Folds of twine spill back into the sea as the boat drifts to leeward.

Wilbert looks up at the tackle; saltwater drips from his thin black mustache. He brings the bulging bag up the rail. Haddock with eyes agog poke their heads out the twine, all shining in the glow of the lights.

Under the strain the line slips on the wet winch head; in an effort to stop the line Wilbert gets a riding turn, and the rope over his shoulder pulls him into the winch. He feels it bind him quickly; squeezing him ever tighter to the relentless drum. In seconds the rope and steel, all driven off the powerful engine, take him around, forcing him into unnatural contortions. It happens so fast the other winch man cannot reach him; the men on deck, Woody among them, cannot hear his throttled scream. Only when the winch pulls the net too far do they turn and see Wilbert. Woody jumps to stop the engine but it is too late. Snookie II, favorite of the fo'c'sle and the bar room brawl, lies jammed and broken under the winch—flesh and bone bound in the heavy line, his head nearly ripped from his shoulders. Seas, still spilling in over the rail, wash his blood out the scuppers.

A photo of Irene aboard the *Ethel B.* in those days shows the ambivalent face of a woman who has accepted fate: one way or another the business that sustained her family would take them from her. After Wilbert's funeral, Bernard went with Sherman Lord aboard the *Jacob Pike,* a long sleek sardine carrier out of Rockland. The sardine industry was still strong when Bernard landed the site; after so many false starts and chasing down blind alleys, carrying sardines appeared to be his ticket. It paid well, and allowed him to work on the water while staying near home most of the year.

In 1968, after much deliberation, he and Eleanor took a chance and bought their own carrier, the *Ruth & Mary.* The eighty-foot boat had been built twenty years before. She was one of the narrow ones in the classic style, and carried her small wheelhouse aft.

Moses Pike, at Holmes Packing in Eastport, had promised to buy Bernard's fish at his company's Rockland plant. The arrangement went well until the manager at the Rockland plant died and a new man took over.

In the summer of 1969, Bernard found himself standing on the deck of his idle boat while the *Jacob Pike* steamed into Rockland harbor with

yet another load of herring. Her wake lapped the bright white sides of the
Ruth & Mary, lying high in the water against the wharf. In bad humor,
Bernard considered that the *Ethel B.* was having a banner year and won-
dered if he might have been better off staying with his father.

He climbed up onto the dock. The rising sun warmed the concrete.
Trucks rolled up and down Tilson Street, and men and women rushed
about; everyone seemed busy but Bernard. He headed for the cannery.

"What's going on here?" he confronted the new manager at Holmes
sardine factory. "Moses said if I bought that boat he'd buy my fish. We
done good for a year, but since you took over we ain't been doing so well.
You call us every night and tell us where to go and then you tell the *Jacob
Pike* to go there, and they get the fish while we wait around."

In the office crammed with stacks of paper, the new manager looked
him up and down, like they had just met. "Well, go find a trip of fish."

"What do you mean, 'go get a trip of fish'?"

The man gave Bernard a cursory look, shrugged, and turned away.

Bernard tried running seventy miles east along the coast, almost to
Canada, to load herring from weirs, vast herring traps that lined the shores
"Downeast." He would tie up to one of the tall wooden stakes that held
the dark circle of twine, pump the fish aboard, and run all night back to
Rockland. It did not work; the trips took too long. After a couple of weeks he
got a call from his cousin Andrew Gove, who was stop-seining, and Bernard
headed over to North Haven. Andrew had told him he'd get him some fish.

In the dark of the moon a huge school of herring moved inshore and
milled in the shallows of Marsh Cove on the northeast side of the island.
Once he saw the fish breaking the surface, Andrew fired up the engine
of his seine skiff and took off across the mouth of the small cove. In the
stern of the boat leads snapped and corks bumped on the transom as two
crewmen watched the long stop seine slip out into the water. When they
reached the further shore, a line of corks marked the top edge of the fine
mesh net blocking any escape from the cove. The leadline anchored the
twine down on bottom, and the net held firm as a hundred hogsheads
of herring, over five hundred thousand fish, all moving as one, charged
against it in a desperate attempt to find open water. Instead they found a
pocket of twine.

Bernard moved in from Hog Island and tied up alongside the corks to wait for low water. They would then seine the pocket and pump the fish aboard. In the pitch black the men talked briefly from boat to boat.

Andrew held a length of wire down into the pocket. "I think I got a good load for you here Bernard, I can feel the way they're hitting the wire."

"Good, we need it," said Bernard.

"Well I'm going to lay down, it won't be low water till after daylight."

Bernard tried to sleep, but only dozed in his bunk. The sound of a familiar engine startled him at dawn. He jumped up and looked out to see the white hull of the *Jacob Pike* emerge from behind Hog Island and steer across the hazy blue sea, right for him. Moments later the *Pike* heaved to and lay outside the cove. Static came from the radio and Bernard searched the channels until he heard the manager at the factory.

". . . those fish aboard the *Pike* and get them in here now! We need'm."

Bernard reached for the mike. "Listen, I been here since last night waiting to put these fish aboard, and they're coming aboard the *Ruth & Mary!'*

He waited for an answer. Nothing.

"Andrew, put those fish aboard the *Pike* and get'm in here."

In the crisp morning air, Andrew raised his hands and looked at Bernard. "I'm sorry cousin, I gotta do what the man wants."

Bernard watched again as the *Jacob Pike* took a full load and he got the leavings. This time he refused to take them. He left twenty hogsheads there that the *Pike* would have to come back for. Disgusted, he steamed home to Owls Head and put the *Ruth & Mary* on the mooring.

"Mother, I think we better rig over to go shrimping," he said to Eleanor when he got home.

"Well, we might as well, we're sure not getting anywhere with that crowd."

Since the late 1950s, after Del died and *Ethel* came ashore, Bernard had rented out the house on Matinicus. A schoolteacher lived in it for a number of years, but the place looked worse every year. One tenant left big piles of trash around the place, and Bernard could not get out there often enough to take care of it. He went out in 1969 though, to meet a man named Chris Russell, a missionary worker who needed a base in the United States. Russell had gone out to Matinicus on a vacation and thought that if he could find a reasonably priced place, he would settle there with his wife and two young daughters.

"Bernard came out and set his price," Russell recalled in 2003. "He said that was the price and there wouldn't be any haggling because that was exactly how much he needed to rig over for shrimping."

They struck a deal, and Bernard came out on the ferry with a rented truck, the family, and a crew.

"They came out and took everything that was theirs out of the house," said Russell. "Anything that had been here when they bought it, they left. That seemed very generous."

"Thirty thousand is what we needed. The *Ruth & Mary* needed a lot of work. She had rot all around under the rails," said Bernard, as he considered the skiff he was building in the barn. He had decided to strip plank her and began nailing the planks over the molds, one plank nailed to the other. He ran each plank through a planer first, to shape it. After he shut down the planer he examined the wood and tossed a plank away after discovering a minor defect in it.

"Meticulous aren't you?"

"More like ridiculous," Bernard said. "The shrimping in the North Sea had gone all to hell, so we had the Norwegian market in them days," he continued, nailing the planks one to the other over the molds. "They wanted'm cooked with salt and red dye, that's how they eat'm over there—like pretzels." He shook his head smiling. "We'd be taking out and the crew would all have red dye smeared on their faces from eatin' them shrimp."

High prices paid by the Norwegian market and abundant shrimp stocks created a boom situation that put Bernard and Eleanor ahead.

Three years after they bought the boat, Eleanor announced that the *Ruth & Mary* had paid for herself—seven years ahead of schedule. Bernard felt like he had finally found his niche; the obstacles looked more manageable, but they didn't go away.

Before getting under way one spring morning Bernard climbed down into the engine room as he always did, and stood between the two big GM six-cylinder diesels—671s that sounded like machine guns in hell, but ran reliably. He pulled the dipstick on the gear and frowned at what he saw: the oil level had been dropping more quickly lately, and now it didn't even register on the stick. Bernard crawled around the engine looking for oil leaks. He checked the plug in the base pan, clean; the seals, clean. He reached down and felt the fitting where an oil line met the gear box, and his hand came up black with oil.

"What's going on?" Marc LeBlanc, who worked the deck for his nephew, called down into the engine room. Bernard wiped his hands with a rag.

"We ain't going nowhere just yet Uncle Marc," he said. With a flashlight he could see the drip, but he couldn't get at it. "Can you come down here?"

Marc already stood on the ladder. "What's the matter, Bernard?"

"This fitting's gone. I got to see if I can't get under there to reach it."

Alongside the battery bank a deep shelf held boxes of spare parts, and Bernard searched around until he found another fitting. "We'll need two nine-sixteenths wrenches, or one and a crescent wrench. Whatever you got there Mr. Engineer."

Marc had the toolbox open and a wrench in one hand. He dug around looking for another wrench, and finally pulled out an adjustable wrench locked tight with rust. He looked at it a moment and found a can of WD-40 and a wire brush, he sprayed the lubricating oil on the virtually useless wrench and scrubbed it with the wire brush. It took fifteen minutes to free it, by then Bernard had the flooring up and a piece of cardboard spread under the engine. Marc passed him the wrenches, and looked at the size of the slot Bernard planned to crawl under. "You going to fit?"

Bernard lay on his back in the cool damp bilge; it smelled of diesel and mildew. He bent his head back and considered the upside down view:

the bottom of the dark oily engine only ten inches from the planks. He tried his best but could not get close to the fitting.

They rowed ashore and headed for home.

At the house Eleanor looked suspiciously at Bernard and Marc. "You want me to do what?"

"You just got to unscrew a fitting on the engine. It's in a tight spot and I can't reach it." He looked at her and smiled, but she stared back. "You're the only one that can do it," he said. "Come on, Mother, put on some old clothes and come along."

Marc opened the passenger side door of the old Chevy pickup and Eleanor climbed in. She sat there, squeezed between Bernard and his uncle like a prisoner with no escape.

Down in the engine room of the *Ruth & Mary,* two bare light bulbs burned on either side of the engines. Eleanor looked at the situation, and back at Bernard. "Bernard, you didn't say, 'under' the engine."

He handed her the wrenches and explained what to do. She lay down on the cardboard and with his palms on the soles of her shoes; Bernard slowly pushed his little wife into the narrow space beneath the engine.

"Bernard, I can't see a thing."

"Just wait till your eyes get used to it."

Marc shone the flashlight down under the engine, and Eleanor scolded him.

"Not in my eyes!" He shut it off.

"No, shine it ahead there so I can see. Goodness gracious!"

"Can you see it?" Bernard asked, but Eleanor had already put the wrenches on the corroded fitting and loosened it. When it came off oil poured into her hair. She tried to move and banged her nose on the greasy engine. "Bernard I'm getting claustrophobia under here."

"Now, don't do that," he said and passed her the new fitting.

But the shrimping did not hold up. The European shrimp stocks had rebounded and the Norwegian market was disappearing; the *Ruth & Mary* had limitations; she was getting old, and her narrow beam made her unfit to go offshore.

"After the Norwegians left, these outfits rented picking machines and used'm all winter," Bernard said as he winched the finished skiff out of the barn. "They were idle in the summer so they talked us into looking around. We found the shrimp out on Jeffries. They were soft, and all mixed up with small stuff, but the processors didn't mind."

The northern shrimp, *Pandalus borealis,* spend their first two or three years as males and then transform into females, the females migrate inshore to lay their eggs in winter, and that had been the traditional season for the fishery. In chasing the shrimp offshore in the summer, where they caught large numbers of juvenile males, the boats destroyed the resource. "We fished'm too hard," said Bernard.

In 1969, Maine and Massachusetts boats landed 11,000 tons of shrimp; by 1972 landings had dropped to seven thousand tons—and would continue to dive until the fishery closed in 1978.

Before things got that bad, Bernard and Eleanor decided to take what chips they had and cash them in on a new vessel: one that could take them where they wanted to go.

When Bernard started thinking about a design for the new boat, and whether to buy or build, he looked at the steel vessels arriving in Rockland: hard chine boats, some of them shoal draft shrimpers from the Gulf of Mexico yards. They sported wheelhouses set forward, great long outriggers bolted to the rails, and paravanes—steel triangles that hung from the outriggers and rode in the water like upside down kites. The paravanes worked to slow the boat's roll, providing only a sense of stability, which the hulls inherently lacked.

Like Ernie Kavanaugh, who left the *Mariano*'s outriggers in a yard near Panama City, Bernard thought little of the modern design. "Once a wave caught hold of one of them outriggers, there's no way you could steer against it," he said. "You think of a gull riding out a storm, as long as he keeps his wings folded he's alright, but if he put one of his wings out and a wave caught it, it could do what it wanted with him. I think that's what happened to that swordfish boat they lost," he said in reference to the *Andrea Gail,* the Western rig swordfish longliner lost returning from the Grand Bank in 1991.

Western rig draggers—with wheelhouses forward and the net set and hauled over the stern—had been developing in southern New England since the early 1920's, and in 1963 Luther Blount built the first one with a net reel—the eighty-three-foot *F/V Narragansett*. Credited with revolutionizing the groundfish industry, the *Narragansett* served as a model for the thousands of steel-hulled draggers built over the next two decades. The Rhode Island-built dragger would see thirty-four years of service before being retired under a 1997 federal fishing vessel buyback program.

Bernard had his own vision of what a fishing boat ought to look like. He had inherited it from Alton, who had listened to the experiences of his father Del, and the other men of the Raynes family—all boatbuilders. Alton also heard of tricks learned from builders in other parts of the world; stories told of how this boat or that boat handled and why. He gathered a sense of what looked right in a hull—the proper compromises between speed and safety; carrying capacity and stability. Working in his shop in the late 1930s, Alton incorporated his observations and accumulated knowledge into a design for his *Ethel B.* She was the boat of his dreams, and Alton worked slowly carving the model. He discarded his first several attempts and settled finally on a schooner hull.

It was Alton who offered Bernard the gulls as examples: they spent every day in the world he needed to understand. "He said there's times when a boat has to take care of herself," Bernard recalled. "He watched gulls ride out the worst weather not bothered at all, and he figured a boat ought to be shaped like them. So that's how he made the model, with a fullness forward, deep in the water, and a little tail coming up out back."

After they laid the keel for the *Ethel B.*, however, they realized the stern would be too narrow to fit the engine. Alton took the necessary measurements to a naval architect in Camden, and came back with new offsets, but the new plan gave the *Ethel B.* too much tail.

"I wanted to build the original design," said Bernard. Alton had sold the *Ethel B.* in 1970, and bought a lobster boat, but he kept his model. "He had it hanging on the wall there. I took it down and looked it over. I didn't want to widen the stern any," he said, "So I had to make the whole boat bigger."

The model was fifty-two inches long; at fifty-two feet the *Ethel B.* matched it a foot to the inch. Bernard and Alton played with the idea of a bigger boat. Alton took out his scale ruler, the next scale he had was three-quarters inch to the foot. He took a scrap of pine from the kindling pile and scribbled on it with his pencil. "That would make her sixty-eight feet. Do you want her that big?"

"No. Ain't there nothin' in between?"

"Not on this ruler." said Alton. "But let's see what it'd be if you went seven-eighths." He did the math. "She'd be right around fifty-nine and a half feet."

Bernard searched around and found a piece of wood that suited him. He ran it through the planer until it came out thin and smooth. He found an awl and a caliper, and pulled a three legged stool up to his father's workbench. Alton left him there and went back to knitting heads for his traps. After the old man emptied his needle he stepped over to inspect Bernard's work. Slowly a seven-eighths scale ruler grew along the strip of wood. Alton considered the model a moment. "If you make her that much bigger, and you're going way offshore, I'd let the bow come up another two feet," he said. Bernard nodded.

Most of the hundreds of new boats that entered the fisheries in the 1970s came out of yards where welding rods sparked against steel, or fiberglass resin poured out of barrels but Bernard trusted wood. No one has ever created wood, as far as building materials go it is a gift. Human technology has unlocked many secrets of metallurgy. Fiberglass resins continue to improve. But wood forms slowly, the same way it always has; made by nature from water, earth, and sunlight, it bears the marks of every moment it has lived.

Twelve miles north of Owls Head, near Camden, great oaks crashed to the earth. Cedars fell in a bog near Thomaston and were hauled to a nearby mill.

The lumber and hardware bills piled up. "How are we ever going to pay for all this, Bernard?" asked Eleanor.

"We'll do what we have to do, Mother."

For Eleanor that meant getting a job. Later that week she filled out some paperwork at the Port Clyde sardine factory and went to work alongside many other fishermen's wives.

Eleanor stood at her station next to the rumbling belt as the herring came down between the rows of women. She watched as arms reached out and swept piles of herring onto the packing tables, each shared by two women. Eleanor looked across her table at the old woman smiling at her. "Hello," Eleanor hollered across the table, trying to be sociable. "How long have you been working here?" The old woman smiled and nodded, half deaf from the noise of the machines.

Eleanor helped her sweep a pile of fish onto their table and began the monotonous process of cutting off heads and tails and putting the fish neatly in the little tins. Her partner worked with lightning speed—piling up three pans before Eleanor had finished her first.

"I said what the heck am I doing here," Eleanor remembered years later. "I used to make good money working for the phone company before I got married, so after one summer in the cannery I went down to the phone company and they hired me back."

The money helped. And Eleanor finally had what she wanted, a steady paycheck coming into the house.

Meanwhile, Bernard and Alton pored over the milled lumber, picking and choosing the best pieces. Eyeing wood for boatbuilding is an art in itself, like selecting wood for a violin. All through high school Bernard had watched his father sort through the lumber piles at various mills. Alton had checked for knots, and eyed the run of the grain seeking the perfect wood for the *Ethel B.* But some defects failed to show until a cut revealed the dark secret of a blemish in the wood. After the building had begun on his boat, the *Ethel B.*, Alton found a bad spot on the stem.

"He told them to take it off," said Bernard. "He told them he'd get another. A fellow down the road took that stem piece and used it to build a boat on father's model."

Alton maintained meticulous standards. He knew a knot often held water and started rot. In a moment of crisis a weak piece of wood could be the difference between life and death.

In the basement of the house they had built a mile from the shore, Eleanor and Bernard put together the oak stem and keel for their boat. While Bernard cut and measured, Eleanor painted the wood with a mixture of linseed oil and kerosene.

"Good Lord, Bernard, this stuff's awful. Why'd you put all that kerosene in it?"

"Kero-seen? I ain't seen nothing," he answered. Eleanor shook her head at the lame pun.

"It helps the oil soak deep into the wood," Bernard told her. "So's the water won't drive it out after she's been overboard a while."

They assembled the frames according to the loftings; drawings made from the model, and stacked them outside. In spring, the doors of the basement opened into the backyard, and the work proceeded. Tourists came and went along the road out front, unaware of what the pile of wood represented.

Bernard and Eleanor set up blocking and started moving the heavy lumber into place. By the time the trees had leafed out the skeleton of the boat Alton had imagined almost forty years earlier stood visible from the road. The backbone lay solid on the blocks. The molds, held together with long rib bands, outlined the shape of the coming hull.

On a late September afternoon Bernard waited by the public boat landing in Thomaston as the clammers came in on the rising tide. He spotted an older man, Basil Burns, a sometime boat carpenter from Thomaston. "Hello, Mr. Burns."

"Hello, Bernard." Basil stood by his wooden skiff, stoop shouldered in a pair of hip boots. The outboard engine was cocked up and Basil had hauled the bow up onto the beach, waiting his turn to back his trailer down. In the skiff sat eight hods—wooden baskets—of clams, a good day's pay, even at the end of tourist season. "What can I do for you, Bernard?"

"Well, we got a boat we're tryin' to build and I thought you might come over and help us put the ribs in and plank it."

Basil looked into the boat at the hods full of clams. "Have you got everything you need? Ready to go?"

"All set. We just need you."

"Alright, Bernard."

"Is five dollars an hour alright?"

Basil looked up. Five was more than most boat carpenters made in those days. "Oh, that's plenty."

As the demands of the project increased that autumn, Bernard hired more help. He gathered an assorted crowd of carpenters. Among them some of his future crew: Donald Pelrine, from Massachusetts, and Glenn Lawrence, whose families also came from Nova Scotia. Under the plastic roof Bernard had set up over the hull, their accents mingled with those of the locals in the daily banter.

Over the winter, the crew followed Basil's instructions. Once the ribs had been steamed into place against the rib-bands the planking began. Basil planed the edge of a plank, and with help from the crew, carefully tried it in place.

Nearby, a tank of boiling water sat atop a roaring propane burner, and a hose ran from the tank into the bottom of a long wooden box that dripped water and leaked steam from its seams. Basil's helpers slid the trimmed plank into the box before sliding a hot one out. Quickly they clamped the pliable wood into place while another fellow drilled and screwed it to the frames. They kept just ahead of the steady rhythm of Milton Greene, a master caulker who pounded oakum into the seams with his ironbound mallet.

Basil marked the inside of the frames for the stringers and clamps—the long wooden braces that would stiffen the hull from bow to stern. Steadily and solidly the boat came together. Bernard cut the pieces for Basil as the old man fit the deck beams and built the bulkheads. "About March we got a big snowstorm and the roof collapsed," said Bernard. "The weather was starting to warm up so we just left it like that and took it down as we needed to."

Basil took his breaks religiously. He would set himself down on the nearest flat surface, unscrew the lid off his Thermos and pour a cup of tea. And there he would sit, usually wearing his tweed cap, and a cardigan over a white shirt buttoned to the neck; eating a cookie and sipping his tea.

When he finished he would put the Thermos back in his canvas sack, pick up his tools again, and commence right where he had left off.

Once they planked the boat over, caulked her and sealed the seams, they started the finer work, the mast step, hatch combings, doghouse, rails, and caps. As the weather warmed, the wood needed to be tended to prevent deterioration before it reached the salt water. They painted all the hardwood with white lead, and slapped a coat of paint on the seams of each plank. Bernard's daughters joined in, cutting and fitting bungs, the little wooden plugs that covered the screw holes—a photo of sixteen-year-old Dawn tapping bungs into place appeared in the local paper.

It took fourteen months to put in the ribs, plank the boat from the keel to the top of the bulwarks, deck her, fit the hatches, and trim her. The community watched with pride as the boat's sea kindly lines, inspired by a bird floating on the water, took shape before their eyes. Toward the end of August the crew hoisted the engine, a GM 871, onto its bed in the narrow stern. GM offered Bernard his only choice of an engine. "It's the only one with a gear that will fit down in there," Alton had told him.

Irene stopped by to visit on the day the sign painter came to put the name on her son's new boat. She stood at the sink helping with the dishes and leaned over to get a better view. The painter worked from a ladder by the bow, and when he stepped down out of the way, there stood the black letters of her own name: Irene. "Oh!" she said. "What did he go and do that for?"

Before going home she went around to see the finished lettering that included Alton. "What is he thinking putting my name on that boat?"

In September 1976, the *Irene & Alton* stood in Bernard and Eleanor's backyard with the paint of the lettering drying. Late in the afternoon the truck from Robinhood Marina backed a trailer under her, jacked her up and drove her down to the shore. They set the boat on the gravel beach, blocked her up, and left her for the tide to float. Later in the night Bernard and Alton stood on deck, and by the lights from the wharf they watched the water rise up the sides until they felt the tide lift her. With flashlights they inspected the fo'c'sle, hold, and engine room. She was dry.

They roped the naked hull in alongside the wharf, and laid an old truck tire against the pilings as a cushion for when the tide set her down. The launching passed quietly; nobody fussed on the outside but on the inside everyone in Owls Head claimed a little piece of her. They had watched her grow and now she had reached the sea. When tourists asked about the beautiful boat in the harbor, the local folks spoke of her with subtle proprietary airs. Over the ensuing weeks, the work continued. The winches arrived from Fairhaven, Massachusetts, and were themselves winched into place. Bernard robbed the wheelhouse from the *Ruth & Mary*, before selling his old boat to a fellow in Gloucester.

"He's going to build a new wheelhouse forward on her and take her swordfishing," Bernard said to his father. Bernard kept with the traditional "eastern rig" style. He put his familiar old wheelhouse aft on his new boat, and rigged up to work his gear over the side as he always had. Eastern rigs, towing over the side, enabled a kind of finesse fishing in tight spots, whereas the Western rigs were more focused on power and towing a net across any kind of bottom they could.

Bernard and his crew hooked up the steering and engine controls, and Bernard steamed over to Knight's Marine in Rockland where they stepped the mainmast. A crane lifted the thirty-five-foot galvanized steel mast, with all its shrouds and stays bound to it, and swung it out over the boat. Basil guided the operator until the mast slipped down through a hole in the deck. From below, Bernard called directions as the butt descended toward its step on the keel. "Move the top a little forward and to starboard." Basil relayed the message with signals to the crane operator. "Good, good, good," Bernard shouted from below. "Let her down, let her down!" Bernard watched the foot of the mast settle on the silver dollar he had placed on the step. He felt a satisfying thunk. "Good, she's in."

They stepped a smaller mizzen mast aft, bolted to the deck in front of the wheelhouse.

The next day Basil and Bernard set up the rigging, tuning it to just the right tension. They tweaked all morning, with Donald and Glenn tightening and loosening turnbuckles, as they were told. Basil stepped back and looked aloft, tugging on the shrouds to feel if they were balanced, until he and Bernard felt satisfied. "That's as good as we can get her," he said toward dinnertime. Bernard started the engines and they cast off for the run back to Owls Head. She emerged from the dock at Knight's and headed out past the new O'Hara boats.

Amid Rockland harbor's increasingly modern fleet, the *Irene & Alton* appeared like a ghost from the past. What she lacked in advanced design, though, she made up for amply in style. The wood used to build her lent its natural form to her lines. It imparted a certain grace to her; and it was almost as if she knew it when she crossed Rockland harbor against a backdrop of wall-sided steel draggers, sporting their ungainly outriggers, towering gantries, and top-heavy superstructures set forward over their bows.

On that clear November morning, the *Irene & Alton* cut gracefully through the water and passed beyond the breakwater. Her rounded gray hull gleamed in the sun, highlighted by white rails, and she showed her dark red bottom paint when she crested the swells of the open water.

Besides building an anachronism, Bernard also deviated from the norm by not installing the latest electronics. Advances in navigation and fish finding technology continually offered competitive advantages to fishermen eager to upgrade. Color sounders showed hard bottom in graphic detail; track plotters hooked to lorans maintained a record of the boat's position at all times and allowed captains to repeat successful tows with lethal accuracy; side scan sonar could create an almost perfect picture of the bottom.

Bernard stuck to the basics, and did not forget the human skills that technology replaced. He set out with a radar, loran, and paper machine— the obsolete depth sounder of the postwar era. He carried little more than his father did, but he carried what money could not buy because technology could not produce it, faith in the knowledge he had inherited. "I just didn't know any better," he said in a subtle play on words. There was no better to know.

Navigation in any form requires continuity, a linear flow of connected points. The navigator maintains constantly expanding and contracting mental images of unseen places, and unknown shorelines: a complex arrangement of here and there, then and now. When Bernard's contemporaries abandoned their abilities to use leadlines, sextants, and dead reckoning, they created a disconnect between themselves and an intimacy with the environment that sustained them.

But the trends of the times did not shake the Rayneses. Alton and Del passed not only their skills, but their worldview on to Bernard, establishing a cultural continuity critical for navigating the shoals of fisheries politics, where many a small fishing business came to grief.

Unlike many boat owners of his day Bernard had also failed to take advantage of lucrative subsidies intended to modernize the fleet—though his boat would not have qualified for them anyway.

"A lot of fellows got in on that," he said. "We never did. The government gave money to O'Hara's to rig up one of them western rigs, they took the gear off another boat, hired a skipper, and made a pile of money. They were supposed to pay the government back."

Instead of taking handouts Bernard had taken a year off from work. Although he had swordfishing in mind when he built the *Irene & Alton,* that was a summer fishery with a lot of financial risk he could ill afford in the fall of 1976. He needed to make the new boat pay, and quickly.

Bernard knew that dragging would be a major component of his fishing plan, and in the late 1970s, the scallop fishery offered the most promise. Everywhere on the east coast north of Virginia, the fishery was rebounding after several lean years. Scallop draggers were landing tons of product and the price sometimes topped four dollars a pound.

Bernard rigged up to tow a pair of nine-foot wide dredges. The crew bolted a set of heavy gallows frames, fabricated from six-inch I-beams, to the deck up forward. One braced to each side of the mast, the gallows leaned out just beyond the rail. Scallop booms loomed up from the base of the mast, angling above the deck on each side of the boat.

Bernard bought a pair of used nine-foot dredges from an old scalloper named Arthur Baine. Baine brought them over on a flatbed truck, dumped them on the beach at low tide and Bernard buoyed them off.

In the parking lot, the crew took the big spools of heavy steel wire and set them up on lengths of pipe supported by pallets. They stretched the five-eighths inch wire the length of the wharf, over fifty yards, and they set up a system of blocks to guide it aboard the boat and onto the winches. Bernard started the engine, engaged the winch, and wound the wire aboard from the spools. He stopped it periodically while the crew on the dock spliced in markers.

With marlinspikes they opened the wire every twenty-five fathoms, 150 feet, and twisted bits of light-colored rag rope in between the strands. On the first mark one piece, on the next mark two pieces, then three, over and over, with an orange marker ten fathoms before the end. At high tide they moved the boat over above the dredges, hoisted them aboard, one on each side, and shackled them to the wires.

Before daybreak on a cold December day in 1976, the *Irene & Alton*'s first crew: Bernard, Donald Pelrine, Glenn Lawrence, Uncle Deke, and Pat "Spic" Wilson; rowed out to the mooring where the new boat lay ready. While Donald fired up the galley, Spic and Glenn struggled to unhook the boat from the mooring. The high bow forced them to lift the mooring chain up in a gut busting effort—it would take a while to get the system down.

They headed out toward the Vinalhaven ferry lane, where the lobster buoys thinned out. Bernard opened the window of the wheelhouse, and signaled the boys to get ready. Only he and Glenn had scalloped before so they took it slow. Methodically they set the drags out, first one then the other, towed them for fifteen minutes, and hauled back. Satisfied that everything was in working order, they headed for the waters east of Isle au Haut, in search of the scallops.

"Not too much went wrong that first trip," said Bernard. "Except we couldn't find any scallops."

Bernard would find the scallops eventually; more important, at age forty-four, he had found his course as a fisherman; the coming challenge would be to stay in a game that had already gone through revolutionary technological changes over a century, and was about to be redefined politically and economically. As Bernard set out with his new boat and his old philosophy, the new two-hundred-mile limit was about to go into effect. Other countries had already extended their fisheries jurisdictions, and the first step in a global change took place. The world's oceans, long regarded as a commons, were on their way to being privatized.

Standing on his front porch, looking out over the harbor, Alton watched through binoculars as the boat maneuvered in the ferry channel.

He smiled at the sight of her sails, small triangles of canvas: one stretched between the main and mizzen masts, another on a boom from the mizzen. From his vantage they looked dark against the rising sun, but occasionally, as the boat turned, they flashed golden white.

"May I look?" said Irene, reaching for the binoculars.

From a separate kitchen at the back of the house, ninety-two-year-old Ethel Raynes also looked out her window. She could not see the boat, but she knew it was there.

Part Four

LIVING IN THE EYE OF THE STORM

Fourteen

GENERATION X

*You know how if you keep cutting the distance in half between you and the
wall you can do that forever and never reach the wall? That's what I hate
about postmodern America; it's like they've fired a bullet at my head, but they
just keep cutting the distance in half so it's never going to get there.*
—*John Mecklin*

The *Irene & Alton* and I started our fishing careers around the same
time: during the boom years when the two-hundred-mile limit went
into effect and the US fleet had the entire continental shelf to itself. It was
fun while it lasted. By the mid 1980s Bernard's boat and I were both in our
prime, but coming up against the same obstacle: a shortage of fish. The
North Atlantic had suffered over a century of boom and bust industrial
harvesting that had cascaded down a declining ecosystem. Each new inno-
vation from hooks to trawls to sophisticated electronics and gear, led to
increased catches in the short term, but damage to habitat and stock struc-
ture in the long run. Every few years somebody had to pull another technological rabbit out of their hat in order to keep the industry productive.

Besides the scarcity of swordfish, landings of groundfish, bluefin tuna, and scallops all declined in the mid-1980s. The creation of the Hague Line between US and Canadian waters shut US fishermen out of what had been the most productive third of Georges Bank and concentrated a still growing number of boats into a smaller area. For Rockland, a port that had relied heavily on access to fish in the areas lost to Canadian control, the new line marked the end of an era. With not much chance of increasing production in wild fisheries, regulators and academics proposed aquaculture as the next technological rabbit, but that did not help an overcapitalized fleet, and we started to hear "too many fishermen, too few fish," repeated with menacing regularity.

After we took the swordfish gear off the *Irene & Alton* in 1985, Bernard too experienced a setback. He had problems with his blood pressure and kidneys, and the doctors told him not to make any more extended voyages. At fifty-three years old, he gave up the helm of his boat and confined himself to the shore side of the business.

Brad took over as captain of the *Irene & Alton,* with Spic and me as crew, and we headed offshore to drag groundfish. Pretty soon life on board became a predictable routine: icing and fueling, setting and hauling, lumping and selling.

One September day we set our net out on the Falls, a well-known fishing ground fifty miles southeast of Rockland. Alton had first explored the area with his tub trawl in the 1930s, and it had since become the favored ground of Bernard and Brad. On the stern, Spic and I stood on either side of the net reel, an eight-foot-wide steel spool that held the net and ground cables. The reel represented Bernard's concession to modern methods, but we still hauled the cod end over the side.

"Okay, let her go," Brad hollered back to us. I climbed on the rail aft of the net and after checking to make sure the cod end was closed, dragged the thick webbing over the side as Spic opened the valve that lowered it into the green water. He unspooled the net until it trailed behind us: the heavy chain and rollers of the sweep hung deep in the water, out of sight, but the cans, round plastic floats tied to the top opening of the net like a string of orange beads, held it on the surface. As Spic let out the ground-cables the cans sunk out of sight. We hooked up the five-hundred-pound steel doors that would spread the mouth of the net, and went forward to the winch, an old Hathaway like the one that had caught poor Wilbert. Spic and I let the wires out until the net reached bottom far astern of us.

After four hours we hauled it back. We brought up the doors and ground-cables and as we reeled the net aboard Spic pointed to a tear in the wing, a long row of ragged meshes. Pulling on the bull rope, tied to the tail end of the net we brought the cod end bulging with fish alongside. With the tackle Brad hoisted it over the rail and we dumped it between boards—checkers we called them—that divided the deck into sections for sorting the fish.

Before setting out again I reached into the wheelhouse and grabbed a wooden box bulging with rolls of twine, of various thickness and color, and a number of twine needles. I pulled out a needle, a thin strip of plastic about eight inches long by an inch wide and wrapped full of green twine and put it in my back pocket. Spic had unwound the net and found the tear. I opened my knife, trimmed the ragged edges of the meshes, tied the twine to the beginning of the tear, and began to knit new meshes that filled in the gaping hole. Brad came out of the wheelhouse, and watched me for a minute. He decided I was too slow and muscled me off the twine. "G'me that," he said, and took the needle. "Better fill another one."

I took a needle out of the twine box, filled it with twine and passed it to Brad after he emptied the first one. I had spent two years learning how to mend nets at the University of Rhode Island—a model net I had built in order to graduate hung in Alton's barn—and I was filling needles. After Brad finished mending the net, we set out again. As we sorted and gutted the fish on deck, the towing wires started to shear off away from the stern at odd angles. Brad noticed first and put the winch in gear to haul back. The wires wound aboard without much apparent strain, the doors came up, and nothing else.

The ground cables that held the net to the doors had sat coiled around a big steel spool, wrapped in the damp net, all summer—they had rusted through, and we had not noticed. When the net dug in the second time, both cables snapped. We lost Bernard's $10,000 net.

After three days of searching—dragging a grappling hook along bottom—we headed home. Bernard said little. He gathered up what twine he had and set us to work building a simple single seam net like the one Alton had used forty years before.

Every morning we showed up at the barn by Alton's "house on the hill," overlooking the harbor. Irene had died six years before and Alton lived there with his mother and second wife. He had an antenna set up on the roof, so he could pick up a Nova Scotia radio station that played Acadian fiddle music all day. You could feel Irene's presence around the place, like she wasn't gone, just in another part of the house out of sight, and you might walk around a corner at any moment and find her standing there.

Most days Alton puttered around in the barn with the radio on, and the lively fiddle music kept us jumping. Brad and Spic shackled together a new sweep, and strung cookies onto the new groundcable. Bernard had me splice the eyes in the groundcable. Brad stood by and watched me bend the steel strands together with a marlinspike. We spread out panels of twine in the yard and knit them together: plying our needles, counting meshes, and calling numbers to each other—and from her kitchen window, 101-year-old Ethel B. Raynes watched us.

On rare days off I would head for breakfast at the Wayfarer Hotel on Park Street in Rockland, where the top fishermen, the highliners, gathered when they were ashore. Captains and crew from the big boats all sat together at a long table in the middle of the dining room, like they would in the fo'c'sle. They were a fraternity born of common experience, but always invited us small boat fishermen to join in. I sat down between Chuck Doyle and Dickey Griffith, both from the one-hundred-footers of the O'Hara fleet, which at that point was steaming all the way to the tail of Grand Bank to find fish.

Chuck smiled. "Hey, how you doing there Paul?"

"Not bad. You guys been down to the Grand Banks?"

Dickey nodded. Dressed in black leather, hair slicked back like James Dean, he twirled a cigarette slowly between tired fingers.

"Hey," I said to Chuck. "I saw the *Enterprise* out on the Falls last trip. Quite a sight: a one-hundred-footer in amongst us little guys."

"She's going to the Grand Banks next time."

"Good. There ain't enough fish left in the Gulf of Maine to keep O'Hara going."

"There's a pile of yellowtail out on the Bank," Chuck said. "Four days steam, load the boat in five days, and four days back."

"I heard you have to gut them."

"That's right, it's the only way they'll keep." He leaned on his elbow, cigarette in hand. "A hundred thousand pounds, Pauly."

"What'd you share up?"

"Over ten grand." He paused to watch the effect on me. "When you gonna make a trip out there?"

"I ain't. I went on the *Atlantic Mariner* last spring. Every tow, I had to jump up on the rail with a twenty-pound steel G-link in my hand and lean out over the prop wash to hook up the doors. I survived one trip on a hundred-footer and that's enough. Lloyd was there."

An old man, Lloyd Richards, a veteran of the *Trinity,* featured in William Warner's classic book, *Distant Waters,* sat at the middle of the table and looked up. He saw me and shook his head. "Jesus Christ. You figured out the difference between a hake and a codfish yet?"

When dressing fish we always cut the heads off the hake, but no other fish, and Lloyd would not let me forget the image of him standing on the deck of the *Atlantic Mariner* with a decapitated cod in his hand. He had known I was the culprit. He shook the fish at me demanding: "Is this a hake? Is this a hake?" The white stripe down its side clearly identified it as a cod, and he threw it down in disgust.

I remembered too, the thousands of pounds of small hake we had dumped overboard that trip. Too small for market, the dead fish floated all around us, their white bellies to the sky were a sign of the captain's desperation to meet the expenses of the big boat and make the trip pay. A Canadian coast guard plane flew over low, close enough that I could see the pilot and co-pilot shaking their heads in disgust. But I didn't remind Lloyd.

I met a guy years later who used to fly for the Canadian Coast Guard, and he told me about seeing boats surrounded by dead fish: discards we called them, or trash.

The waitress stood by waiting to take my order. The Wayfarer still served fishcakes for breakfast, a traditional delicacy found in no other

local restaurant. They fried patties made from boiled hake, mashed potatoes, eggs, and cornmeal, and served them up as a side dish; I ordered two.
"That's all?" asked the waitress.

"That's all I need."

Belly full, I smoked a cigarette, drank a cup of coffee, and talked with
the other fishermen. "When you going out again?" I asked Chuck.

"Gotta wait for this hurricane to blow by," he said. "We're supposed
to be aboard standing by in case we have to take the boats out to sea."

I went along with him down to the end of Tilson Street, where all
of Rockland's big boats lay rafted along the wharf: the O'Hara fleet: the
Enterprise, the *Araho*, the *Freedom*—ninety- and hundred-foot steel boats
ready to go to the Grand Banks; the new groundfish longliners: the *Jessica
B.*, the *Rebecca B.*, and the *Cecilia B.*, bankrolled by the State of Maine and
designed to increase net profit on a dwindling number of fish. The heavy
boats bumped slowly against each other and the dock as Hurricane Gloria
churned along the coast. All their crews milled around the dock, ready to
take the boats to sea if waves started to bang the two-hundred-ton hulls
against the wharf too hard. A few other fishermen joined them, standing
around telling lies and smoking cigarettes.

One group ringed a short stocky guy going on about the old days. I
listened. ". . . used to get dressed when we came ashore. I'm talking suit, tie,
soft hat. Well, Eddy come back to the boat so drunk and he comes down
the ladder and he keeps going right past the boat till he's in the water up
to his balls, and then he kind of wakes up, and starts climbing back." The
gang all smiled and laughed, and dragged on their smokes. The cook from
the *Araho* passed Styrofoam cups full of coffee up from the galley and we
all got one. The tide ran higher than normal with the storm surge and he
passed them right across to us on the wharf.

"What are you doing?" the stocky guy asked me.

"Fishing with Bernard."

"He runnin' the boat?"

"No, Brad is."

"How you doing?"

"All right."

"Did you see my new boat?"

"I heard about it. I thought it was in Portsmouth."

"She's down at Stinson's now. You wanna have a look at her? I gotta go check on her anyhow."

"Sure." I raised my cup in farewell to a friend of mine from the *Araho* and walked up to the parking lot. We drove around to the south end of the harbor in his new used Ford.

"Nice truck, Billy," I said, touching the clean black dash.

"I wanted four-wheel drive, but I got a hell of a deal on this."

We passed the watchman at Stinson's. He waved from his little gray shed, and Billy waved back. Half a dozen boats bucked at their mooring lines and bounced against the camels, log fenders floating along Stinson's wharf.

"That's her there." He parked right in front of a little gray boat named after his daughters.

"She's small," I said, as I took my first look at the stubby fifty-footer.

"Listen, Cap, there's a lot packed into her. I can fish her right along-side an eighty-footer and tow the same gear."

We climbed aboard. "She's fiberglass?"

"An inch thick. This is a tough little boat, Cap. And everything on her is the best."

He showed me the gear on deck, split winches controlled from the wheelhouse, the safest design. "This way I can run the winches and watch they never slip." He put his hand on the tackle that would lift the cod end. "This line cost two dollars a foot, Cap. Look at it."

I reached out and touched the clean white Dacron.

Inside the wheelhouse he invited me to sit down in the plush captain's chair. "Hundred thousand dollars right here," he said sweeping his hand around the array of electronics. "Color digital plotter, I can tape my tows onto a cassette." I looked at him, wondering what the point was. "That way I could put a trip together on tape, hook the auto pilot to the plotter and the boat would just about fish itself." He went down his list of new toys: "Color depth sounder, sonar, GPS, two lorans, two VHFs, a single side band, and a radio direction finder."

"What's that for?"

"If somebody's on fish I can zero in on their radio signal and find'm."

"Clever."

He looked at me. "I want to get somebody to fish with me, someone who can run her sometimes."

I looked at him and then at the boat again.

"I had everything built for guys our size," he said. "No reaching, everything's right there. The guy at the yard asked what I'd do if I got somebody six-foot aboard. I told him I wouldn't."

He showed me down forward, the galley, and the engine: a six-cylinder Volvo four cycle—much smoother that the two-cycle GM on the *Irene & Alton.*

"You see the size birds on the outriggers, she'll ride as smooth as any big boat." I looked over the spread of electronics, and back out the window at the deck. "What'd ya think?" he asked. "Ya wanna make a trip?"

I owed Bernard, but the same seduction that pulled Doug Anderson and many others away from their traditions, overpowered my loyalty. A few days after Billy made his offer, Bernard nodded as I made my excuses. I rowed alone in the dory out to the *Irene & Alton,* laying silent on her mooring. Down in the fo'c'sle I rolled up my sleeping bag and gathered my clothes. In the doorway to the engine room I found my oilskins and gloves. As wavelets from the harbor slapped the sides of the *Irene & Alton,* I piled my dunnage into the stern of the dory, and on a gray autumn day I rowed away from Bernard's boat, the best I ever worked aboard.

"You're a professional now." Billy had said before we left on our first trip. "Get a haircut."

He started up his new boat at midnight. "I ran out of money so we skipped the muffler," he hollered over the noise of the engine.

"Well at least it's not a 671," I hollered back. We pulled away from the dock, and as soon as we stowed the lines I turned to see him standing in the door of the wheelhouse, screaming over the roar of the engine.

He pointed to three buckets full of oil from the last change, all jammed into the corner of the stern. "Dump that shit over!"

Billy came from a fishing family. His stepfather had run one of the beam trawlers out of Rockland, and Billy had gone on to fish aboard some of the most famous trawlers out of New Bedford. He intended to run his boat like the big ones.

"Clean those buckets out when you're done." He tossed a bottle of Dawn dishwashing detergent across the deck. Eddy, my new dorymate, shrugged, and went down forward to see about his galley. Almost everyone that Billy brought aboard to fish with us came from the big boat fleets of Boston, New Bedford, or Rockland. Lloyd Richards and Dickey Griffith each made a trip with us. They shared a common history with Billy but they fought with him as a captain.

In the morning we set out our gear, rolled the long net off the reel and watched it trail behind us, sinking slowly into the dark blue. The rollers of the sweep fell crashing to the deck when the net reel rolled around. "Tie that next time!" Billy screamed. Eddy and I kicked the sweep down the ramp. The net disappeared and we hooked the doors up. Like Billy said, everything fell within easy reach. I pulled the lever on the net reel and watched the doors and the wires from the winches take on the strain.

Eddy and I moved to the winches, and from our stations we waited for Billy to give the signal. "Two hundred and twenty five fathoms," he hollered from the door. From the wheelhouse Billy backed my winch, and I disengaged the clutch so the drum would free wheel. Eddy stood by, hand on the brake of his winch, and we looked at each other.

"Okay, let her go!" Billy screamed from behind us.

We loosened the brakes and let the doors sink slowly to the ten-fathom marks.

"Okay, hold'm there a minute. Let'm spread."

Eddy and I braked simultaneously. The doors caught the water like kites and drew out to either side. "Okay, let'm go!"

We eased off the brakes and let the wire spool out with increasing speed. "Twenty-five," Eddy called off his marker.

"Twenty-five." I answered a second later, as the weight of the sinking net and doors tore the heavy wire off the winch. A pair of white blurs whipped past.

"Fifty."

"Fifty."

The wire flew of the spool. The engine hammered rhythmically, as black exhaust poured out of the smokestack and swirled around us in the back draft. We set and hauled the net without incident most of the trip.

On one occasion my attention drifted as the wire spooled off the drum. I thought about a woman I'd met in Rhode Island.

"Who the hell are you fucking?" Billy's scream snapped me out of my daydream. "What mark are you on!"

I had no idea.

"And you want to run this boat?"

He closed the wheelhouse door and stood looking out the window. "There's your mark," Eddy shouted, and I braked my winch. We evened up our marks and tightened down our brakes.

"Jesus Christ," said Eddy, cigarette dangling out his mouth. "I thought he was going to blow a gasket."

We laughed, and stood on deck smoking our cigarettes, watching the wires as the boat rode up and down over the swells.

A brisk northwest wind followed the last hurricane of the season. The autumnal sea boiled, the cool surface water sank, and warmer water, rich in nutrients, rose to the surface fertilizing the secondary plankton bloom of the season. It started a feeding frenzy as seabirds fattened up for their flights to South America, or the long winter offshore. Over the starboard rail, I watched the birds that seldom touch land: sooty shearwaters, petrels, and fulmars. They landed on the surface, and dove below, flying underwater after small fish that fed in the rich zooplankton.

Pop! I turned and there stood Eddy laughing, a .22 rifle in hand. Billy took it from him and aimed at a shearwater floating thirty yards off to port. *Pop*!

"You want a try?"

"Sure."

I took the .22 and aimed it at the bird. It floated on the water oblivious to its danger.

"You ain't going to hit it anyway."

I pulled the trigger and watched the bird jolt. It tried to fly, but it could not.

"Damn, you're deadly ain't you?"

I stood there, looking at the wounded bird flopping in water. Seventy-five fathoms below the boat, and a quarter-mile astern, the net bounced, dug, and skirted along the bottom at two knots.

Unseen by us, the long ground cables, wires running from the doors to the wing ends, rolled through the mud creating clouds that herded the fish toward the gaping mouth of the net, held open by the cans above and the sweep below. The fish swam ahead trying to escape, but flounders, cod, and haddock have little endurance; the skates and dogfish, cartilaginous forebears of the modern fish, have less. For a short while they all swam in the wide mouth of the mesh but gradually drifted further back, until finally they turned and disappeared into the dark funnel of twine leading to the cod end. They landed there pressed against a growing pile of fish. In their turn they were pressed, squeezed, and suffocated.

A few cod dove under the sweep at the last minute, and those that survived the sharp edged rollers passing over them, escaped out into the thinning cloud of mud. Behind the net the water teemed with feed torn up by the sweep. Cod and dogfish gorged on sand eels and dazed small fish that escaped through the meshes of the cod end.

After four hours the net slowed, then stopped and began to rise. The groundfish in the cod end were unable to expel the air in their swim bladders as the net hauled them higher into the water column and the laws of physics came into play. Water pressure decreased and the expanding air in their bladders forced the fishes' stomachs out until their combined increasing buoyancy began to lift the cod end past the rising net.

Gulls hovered over a patch of bubbles behind us. As the yellow and orange cans from the headrope gathered toward the stern, the cod end full of fish burst to the surface behind them, bobbing there while the birds dropped down to pick at it.

"Not many flats in there," said Eddy. The flounders, with smaller swim bladders, would never float the cod end.

We wound the net aboard. With the bulk of it wrapped around the reel, I hooked the tackle to the cod end and Billy hoisted it up the ramp.

The bag bulging with fish hung in the air. I gaffed the pucker string that held the cod end closed and wrapped the tripper line quickly round a cleat. As the heavy bag swung away, the tripper, a bronze trigger device, snapped open and the fish poured out on deck.

The cod, hake, and cusk wriggled weakly, gagging on distended bladders that bulged out of their mouths like balloons. Skates and dogfish mingled with the marketable fish in the pile of mud and debris on deck.

I drew the cod end closed with the pucker string and reset the tripper. We set the net out again and waded into the pile of fish on deck, flipping the flats into baskets and the groundfish into another checker. We stepped thoughtfully, mindful of the wolf eels with their long sharp teeth and powerful jaws.

I spotted one and tossed it squirming into the checker with the cod. "I seen one of them bite right through a guy's boot," said Billy. We sorted everything of value from the pile and washed the unwanted species out the scuppers with the mud, and small fish; all dead except for the skates and dogfish. A trail of dead groundfish floating belly up stretched out behind us.

"They say there are more skates and dogfish now than there are groundfish," I said to Eddy.

He lit a cigarette and picked up a ripper, a short-bladed knife that he sharpened quickly on a honing stone, and together we began cutting and gutting the groundfish.

"The boats going to the Grand Banks have to gut the yellowtail," I told Eddy.

"Well they're sharing up fifteen grand a trip. I guess I'd dress flats for that."

Fish blood covered us to the elbows and sprayed across our faces. Eddy's cigarette bore a smattering of red dots. We hosed the fish down, washing the blood away.

"Clean'm good!" Billy hollered from the wheelhouse.

Eddy and I lifted the top hatch cover and set it down right side up, we pulled off the insulated covers and I climbed down into the hold.

"Put the lights on," I hollered up.

I lit a cigarette and leaned against a bulkhead in my sanctuary, the only place on the boat I had all to myself. After a few minutes the lights came on.

I stood in an alley that ran down the middle of the hold—the slaughter—and breathed the cool damp air, heavy with the smells of ammonia, ice, and old bile. Eight fish pens: four- by five-foot compartments about six feet high, opened into the slaughter like rows of walk-in closets: four on each side, some full of ice, the others partially full of fish. I tossed my cigarette into the bottom of an empty pen and shoveled ice on top of it and then slid two thick wooden boards into slotted stanchions at the opening, building a wall that would rise as I filled each pen with ice and fish.

"Ice'm good," Billy hollered down.

"They are."

Eddy handed down an eighty-pound basket of flats and I tipped it into a forward pen as it fell into my hands. He passed more down, and in between baskets I tossed ice across the slimy flat fish, mostly dab and gray sole. Then he pitched down the several hundred pounds of ground fish. "That's it," he hollered.

"Okay." I lit another cigarette, and stood considering the pile of dead fish at the forward end of the slaughter. Using a short-handled, two-tine pitchfork, I threw them into their pens, icing them down at intervals until they all lay snug.

In the wheelhouse Billy accosted me on my way down forward. "That took you nearly two hours to handle a thousand pounds of fish. We used to get five thousand pounds a tow out here, and put them down in an hour."

"They were bigger fish back then, you didn't have to handle as many," I said, and went below. A minute later I came back up. "And you had four or five men on deck." As always, Billy had the last word, but I cannot remember what it was.

Out on the Falls one night, I stood watch while Billy slept. I saw a blip on the radar, and in the distance a light. As we drew closer I could see the arrangement of the decklights on the other boat, and recognized her: the *Irene & Alton*. I talked to Brad on the VHF. Nobody was catching much that year, but high prices more than made up for the lack of fish. As the fish stocks declined, net profit continued to increase, masking the problem and creating an incentive for more effort.

"How high will the price have to be when there's no fish?" I asked, but Brad didn't think it would get that bad. Using the net we had patched together in the barn, he and Spic, and our old swordfish pilot, Fred Brooks, were making more money than I was on Billy's $300,000 high-tech wonder.

I stayed aboard with Billy, though, because I wanted a chance to run his boat, but as the months went by, he became more and more stressed by the payments he had to make. He changed the share system so that he took a bigger percentage of our gross, and he got meaner. One cold night in December he shook us from our bunks. "Hung down!"

The net had snagged on some immovable object below. In minutes we donned our boots and oil gear, found dry gloves and stepped out the door to survey the ice-covered deck. The boat churned the water behind us but we went nowhere.

"Didn't you feel us hang down?" Billy demanded, squinting at me. I said nothing. "You're not even here, are you?" He elbowed past me out onto deck. "Put that fuckin' winch in gear!" he screamed. He tried to reach past me, but I pushed his arm away. He grabbed me, spun me against the bulkhead, and drew back his fist, about to hit me. The boat rolled, and we braced ourselves in that momentary tableau.

He dropped his fist and put his face in mine. "Don't you ever get slatty with me. I'll throw you the fuck over."

After we broke free and hauled the doors up, I stood in the stern by the net reel, holding the lever—easy to reach—and watched sheets of water slough off the ground cables as they broke the surface. In the black beyond I saw stars, pinpricks of light in cold space. The net reel turned, and water splashed up the ramp, coating the deck with ice.

I turned suddenly at the sound of someone calling my name. But it was only the noise of the engine.

"Did you hear someone call you?" Lloyd Richards had asked me one night, after he saw me startle like that.

"Yeah."

"Be careful. They'll call you right over. I watched a guy walk right out the stern ramp one night. Never saw him again."

I almost made another trip with Billy after that. I went down to the wharf at midnight, but the wind whipped through the rigging, and he decided to wait until dawn. Back home at one a.m., I called a friend in Alaska—it was only eight in the evening there. We talked for over an hour. "You're working with a crazy-maker," he told me. "You're never going get it right for him, so get as far away from him as you can—before you do something you regret."

I had found three shells for the .22 rifle and put them in my pocket, thinking they might come in handy if Billy threatened me again. The next morning aboard the boat I handed Billy the bullets and said, "These are for you. I'm all done."

He looked down at them, and back at me. "Okay."

I sat on the dock watching the boat steam away. I needed to step away from fishing for a bit. Even Bernard did that occasionally. I recalled him talking about a trip he and Eleanor once took to Amish country, in Pennsylvania; a place where an American subculture thrived by hanging on to the past.

I'd grown up on the fringes of Amish Country and knew what it looked like: Black wagons, shy women, and an old man with his gray beard flying in the breeze as he plowed a field behind six Percheron horses hitched abreast. Nice, but I needed to go someplace less domesticated.

Thinking I could escape noise, diesel fumes, grinding machinery, and patterns of destruction, I got in my truck and drove north toward what I thought was wild country. I crossed the Canadian border at Madawaska, and continued on across the Gaspe Peninsula. At Matane, Quebec, on the St. Lawrence River, I left my truck and took the ferry to Godbout; from there, the bus to Sept-Isles, moving deeper into Canada.

On a bitter cold December morning, I climbed aboard a strange train, unlike anything I had ever seen: two passenger cars hooked to the tail of a string of boxcars and gondolas, pulled by an engine with a big snow-plow on the front. Diesel stoves surrounded by metal screens sat at the ends of the passenger cars. They emitted intense heat, but failed to warm the car, which had filled to brimming with Natives: Naskapi and Montagnais. The only other white passenger was a fellow about my age with hair down over his shoulders and a beard neatly trimmed in the old French style, a mustache separated from a wisp of a goatee, like the Three Musketeers.

I sat down across from him, and we struck up a conversation. His name was Sylvain. He worked as a guide and trapper, he said. He had left Gaspe the day before with a load of goose decoys. He pointed to them: half a dozen plastic geese shoved into the overhead racks in a confusion of heads and tails.

"Why you go to Shefferville?" he asked.

I had no answer for him. If I had said I wanted a break from cultural disintegration and watching natural resources wiped out, he might have told me I was on the wrong train. The tracks had been laid to reach iron deposits and other resources in northern Quebec and western Labrador. The iron mines had played out, but the train continued to bring supplies to the Native people who had come to depend on them.

We rolled north along frozen rivers in valleys between gumdrop-shaped mountains, on into Labrador and the taiga, where wispy patches of stunted black spruce grew on the verge of the tundra. Sylvain showed me a stack of photos from hunting trips. Periodically a face would be smiling up from a picture and he would tap it with the back of his finger and say. "This one. He commit suicide." There were about three or four of them in that one stack of photos, all young guides, most of them Natives. I wondered what made them do it, but did not ask—hopelessness beyond words I figured.

Half a dozen caribou galloped alongside the train. A willow ptarmigan flew from the bush, and disappeared out over the snow. Further along I saw snowshoe tracks that crossed the train tracks and headed off toward the empty and frozen horizon.

All along the route I saw two types of Natives, those who lived by their old ways, hunting and trapping in the bush—one such group came aboard the train dressed in moosehide moccasins and carrying bundles of skins—and those who lived in the system, close to town where they cashed their checks and bought supermarket food. A family of four assimilated Indians sat next to me, and the father, I presume, asked for a cigarette. I gave him one. He passed to his wife and looked back at me. He repeated this until everyone in the family, including a little girl about six years old, smiled back at me as they puffed on their cigarettes. I thought there might be two types of fishermen too, the ones who held on to their traditions, and those who became dependent on a vicious cycle: constantly forced to upgrade their technology in order to catch more fish to pay for more new technology.

We reached Shefferville after dark. A green curtain of light filled the northern sky: the aurora borealis. A Naskapi man on the platform looked at my sheepskin gloves. "You need these," he said and held up his moose-hide and beaver fur mittens. I smiled and offered to buy them from him, but he shook his head and told me to take a taxi into town, that I would get hurt trying to walk.

I took a taxi from the station to the Hotel Royale and checked into a stark room where I lay on my bed in the dark, thinking about Bernard and Billy, the snowshoe tracks across the taiga, and how a culture can endure and decline simultaneously. I drifted into a waking dream.

Somewhere in the Gulf of Maine, a big cod glides through the cold viscous pressure. Night at forty fathoms: a world as dark as the womb, and every bit as sensuous. Searching for its own cohorts, the lone codfish snakes through the murk—seeking the submarine landscape of her past and finding only fragments.

She joins a meager school of middling sized cod, eleven-year-olds that weigh around twenty-five pounds. In the past she would have guided the school to known places, but fragmentation of the ecosystem leaves no path from one feeding ground to the next. Around her, undersea barrens lie between smoothed-over ridges; her old migration routes have been altered beyond recognition.

The smell too has changed, the scents of deep-water coral, and the gravely mud it held in place, have vanished. Her tail flips and she surges forward, the weight of her, fat with roe, carries her into a boulder field amidst the gravel and sand. She feels the emptiness beneath her and drops down, and there in a small depression finds an oasis of anemone and coral. The bottom writhes with sandworms feeding in the night, and she charges through the undulating forest, her streamlined nervous system categorizing every subtle shift around her, her barbel, the little whisker on her chin, tastes the difference between anemone and worm, and she snaps up the latter. She leads the diminished school through the remnants of the environment in which her instincts evolved.

Then they glide past a glacial boulder, left thousands of years before for their protection, and back into the barrens. She snaps her tail again and surges weightless through the darkness. In the night, she lives by smell, and feel, and sound, touched by every pulse that strikes her lateral line, like notes plucked on a tight string. The music plays continuously, but the range of octaves has changed, the notes diminished, and she is going deaf. Less pummeled by ambient noise twenty years prior, her otoliths, ear bones, developed far more complexities than those of the young fish surrounding her. At one time she could hear much more than the small cod. But the variegations of her otoliths left them more vulnerable to damage from seismic surveys and sonar. Even ships' engines in close proximity have had an impact on her senses, and now she can hardly hear the grunts and serial knocking of the eleven-year-old males seeking to attract her as a mate.

But the muffled calls of the males strike old synapses, and somewhere in her nervous system may echo the memory of larger males over rich feeding grounds, the volume of their grunting and knocking, demonstrating their strength to fecund females, plump with millions of eggs. It is enough, and she expels her eggs amid a cloud of the competing young males' sperm.

The sand lance she feeds on grow only half the size they used to, stunted by PCBs. The toxins, endocrine inhibitors, have accumulated in her system and taken their toll; many of the eggs she lays develop poorly, the hearts and nervous systems of the larvae are often malformed. By the time the larvae wriggle out of their egg cases the yolk sacs meant to sustain them have long since disappeared. The malformed larvae float in darkness and perish.

The young that survive mill about in isolated areas, unable to follow the old migration routes, now forgotten or useless. Few old fish are left to lead the way. Their indelible memories, gifts of millions of years of evolution, have become obsolete. No reason remains for the cod to know when the herring will be near shore, if the herring are gone, or to know where the sand eel bottom is, when draggers have scoured it. Too much has changed in the ecology that once sustained them in abundance.

In the altered world beneath the surface, rapacious dogfish compete with and sometimes eat the smaller cod. The small cods' own parents hunt them down. The rumbling nets, clinking chain, and banging doors drive them from their last strongholds. Fish bodies hang in gill nets, and discarded cod litter the seafloor, covered with crabs.

The already fecund two- and three-year-old females linger above the offshore shoals, or concentrate in their ancestral breeding grounds in the western Gulf of Maine. They cannot expand to their old numbers; the ecology they depended on has shifted and grown less hospitable.

Back in Rockland a similar shift had begun. The O'Hara boats disappeared, some to Gloucester, others to Alaska, and in Rockland the once bustling waterfront became a scene of intermittent activity. The *Irene & Alton* continued to unload there, but she offloaded her fish into trucks bound for Portland. With Bernard's charts, Brad managed to find enough fish to keep the boat going, but the situation looked bleak. Most fishermen had seen their share of dead fish, floating in long trails behind the boats, with white bellies to the sky.

I did not try to get back aboard the *Irene & Alton;* I enjoyed fishing with Bernard, listening to the odd jokes and songs he no doubt had gotten from Del. With Brad it became just a job.

Not many options remained in Rockland so I wandered down to Point Judith, Rhode Island, and landed a site as mate aboard a sixty-five-foot dragger, the *Ian Keyes*. A young guy came out with us and while we worked sorting through a tow of whiting, he started to tell me how to pick deck. He made that mistake three times, and even though he outweighed me by a few pounds, I threw him into the shrouds and pinned him there with my fish pick across his throat. "Don't fuck with me!"

"Ungh."

The brotherhood that I sought, the mutual benevolence I first learned on Kerr's Pond, had vanished.

I drove back to Maine and moved downeast to a remote part of the coast near the Canadian border. I came ashore and worked for the

Passamaquoddy tribe for a while, running a processing plant that handled Canadian fish.

After that collapsed due to a lack of financing, a friend called from Alaska. "Paul, do you know how to salt codfish?" I knew the basics. "Yeah."

"Well, we need somebody to come up to Alaska and teach the Yupiks how to salt cod. You interested?"

"Sure. Who are the Yupiks?"

"Eskimos."

We talked out the details and clicked off. I dialed Alton in Owls Head. "Hello, Alton. You know how to salt cod right? Can you teach me?" Down in Owls Head, Alton and I split cod that Brad had brought in. I took notes while Alton gave me recipes for salting.

"How do you like it Downeast?" he asked as we worked.

"Nice."

He reached for another fish.

"Have you ever been out to Cross Island?"

"No." I looked up at him. "Where's that?"

"Near Cutler. My grandfather and grandmother used to sail down there in the summer to salt cod. They'd set up their flakes on the beach and dry fish there all summer."

"No, I ain't been down there. Mostly I've been around Pleasant Point, Eastport, and the Saint Croix River."

"Well, if you go down there, be careful," he said as he slid his knife along the cod's belly and laid it open. "My grandmother would go clamming at low tide and she had to watch out for what they called honey holes. It's like a spot of quicksand and there's no way to tell it."

Three weeks later, after changing to smaller and smaller planes, a Cessna landed me in Toksook Bay, Alaska, on the Bering Sea. The pilot pointed out the house of one of my contacts, David Bill, the village headman.

David Bill had a musk ox skin spread out on a rack in front of his door; a pack of sled dogs stood stiff-legged on top of their houses and howled when I knocked. Nobody answered. I heard the sound of the plane taking off, and stood on the porch looking around. The village, a mix of pre-fab and patchwork houses, spread out down a slight grade and ended at a beach where a few small boats sat on the sand. Beyond that stretched the Bering Sea, a wide expanse of slate-colored ocean dotted with white caps. Because I could see so much of it, the sky appeared low. Shrouds of gray rain hung under distant clouds, moving hither and yon with the wind. They passed over the village just often enough to keep the streets muddy.

"What are you looking for?" asked a young guy as I wandered deeper into the village. He wore a too tall baseball hat, and the brim sat down low over his eyes.

"I'm looking for David Bill."

"He's not around much. He's fishing out of Mekoryuk."

"How about Willy Wasson, of the Bering Sea Fishermen's Association?"

"He's down at the Co-op. You here to work with him?"

"Uh huh."

"Come on."

"What's your name?"

"Sam."

We walked down toward the shore, our rubber boots sinking into the soft earth. We passed an open field with an earthen dome in it. "What's that?"

"You know Robert Redford? He came here about three years ago and hired some people to build him that sod igloo for a movie. They never made the movie and those people never got paid."

"What do you know about this great cod stock out here?"

"I heard the government boat caught fifteen thousand pounds in a fifteen-minute tow."

"Dragging?"

"With a net."

I could hardly imagine, but when I checked the number later I found Sam had understated the case. Although the Pacific cod lacked the quality—the firm flesh and flavor—of Atlantic cod, they made up for it in quantity.

I met my contact, Willy Wasson, and he took me on a tour while explaining the project.

By late afternoon the fishermen had returned and their little skiffs crowded the shore. Willy explained that these boats would have first crack at the new cod quota. "What they don't catch goes to the Japanese."

"What do the Japanese have for boats?"

"One-hundred-fifty-foot automated longliners."

"I see. Who orchestrated this deal?"

"We worked it out with the state, and David Bill."

In the processing plant, four women watched while I showed them how to split cod. I cut the fish the way Alton showed me a few days before and they nodded in appreciation. I tried to give them the knives I'd brought but they pushed them aside and brandished their ulus. With those traditional crescent shaped knives they cut the fish exactly the way I had learned it from Alton, but they did it faster and cleaner.

"I haven't got much to teach you about cutting fish," I thought to myself.

On the other side of the building more Yupik women cleaned halibut and packed them in iced boxes. A white guy stood nearby, overseeing their work. Willy introduced me to Mark Ernest.

"What's going on?" I asked him.

"We're flying these to Anchorage," he told me.

"No kidding? Does it pay?"

"Oh yeah, we're doing all right. It's the best market these guys have ever seen."

With Willy, things did not go as well. I may have been ad-libbing on the salting, but I knew how to run a processing line. I told him what he needed if he wanted to create a smooth and competitive operation, but he preferred to improvise on so many aspects it started to look like a Rube Goldberg project. I realized I was participating in a sham, a bone tossed to the Yupiks while the industrial scale boats took the resource.

A few days before leaving I stood on the village beach looking out under the low clouds. Half a dozen big halibut lay rotting in the sand.

Sam leaned against the tailgate of a truck. "Mark lost his market," he said.

"Will he get it back?"

"Maybe next year. We did okay."

"That's good. What are you going to do with all your money?"

"Buy a truck, man."

"But there's only one mile of road in this town, and gas is $5 a gallon. What the hell are you going to do with a truck?"

"I can lease it to people," he said and tapped the tailgate. "Mark had to lease this one."

An old woman from the more traditional village of Nightmute stepped out of a boat that had just landed. She stood in her sealskin boots and fur parka amidst several hundred pounds of rotting fish. Her toothless jaw hung loose as she took in a scene she could hardly contemplate. At her age she had survived many famines, and the halibut-strewn beach was a grave sin. She cried and pointed at the fish, speaking harshly to Sam.

"She says a curse will come from this," he translated for me.

"Tell her it already has."

Home in Maine, days came when all I wanted to do was drive to Owls Head and beg my way aboard the *Irene & Alton*. I satisfied myself by stopping to visit Bernard whenever I went down to Rockland; on every occasion, the groundfish fleet had grown smaller and more processing plants closed. Brad kept the boat going by fishing two-handed, and I knew there could be no return. But many of us who had fished on the *Irene & Alton* never got her out of our systems. I saw it in others.

Glen Lawrence bought a sardine carrier in the late 1980s: the *Double Eagle*. The first time I saw her coming across Rockland Harbor, I thought she was the *Irene & Alton*. She had the same sweeping sheer and high bow, her wheelhouse sat aft, and Glenn had painted her the same gray and white Bernard used on his boat.

"When I found her she had grass growing on her deck," said Glenn. He bought her and brought her back to Rockland where she sat on the rails at North End Shipyard for almost a year. "Once we got going we saw almost everything had to be replaced, frames, bottom planking. I put over a hundred thousand into her," he said. "It's basically a new boat built on the model of the old."

The *Double Eagle* had a slightly checkered history in becoming a new boat. Fish landed in US ports have to come out of US-built hulls, but the

Canadians can build boats cheaper. In 1949 the *Double Eagle's* owners took her to Nova Scotia to be rebuilt. She left Rockland as a fifty-foot boat with a square transom, and returned as a seventy-foot double ender.

"It was a new boat," said Bernard, who remembered the boat's return. "Folks said the only part of the old *Double Eagle* that come back from Nova Scotia was the deck beam with her [documentation] numbers on it." But the ruse worked, and in 2004 she was still carrying sardines around Penobscot Bay, and Glenn still paints her up gray with white trim every year.

Another veteran of the *Irene & Alton,* Georg Hinteregger, built a Swampscott dory under Alton's supervision. The Swampscott dory marked the high point of dory development; it fit the definition of a dory: a small, hard chine boat with the bottom planked lengthwise, and a tombstone transom that tapered to a point where it met the bottom. The Swampscott was intended to sail; it had a somewhat rounded hull, an extremely narrow bottom, and a steep rake to the transom, which lay far back over the water.

Georg and I sailed his dory one day near his home in Rhode Island. As we tacked down South Pond, I ran my hands over the wood, painted gray with white trim.

"Alton was so precise," Georg said of the building. "He was one of a kind, Bernard too. When they're gone they'll take a lot with them."

I nodded, not wanting to think about it. We headed back up the bay. "How many feet in a nautical mile?" Georg asked; it was a quiz.

"6,076," I said.

Georg never let go of swordfishing; he made a career of his job as an observer for the National Marine Fisheries Service. In 2004 he was still working, steaming to the Grand Banks on US swordfish longliners to monitor turtle bycatch.

Donald Pelrine took off to Nantucket after the scallop bonanza ended in the early 1980s, but he never lost touch with Bernard. He too had a soft spot in his heart for the *Irene & Alton.* "In Nantucket everything is gray and white," he said. "I never had a boat, but I put those colors into my life."

Brad, of course, lived close to the heart of the matter. Unsentimental, he fished the *Irene & Alton.* In spite of numerous battles with Bernard over whether or not to put outriggers on the boat or upgrade the technology, he never quit, and Bernard never fired him. Over the years he had transferred the marks from Bernard and Alton's charts onto newer charts and into the computerized plotter Bernard finally bought him. Brad absorbed the Rayneses' ways, at least on a practical level, and he still helped paint the boat gray and white every year.

For me, I withdrew from modern fishing and sought to reclaim some things even Bernard had left behind. I built a dory, not as precise as Alton and Georg's, but sturdy—an ocean worthy rowboat. Without a thought I painted it gray and white, moored her in Haycocks Harbor, and fished the fogbound shoreline of Downeast Maine. As the world got more complicated I escaped toward the refuge of simplicity.

Working the intertidal zone and watching the ways of the tides and the moon, I picked periwinkles, "wrinkles," little sea snails that sold for forty cents a pound. Perhaps if I had had Bernard's background and teachers, I might have built a fifty-seven-foot dragger. But all I had was a patchwork of ideas and experiences. I did not have the resources or confidence to attain what Bernard had, so I recreated what I could of it on a smaller scale.

"A dory?" Bernard said when I told him what I was doing. "That was all over in Father's time."

But Bernard talked about how his grandfather found his way among the islands in the fog. "He'd get the wind blowing from one direction on the boat and that would help'm keep straight, and the way the swells came at him. If he could keep them coming from the same direction that'd help too; and he could hear the different horns."

In 1985, Bernard had found his way home from Georges Bank by dead reckoning. He set a course from his last known position, where the loran went out, to Matinicus Rock, factoring in how the wind and tide would affect his run.

He knew the tides offshore, he proved that by finding the last fish on the night of the storm; calculating its drift from where we struck it and tracking it down.

The tides of the Bay of Fundy, where I worked, presented a different challenge. From the mouth of the Bay up to Minas Basin the tide range runs from twenty-seven to over fifty feet, rising and falling twice a day. Every twelve hours the ebbing tide runs out, sometimes at 5 knots, exposing vast flats in the bays, and a wide variety of seaweeds and other marine life.

On the full moon and the new moon, roughly when the sun and the moon are in line, the tides rise and fall to their greatest extremes, known as spring tides, which come any time of year. In the summer the sun arcs high and the full moon arcs low. In winter it's the opposite. When the sun and the moon do-si-do in the spring and fall, they align themselves to give an extra tug, drawing the tides far up the beaches on the flood, and ebbing away to expose parts of the ocean floor that only breathe air once or twice a year. The high spring tides occur around noon and midnight, with low water in the morning and evening.

As the earth turns the Bay of Fundy away from the new moon in the wee hours of a March morning, the narrow bay essentially spins out from under a bulge of water permanently drawn toward the moon and sun, high tide, and into a thinner layer of water: low tide.

Seaweed-covered rocks emerge. The rockweed and bladder wrack that grow just below the high water mark show first. Below that, patches of Irish moss, like little red trees, hide handfuls and handfuls of wrinkles. Below that, dulse, short maroon mitten-shaped leaves, layer over the rocks like shingles. Green and purple laver adheres like bits of wet cellophane tossed against the boulders. Below the short-leaved seaweeds, which survive the worst beating from the surf, live the horsetail kelp—smooth dark fans floating in the deep tide pools—and the thin and fragile alaria, its golden midrib and light brown feathers visible from a distance. Thick forests of long kelp, *Laminaria longicruris,* grow below the reach of the tide, rising up more than twenty feet from the bottom. As the mounting swells approach the shore they sweep up great mats of the kelp, holding the long fronds outstretched before tumbling in white foam on the rocks.

In the gray light before dawn I stand at the head of Haycock Harbor, and pull my dory into shore on a haul-out like Bernard has for his dory I untie the boat, drop my oars in, and shove off, slipping the oars in between the thole pins, two oak pegs on either rail, which act as oar locks. In the fog, the dull wooden thuds of the oars banging between the thole pins, the songs of the chickadees and the "peents" and whirring courtship flights of the first returning woodcocks all echo between the steep walls of the harbor.

Rowing with the ebb tide, it carries me swiftly down the narrow fjord, a mile to the mouth of the harbor. Fog and lingering darkness obscure the rocks along the outside shore, but the swells rolling in from the ocean break foaming white on the headlands and wash into the coves, creating maps through a cartography of sound. I row blind for two miles down the coast, listening to the crashing of the waves on rocks I have grown familiar with, creating a picture in my mind that, along with the swells coming steadily out of the southwest, enable me to maintain my direction and position. It is important, though, that my attention never wavers. If I lose the continuity of images building in my mind, I will get confused and lost.

Closing with the shore in a broad cove called Bailey's Mistake, named after a misguided navigator who lost his ship there, I watch the big seas break at the opening of an extensive tide pool. The big ones usually come in sets of three; they roar through the narrow gut and crash into each other as the receding wave meets the next oncoming. They heap foam on each other and fill the air with spindrift, then calm down for a few moments before the next set arrives. After a series of waves rolls under me and blasts back and forth in the gut, I row furiously through the settling foam, reaching the safety of the pool before the onset of the next tumult. I beach my boat, toss my anchor, and set off with a small pail and an empty onion bag, searching for snails in the intertidal zone, a world between two worlds.

I had started wrinkle picking in 1988, crawling over the rocks around Moose Cove, Sandy Cove, Haycock's Harbor, and Bailey's Mistake. I steered clear of the honey holes Alton had warned me about, and learned to fall on the slippery seaweed without getting too bruised up. I became intimate with the shape of every crack that held a wrinkle and how the tide ran and waves acted over a submerged landscape. I developed the ability to hear the tide change. The topography became a part of my own mental landscape; like abstract art, it communicated with me, and I came to view it as having a personality, which became part of mine. I used to tell people, "I know every rock between Moose River and Bailey's by name." I grew deeply intimate with a small area, a seven-mile stretch of coastline that I could sometimes see, and it gave me an idea of the vision Bernard had to build in his mind when he imagined a vast submarine landscape.

He had an advantage—he built on an old foundation. Bernard's father had shared with him what he knew of the bottom around Penobscot Bay and the Gulf of Maine, and that was a great deal of knowledge. Alton had an incredible memory; he could describe the entrances of harbors he had never seen; he had memorized their descriptions from coastal pilot books and word of mouth—on the off chance that in an emergency he might have to use them.

Bernard added to that knowledge through experience and close attention to the sounding machine, essentially an electronic leadline that showed him cross sections of the sea floor. Through the signal intensity displayed as different colors on a screen, the sounder showed whether he was over rock, mud, gravel, or sand. The display showed a thin line across the bottom, but the narrow slice of depth contour could miss entire underwater mountains, or fertile valleys full of fish. Over the years of putting those lines together, however, Bernard had created a mental chart far more detailed than the ones he bought, and he learned how the unseen landscape guided the movements of fish.

"We always found the fish preferred the west side of any rise. I don't know if that was because things grew better on that side, or if it gave'm a lee from the tide coming out of the Bay of Fundy," he said.

"The man on deck doesn't think the same as the man in the wheelhouse," he added, recalling his transition from crewman to captain. "When I went on deck with Father, all I thought about was how I could do my work better and faster so I could go back to my bunk. Then when I got into the wheelhouse, I had to start thinking about how to make a trip.

"I realized that in order to put a trip together I had to learn to think like a fish. I'd imagine the bottom and try to figure what it looked like and how the fish would move on it," he said. "I'd get so caught up in that, the days would run together. I didn't count days, I counted fuel and grub, and water. Sometimes we'd have to melt ice for water. Ernie Kavanaugh used to do that on the Grand Banks, melt ice for water."

Listening to Bernard, it occurred to me that his were only a few of the observations accumulated by generations of people who had grown intimate with fish. When those fish vanish and the places like Haddock Nubble disappear, all that knowledge becomes obsolete.

I think about these things and others as I work in the quiet tide pools, the crash of the surf in the background. In my first years I have the wrinkles all to myself. On spring tides I can fill seven bags, almost three hundred pounds—$120 for six hours work. Following Bernard's example I keep my expenses low by building my own boat and relying more on my strength and senses than on technology.

One of the two lobstermen working out of Haycock's asks me why I don't put a motor on my dory. "You're going to end up over on Grand Manan one of these days," he says, pointing toward an island ten miles off-shore. "Trying to climb them cliffs like Billy Jones." Jones and his brother had been swept across to Grand Manan, where they spent a night at the base of the three-hundred-foot cliffs on the west side of the island. Their story had been immortalized in *Reader's Digest*.

"They had a motor," I remind the lobsterman. "Besides, I want my money in my pocket. A motor costs five hundred dollars for something decent; then I have to register my boat; there's another twenty bucks; plus gas and all that. That all has to be paid for in product, and that adds up to a lot of goddamn wrinkles. Then I'd have to go further to get all those wrinkles, and when I used them up I'd have to get a bigger boat and probably get into lobstering to help pay for it."

I watch them swallow that one.

"It's a slippery slope," I say. "Plus, if I had an engine I wouldn't be able to hear the breakers, and then I really would get lost."

I am content with keeping my enterprise simple, and I figure that even if I do not get as many wrinkles as pickers with motorboats, I realize more profit from the ones I get. It is the same principle Bernard operates on, and it makes sense. Although he has a motor, Bernard built his boat so that she could be rigged for sail if need be.

Working around the tide pool, I fill six bags and leave them jammed into cracks in the rocks, safe from the crashing waves. I will take them aboard another, hopefully calmer, day. As I sit on a rock waiting for the returning tide to float my boat, an eagle comes screaming out of the sky driving off some gulls that had gathered around a lumpfish stranded by the ebb tide. The gulls circle the eagle and his trophy, but he holds them back, wings spread, his screams filling the whole cove.

Besides picking wrinkles, I sometimes head down the coast to Cross Island to jig for cod, the remnants of the coastal cod stocks that Bernard's great-grandparents Horace and Ada would have salted back at the turn of the century. I study the charts, trying to think like a fish, looking for the likely spots on the west side of underwater knolls.

In 1988 the fish showed up, and one of the lobstermen from Cutler caught several hundred pounds in a morning. There were no fish buyers left in town so he gave them all away. The school has yet to return.

Fisheries scientists suspect that localized stocks that frequent particular spawning grounds can be wiped out far from those areas. The school from around Cross Island may have been decimated in one winter day's fishing by one of the big boats on Georges Bank, or a fleet of gillnetters may have caught them migrating inshore in the spring.

Rocking my dory back and forth in the fog, I work my three hooks, listening to the horn on Little River Island—the entrance to Cutler Harbor. Nothing bites. Horace and Ada would have starved there. After a few fruitless seasons I give it up.

I take what is left to me and continue to work the shore from Moose River to Bailey's Mistake, picking wrinkles, hauling a few dozen lobster traps by hand, and picking seaweed in the coves. I row through the fog, listen to the waves smash into the rocks—and for a few more years, I seldom leave those haunts.

Fifteen

DORYMATES

Some years I would have to make trips offshore to get by, and I passed through Rockland often enough to watch the old guard—Bernard's mentors and competitors—vanish from the waterfront. In September of 1990, 1 made a trip to Georges Bank aboard the scalloper *Master Joel,* a sixty-five-foot steel boat out of Southwest Harbor. On the way to Georges we put in at Rockland to pick up more crew and ice.

The *Irene & Alton* lay under the ice machine at O'Hara's. Brad was still running her and they were icing up for another trip. An eight-inch diameter hose snaked down into the hold, and Brad aimed the stream of crushed ice shooting out of it into the various pens.

I saw Bernard standing on the wharf. "How's Alton?" I asked.

"Not very well."

"What ails him?"

Bernard shook his head. "He's not at all well."

We had a few hours before we left, so I borrowed Bernard's truck and headed over to Owls Head. I pulled up into Alton's driveway and walked up to his door. "The House on the Hill" overlooked all of Owls Head Harbor. His little white fluff dog, Polar, sat on the stoop, but refrained from his usual yapping. Alton's second wife, Anne, let me in, and I found him lying on a day bed in the kitchen. He tried to rise but couldn't, his skin hung sallow on his face and hands. He looked up at me, and I could see his eyes were all clouded over.

"Hi, Alton, how you doing?"

"Not good, not good." He paused. "I don't believe I know you." Anne shook her head.

"It's me, Paul. I used to go swordfishing with Bernard." He did not react. "I used to have a pair of Redwings like yours."

He stared at me, but nothing registered. "No. I can't remember you, boy. I'm sorry. But good luck to you." He lifted his hand a little, and let it back down.

I left him there, and headed back to the *Master Joel*. We went out to the southeast part of Georges, cut "peanuts"—illegally small scallops—for two weeks, and headed back in to Southwest Harbor.

I didn't get back to Rockland till New Year's Day 1991. Lonny Raposa, brother of a guy I once fished with in Rhode Island, had brought his boat up to Maine. He had called me from Rockland. Did I want to make a trip with him? Sure. The wrinkle picking was slow, and my dory was upside down under the snow.

Lonny's boat, a seventy-foot trawler, the *Amethyst,* lay at Stinson's on the south end—though it wasn't Stinson's anymore. A new outfit owned it, and they did not stay in business long. I walked down to look the boat over and did not like what I saw. She had a long cabin on deck, a low bow, tall outriggers, and small birds—all the marks of a southern-built shrimper with no business in northern waters. Her steel hull needed paint, and a diver, who had just finished clearing rope out of her wheel, told me she had no zincs left that he could see. Depending on how long they'd been gone, the welds that held the hull together might be as soft and weak as jelly.

She's a slab, I thought, and was about to leave when an old man poked his head out of the wheelhouse. "How ya doin' t'ere, b'y?" he asked with a Newfie accent.

"Alright."

"You comin' wit' us."

"Maybe."

"You been out before."

"Yeah, I used to fish with Bernard Raynes out of Owls Head."

He smiled at Bernard's name. "By the Lord t'underin' Jesus, bring yer gear aboard," he said. "What's yer name?"

"Paul Molyneaux. You?"

"Ernie Kavanaugh."

There he stood: the living legend of the Grand Banks, Georges Bank, and the Gulf of Maine—Ernie Kavanaugh, swordfisherman, draggerman, and wild pirate of Canadian waters. Since the first time the Canadian Coast Guard hauled him into Halifax in 1985, they had caught him poaching on two more occasions. The last time, under hot pursuit with the Canadian Coast Guard cutter *Chebucto* firing shots across his bow, he raced for the Hague Line. He let his wire run right off the winches, slipped loose of his net and doors so they could not prove he was fishing.

"Come on'n make a trip wit' us," he said. "We need a good man. T'is fellow ain't much."

For Ernie's sake only I threw my sea bag across onto the roof of the wheelhouse, and climbed down after it.

"We'll tell a few yarns anyway," Ernie said, and he took my bag into the galley.

A few hours later Lonny lumbered through the cabin door from deck, followed by a young guy from Rhode Island. "You Paul?"

"Yep."

We shook hands.

"You fished with my brother huh?"

"Yeah, aboard the *Northern Lights* in 1984."

The *Northern Lights* had been a seventy-foot eastern rig with a four-man crew. We had worked her the old way, all of us pulling the net in together, hooking our fingers into the meshes and hauling the twine in handful by handful, every tow.

"Was you on her when she went down?"

"No. I had a bad feeling about her, and I quit just before."

"How'd you like Tony?"

I remembered his brother Tony and I going nose to nose on deck, in a shouting match about what size fish to keep, and the crew all laughing about it later. "He was alright, we got along."

"Yeah right. Nobody gets along with my brother. I'm not like him, okay?"

I shrugged. "Okay."

Ernie leaned over to me after Lonny went forward. "He lays in his bunk all day."

The next morning, New Year's Day, we steamed over to McClellan's Wharf to fuel up. Bernard was in there fueling and icing the *Irene & Alton*. I asked about Alton, and learned that he had died a few days after my last visit, just shy of his eighty-third birthday.

Bernard looked over at the *Amethyst* and then to Ernie and me. "You fellows going out on that?"

We smiled, embarrassed. "Oh, she's alright, Bernard," Ernie said. "Say, can you spare any oil? All the stores are closed."

Besides going to the Grand Banks together in the 1960s, Bernard and Ernie had a long history. They were among the minority of Catholic fishermen in Maine, and when Bernard first started out with the *Ruth & Mary*, he had learned a lot from the old Newfoundlander.

The stars burned bright at five o'clock on a December morning. Uncle Marc and two other crewmen worked the frozen mooring line off the bit on the fore deck of the *Ruth & Mary* and dropped it into Bernard's dory. In 1969, the winter the Stratton Report came out, Bernard had been working the shrimp grounds below Monhegan, twenty miles west of Matinicus. New to shrimping, he met his old friend Ernie Kavanaugh on the grounds.

As they steamed out to Metinic, Ernie plotted a similar course for the *Sachem*, a small Eastern rig steamed out to Metinic in the *Sachem*, owned by a man in Boothbay Harbor. Unfettered by the worries of ownership, Ernie set his net as the sun's first arc cut open the horizon and the spawning aggregations of Maine shrimp settled down to bottom. Bernard set his net behind his old skipper and followed along a quarter mile off Ernie's stern.

The wily Newfoundlander towed his net into an underwater cul-de-sac, throttled back, turned his boat on its heel and towed right out again.

Bernard followed; it looked easy enough. He towed into the dead end, brought the *Ruth & Mary* 'round into the wind, and headed back along his own wake. But the wires never spread, and in a moment the doors dug into the mud. Bernard hauled back the mess and dumped a meager cod end full of muddy shrimp between the checkers.

They set out again, and as the crew picked through the pile Bernard called Ernie on the VHE.

"How the heck did you do that there? I seen you go right up into that crack, turn round and come right out again."

"Dere s no trick to it, b'y," Ernie radioed back. "Just let yer doors lay down, t'en pick them up again as you go by t'e ot'er way. Dey sorts 'emselves out, and you save a haulback."

Bernard tried it once more and got his doors crossed. He hauled the five-hundred-pound doors up between the gallows on the starboard side, where they hung tangled together. It took an hour to sort things out, and he was not sure how he did it, but the doors parted and they hauled back another small bag of shrimp. Uncle Marc gave him a short look before they set out again.

"I guess you're going to have to explain that to me another time, over," he said to Ernie. "The boys ain't going to appreciate it if I go up in there again."

Ernie stopped to visit after Christmas, and Bernard had him draw out the maneuver on a piece of paper that he took aboard next time out. They steamed down to Metinic in mid-January of 1970. With the crew looking grim, Bernard set out to tow into the crack again.

Less than a mile to the northwest, the *Sachem* had her doors up and a full cod end rising over the rail. Glancing up from his compass and depth sounder, Bernard could see the orange red tinge of shrimp in Ernie's net.

The black line on his sounder began a steep climb, an underwater wall rose ahead of his net. He throttled back, let the cables slacken, and then made his hard turn to starboard. He watched the wires; Marc watched the wires.

They did not look at each other, no need; each knew the other's thoughts. When the doors caught and the wires spread, Marc nodded in surprise. They hauled back a one-thousand-pound tow—pretty good for shipping.

Bernard came out on deck and looked at the shrimp, their tails snapping. He picked one up: it fit in the palm of his hand, bright reddish orange, its tail curled around the mass of turquoise colored eggs on its belly. Two delicate antennae, about six inches long, moved slowly, searching for what they would never feel again.

For his old mentor's sake, Bernard handed over a five-gallon bucket of thirty-weight oil. But he looked pained to see Ernie in such straits. Ernie had aged, the rum had taken its toll on him, and the *Amethyst* was the best site he could find. I didn't have a good excuse, but I was glad to be there.

We headed out on a January night. The young guy cooked, and Ernie ran the boat. I sat in the wheelhouse with him and talked. He asked me about my experiences fishing with Bernard, and he told me a bit of his story. He had come to the states during World War II.

"I was runnin' t'e *Wampanoag* for 40 Fathom," Ernie said, referring to a Canadian company operating in Rockland during the redfish boom. After a few years he immigrated and ran numerous US boats including the *Mariano*. In those days there was no line and he fished wherever he liked, from the Gulf of Maine to the Grand Bank almost a thousand miles to the northeast.

As we approached the waters off Mount Desert Rock, Ernie pointed to the chart. "Bernard come along wit' me down here when I had me own boat and he first got t'e *Rut' & Mary*," he said. "Alton never fished down here, so's I showed Bernard all t'is bottom."

In the galley we ate the poor grub the Rhode Island kid cooked: macaroni and cheese, and frozen hamburgers.

"Rather have hardtack and salt pork?" I asked Ernie. I knew that's what a lot of Newfoundlanders had lived on when Ernie was growing up.

"By Jesus, dat's all we used t' have," he said. "No, I don't want no more a dat."

The fish came slowly, and we mulled over the chart. He took us to all his favorite spots, but the fish had disappeared. Our conversations dwelt on the old days, not so long past.

"Oh me b'y. We used to chase t'e redfish right up t' t'e Straits of Belle Isle before t'ey come up with t'is Chris'less line."

We worked a spot about forty miles off Jonesport, close to my home. The net came up and the cod end rolled right up the stern ramp and onto the reel like an empty purse.

"Did the tripper open up?" Sometimes the tripper would slip, and the fish would pass through the net and right out the open cod end.

"No by Jesus, she's closed."

We put a board across the stern ramp and opened the cod end hanging limp on the reel. A basket of flats spilled onto deck. "Four hours for that eh?"

"Ain't enough t'ere t' feed t'e Chris'less cat."

We checked the doors, and they shined along the bottom edge like they'd done their job.

"She's fishin'," said Ernie. "Just ain't no fish." He shook his head at the meager pile on deck. "We used to be waist deep in'm here in t'e winter b'y. Must have t' get offinta deeper water."

Ernie wanted to run down to Larkin's Ridge on the Hague Line, but Lonny stayed on top of things enough to nix that idea. He didn't want Ernie to take his boat prospecting in Canadian water. We started working toward the southwest when storm warnings came up. The weather report called for fifteen-foot seas. We did not have much to show for five days fishing, and Lonny wanted to hang tough, hopefully finish the trip. But I told Ernie about the zincs and let him know I wasn't interested in finding out how much the old *Amethyst* could take.

We kept the net aboard and headed back to Rockland.

As soon as we tied the lines Lonny disappeared up the dock to a hotel room. We made the most of his absence, and sold off half the trip. Ernie stood on deck hollering encouragement down the hatch to the Rhode Islander and me while we ravaged the hold.

"Take some of t'at hake," he said. "T'ey'll want some hake. Go on fill anutter basket b'y. Get all t'e big graysole, that's damn near four dollars a pound. Oughtta shack t'e whole fuckin' trip by Jesus." At the time Doug Anderson, of *Sea Trek* fame, had come ashore and bought a fish market in Rockland. We loaded Ernie's pickup till the back bumper nearly touched the road and took it to Doug. He bought it all and paid us cash.

"You're Doug Anderson, used to run the *Sea Trek?*" I asked, meeting another figure from Bernard's past.

"Oh jeez, that was a long time ago," he said as we weighed up the boxes of dead fish, their eyes ever open.

The next day we sold what fish remained in the hold at Stinson's, but Lonny got his revenge by loading the expenses on the settlement.

"Fifteen tons of ice?" asked Ernie. "Since when does it take fifteen tons of ice to ice two t'ousand pounds of fish? T'em fish was well iced b'y."

"Look at this grub bill. For the swill he's got aboard?"

We took it in stride. Ernie tried to talk me into another trip, but I begged off.

"Here," he said before I left. "Take t'is jacket. My son give it t' me but it's too small." He handed me an almost new Carhart jacket, lined, and with a hood. It fit me perfect.

I headed out of town, a very different town than the one I had arrived in a decade before. For most of the twentieth century Rockland treated its fishermen as heroes, the crews commanded a high degree of respect for making sacrifices, often their lives, to bring in the fish that made Rockland prosper. The fishermen's wives carried a certain pride in the difficulties they faced as well. In the early 1990s, however, real estate development took fisheries place as Rockland's economic engine. The city began to look at its remaining fishermen as liabilities; we were a rough bunch, and we made the town smell fishy. The City raised taxes on all fishing boats in the harbor.

I stopped at the Wayfarer, the big table still filled the back of the dining room, but it sat empty. Chuck Doyle, Dickey Griffith, Lloyd Richards, and the rest had all gone to other ports or to the grave.

Even my psychopath captain Billy had come ashore and found a job selling marine supplies. "I had to quit," he said when I ran into him in town one day. "That boat was going to kill me." He owned that he had done a lot of things he regretted, an apology of sorts. But I reminded him of the bullets and said it was a mutual mistake.

Boats still landed thousands of pounds of fish in Rockland, but most of that was low-value herring used for lobster bait. Much of what remained of the groundfish fleet followed the O'Hara boats "up to the west'ard," as they said: to Portland or Gloucester, or through Panama to Alaska.

By the time I went fishing with Ernie on the *Amethyst*, the Rockland waterfront had already lost its fisheries infrastructure. Then came the closing of Sea Pro, the rendering plant that turned fish processing waste into meal and oil. The odiferous process gave the city its place in the ditty: "Camden by the sea, Rockland by the smell . . ." For those to whom fish had the smell of money, Rockland would never be the same without Sea Pro.

By the early 1990s, even the most pathological optimists could not deny the fact that the industry we knew and loved had all but disappeared. The groundfish decline might be cyclical, as even Bernard once professed, but it looked like it might take a lot longer to cycle around than anyone had imagined. In 1992, when the Canadian government closed the Northern cod fishery off Newfoundland, the hallmark fishery of the Northwest Atlantic, the future reality hit home: we had the capacity to fish abundant stocks to oblivion, and we could exhaust the natural resources we needed to support our technologically advanced, economically efficient fleet.

As the old dorymates of the highline fishing days disappeared, the ideas that supported them vanished too. The days of open access to abundant resources had ended.

Sixteen

POETS AND WARRIORS

In 1991, conservation groups in the US filed suit against the New England Fishery Management Council (NEFMC). The Conservation Law Foundation, Audubon Society, and the Center for Marine Conservation claimed the industry-dominated council had failed to protect the region's fishery resources. A consent decree a year later forced the Council to create new regulations, including limited entry into the fishery and a reduced number of fishing days. Fish stocks continued to decline, more lawsuits followed, and fisheries management soon turned into crisis management. In an emergency action in December 1994, the Secretary of Commerce closed over a third of Georges Bank to all fishing gear capable of catching groundfish, particularly trawls and scallop dredges.

When the resources supporting an industry reach their ecological limits, say some economists, the only option for further expansion within that industry is through redistribution. That began to take place in fisheries all over the world, as various components of the fleet vied for the existing fish. Allocation battles broke out primarily between small boat fishermen from the old school, and those who supported the idea of consolidating access in the hands of the most economically efficient vessels.

"There will be winners and losers," said the bureaucrats from National Marine Fisheries Service (NMFS) as they advanced the Stratton Commission agenda of privatizing the nation's fisheries through individual quotas and aquaculture leases. NMFS tended to support the overall idea of letting the market allocate fishing rights to the most economically efficient enterprises. Federal regulators and prospective winners repeatedly recommended individual quota systems as the key solution to fisheries problems. "Rationalization" of fisheries, as the neo-classical economists called it, rewarded those who had the greatest impact on stocks, allocating harvest rights to fishing entities with enough capital to buy the most advanced technology—not necessarily those with the longest historical participation in a fishery, or the greatest need.

While the movers and shakers in the world of fisheries management strove to create regulations that would give capital the advantage in acquiring harvest rights to increasingly scarce fish stocks, I was reaping an abundant resource. In 1995 I made more money than I ever had, diving for sea urchins from a sixteen-foot boat in twenty feet of water. My position on the cutting edge of a new fishery for an underutilized species enabled me to pay off my mortgage, and for the first time in eight years, I took a vacation.

In County Kerry, Ireland, I met some fishermen lobstering out of a canvas boat, a curragh. They told me Ireland used to have a sea urchin fishery in the 1980s, but they fished it out in about twelve years. "T'ere's a few still goes out and gets a box or two," one said in an accent a bit like Ernie Kavanaugh's. "But not like t'ey used to."

After a month on the old sod, I came home to a stack of bills, and so, rowed out to the wrinkle rocks to pick up a few extra dollars before urchin season opened. After an hour's work searching all the old cracks and tide pools that had become so ingrained in my memory, I still had not filled a bag. The number of wrinkle pickers had at least tripled, and the novices took everything, even the smallest. I looked at the distance I had covered in my search: more than I would have in a week in 1988. 1 emptied my sack back on the rocks, rowed home to Haycock's Harbor, and sat in my truck reviewing my catch records. The battered pages of my little notebook told a by now familiar story: like everything else, we had fished out the wrinkles.

I knew from what I had heard in Ireland that diving for sea urchins would be short-lived too. The people charged with safeguarding marine resources seemed incapable of learning from the past. The urchin regulators sought input from the most productive fishermen—those least interested in sustainability—and short-term interests guided policy in the urchin industry, as it did in most other fisheries.

As I sat in my truck on that late summer day, listening to the thrush song echo around the harbor and jotting down an epithet for the wrinkles, the thought struck me that I was not on board with the "winners." I was a loser, at the end of the line with the urchin fishery and with no alternative resources to exploit, and I realized I had better find something new to do.

To compensate for the hardships caused by increasing restrictions on the industry, the federal government had instituted the Fishermen's Retraining Program in 1995, offering qualified fishermen two years of training in any field they chose. I walked through the door of the program's office in Washington County. Dan Molinski sat behind the desk and asked what my wildest dreams were, to be a welder, or an electrician, maybe.

I said, "Writer." Dan expressed some skepticism. "Why a writer?" he wanted to know. I told him it would be like fishing, I'd be self-employed, a hunter-gatherer of sorts, and I would only get paid when I produced a marketable product, provided I could find a market. The Feds put up the money and I headed back to school.

By late 1997 I had earned a BA in writing and literature. Although I planned to abandon fishing and write novels, the industry would not let me go. My first sale, a story about sea urchins in Ireland, went to *Fishermen's Voice,* a monthly paper put together by a desperado fishmonger named Bill Crowe, and distributed free up and down the coast of Maine. That first article led to more assignments, which cinched me into writing about fisheries. In March 1998 Bill sent me down to the Maine Fishermen's Forum, at the Samoset Resort in Rockport, where I reconnected with Bernard.

They say the ancient Irish took poets with them into battle to write about the feats of their chieftains and warriors. The great battle between two worldviews of the ocean reached its height in the last decade of the twentieth century. Those with money enough to buy a privatized ocean came up against the last significant constituencies of what the Stratton Commission called, "practitioners . . . less concerned with economic efficiency than with the simple fact of making a living from the sea." I was on the battlefield as a reporter, though not necessarily an objective one.

Most of the fisheries "stakeholders" in the fight: academics, scientists, economists, environmentalists, regulators, legislators, public and private corporations, and fishing families had plans and manifestos of sorts, and chronicling the feats of the various heroes became my full-time job. I had been in the industry for over twenty years, but had spent most of that time catching and processing fish, and largely ignoring the politics. The complexities of fisheries management and the economic theories driving it presented a steep learning curve; I started reading reams of policy analysis and scientific reports, attending management meetings, and churning out copy for the *Fishermen's Voice*.

In 1998, "The Year of the Ocean," there was plenty of material. Saving fish had become a cause célèbre, and people and money poured into the fray. TV stars past and present vowed to not eat lobsters or lobbied to end overfishing. Representatives from organizations such as the National Audubon Society offered to "save the fishermen from themselves." Many of their plans for salvation came from the Stratton recommendations of thirty years prior: they called for a reduction of the fleet and privatization of the resources. Other plans, such as the call for Marine Protected Areas— nature reserves in the sea—and the Code of Conduct for Responsible Fisheries—a template for global fisheries management—emanated from the United Nations.

Each NGO unfurled its own particular banner: the Center for Marine Conservation championed Marine Protected Areas; Environmental Defense claimed individual transferable quotas would automatically lead to fisheries conservation; Greenpeace supported small-boat owners and community-based management.

The fisheries managers sought to protect the economic interest of fishermen, and at the same time reduce the size of the fleet through permit and vessel buybacks. Initially, the buybacks enabled some fishermen to sell their older boats at inflated prices and use the money to build new boats under existing subsidy programs.

As fisheries production stalled and prices rose, previously unaffordable aquaculture production increased, and quasi-government development agencies, such as Sea Grant, explored the idea of turning fishermen into fish farmers. Like the industrial fishery prospects of the 1970s, the fish farming industry offered promising returns to venture capitalists. Fueling new hopes, the National Marine Fisheries Service, Sea Grant, and private speculators sought a fivefold expansion in the value of the US aquaculture industry by 2025. In the excitement of saving the fish and farming the ocean, old fishermen in wooden boats were all but forgotten.

I had not seen Bernard since the year I went fishing with Ernie Kavanaugh aboard the *Amethyst*. Ernie was four years in the grave, and Bernard had nearly died after a failed kidney transplant. I stopped at the house on my way to the Fishermen's Forum on a snowy March morning. "We nearly lost him, Paul," Eleanor told me. "It was scary."

I caught up with Bernard at a crowded groundfish meeting held at the forum. He surprised me by standing up to speak, but I watched painfully as the man who had built the *Irene & Alton* struggled to put his sentences together. His hands shook and his voice quavered. Whatever point he had set out to make was lost on all but those who already knew what he wanted to say: he wanted to fish in peace, in his rational way, but the policies aimed at restoring the stocks inevitably favored the highly mobile industrial fleet, and regulations targeted the shrinking number of fishermen like him.

The moderator thanked Bernard and moved on to the next speaker. Bernard's words vanished like the snow falling on the water outside. Eloquent scientists, environmental activists, and academics fed the press, framing the debate in sophisticated language that often fogged the issues. In their jargon, they called all the flatfish by names many fishermen had never heard: blackbacks became "winter flounder," dab became "American plaice," and graysole became "witch flounder."

Sitting in one such meeting, even the editor of *National Fisherman* Magazine leaned over to me and asked, "American plaice is dab, right?"

"I think so."

Much in the way the English government forced Bernard's ancestors to travel far from home and negotiate in a foreign language, regulators forced fishermen to use a language not their own and negotiate in places far from their comfort zone—the sea.

Using the hierarchal language of science and policy—a subtle form of oppression—served to disadvantage fishermen already losing ground in a discussion framed by those on top. A situation repeated what Bernard's French-speaking ancestors experienced when they had to negotiate with the English, in English. But no one complained about cultural degradation or semantics as the New England Fishery Management Council and the National Marine Fisheries Service promulgated increasingly complex regulations designed to rebuild fisheries while continuing to exploit them.

In 1996 The United Nations Food and Agriculture Organization (FAO) presented the Code of Conduct for Responsible Fisheries as a blueprint for fisheries regulations worldwide: It called for the now familiar measures of reducing fleet size, maximizing economic efficiency, and promoting aqua-culture, and the US Congress had passed its version when it reauthorized the Magnuson Act in 1996. The amended Magnuson, titled the Sustainable Fisheries Act (SFA), imposed ten-year rebuilding schedules on all overfished species, including cod, haddock, yellowtail flounder, redfish, and others.

The new legislation acknowledged the interests of fishing communities, but again, the economic theory driving implementation did not. The drastic cutbacks led many big boat owners to alter their fishing strategies—consolidating operations and infrastructure in urban ports—and pushed many small owner operated boats, which lacked mobility, into bankruptcy. According to many spokespeople from the small ports, divorce and domestic strife became rampant in their communities.

Some economists looking at the fisheries problems in New England went so far as to question whether the US could afford a fleet. The rationale of the global economy suggested it might be better to buy fish from more efficient foreign producers than harvest our own: the theory of comparative advantage, it was called.

The New England Fishery Management Council, seeking to preserve a competitive industry, crafted most of its fishery management plans with fishermen's input. But the participating fishermen often came from the industrial fleet; they knew the economic efficiency equations and held control over substantial harvesting power. Fleet owners, with time to sit in meetings, secretaries to fill out trip reports, and lawyers to explain what the regulations meant, exerted their influence on the council. They were the "winners," and designed regulations that would help them to stay that way in the short term. In the long term everyone lost.

At the Raynes's house, Eleanor had held up a fat file, and a sheaf of recent mailings from the National Marine Fisheries Service, the Atlantic States Marine Fisheries Commission, the New England Fishery Management Council, the Federal Communications Commission, and other government agencies. "I don't know what to do with all this Paul. Half of it I don't understand, and then I call down to Gloucester and they put me on hold forever, or they send me the wrong stuff."

Among other things, Eleanor fills out the regular trip reports, which require her to translate legalistic terminology into plain English. She has gotten good at it, but sometimes she does not get it right, and NMFS returns the reports for her to revise. Her file holds numerous examples of the problems she must resolve and explain to Bernard and Brad.

Among them a letter from NMFS regional administrator, Andy Rosenberg, informing her that regulations for net stowage on vessels transiting closed areas have been changed because they are "not practically feasible."

Another letter explains that in order to qualify for an initial limited access permit for the swordfish fishery Bernard would have to demonstrate "current and historical participation" in the fishery between the years 1987 and 1998. Bernard struck his last fish in 1985. The regulation, crafted with input from the longline fleet, created a history window that, for all intents and purposes, ignored the century-long existence of the harpoon fleet.

After sorting through the criteria, Bernard qualified for a harpoon permit on the same basis as I did: 50 percent of my income came from fishing during one of the preceding three years. His having harpooned scores of swordfish from the pulpit of the *Irene & Alton* meant nothing to NMFS. Bernard failed to qualify for a shark permit because his application arrived a month late. Buried in a document full of numerical references to the federal register, Eleanor had missed the announcement that the deadline for shark permits was two months earlier than swordfish. Rebecca Lent, Chief of the NMFS Highly Migratory Species Division, signed the letter bearing the bad news.

Another letter informs Bernard that he has lost access to the scallop fishery because he did not have any landings after 1983. He had missed the history window for that fishery as well. One by one, the system denied him access to the fisheries that once supported not only his boat, but his community.

In addition to following the regulations that apply directly to the fisheries they participate in, Eleanor must keep up with revised definitions, regulatory terms, and catch limits for certain species, which can change several times a year.

She also has to review and digest volumes of complex regulations for species that the boat only catches small amounts of incidentally: such as monkfish. Item #2 in a NMFS monkfish notice states in one sentence:

"A trawl vessel may fish in the SNE Monkfish Fishery Exemption Area when not under a NE multispecies day-at-sea (DAS) providing such vessel does not fish for, possess on board, or land any species of fish other than monkfish, except that such vessels may retain and land exempted species, and amounts specified, for the SNE Regulated Mesh Area." Eleanor not only has to read such mind-boggling sentences, she has to try to understand pages of them.

Inevitably, she must straighten out any bureaucratic mistakes, such as the shocking notice that allocated the *Irene & Alton* zero fishing days for 1995. An unapologetic letter from NMFS later acknowledged that there was "sufficient evidence to support an upward revision to the initial allocation of days. The initial allocation of zero days is hereby adjusted to 219 days."

Another letter from the Department of Commerce Office of Sustainable Development and Intergovernmental Affairs invited Bernard and Eleanor to join the Fishing Capacity Reduction Program, with "voluntary sinking" as a disposal option for the *Irene & Alton*.

I met Bernard in the hall outside the meeting, and he and Dawn's husband, Steve, invited me to join them for lunch. In the sumptuous banquet hall of the Samoset Resort, a waitress served us fresh cod and new potatoes on real china. I spread my napkin in my lap and looked at the silverware.

"Who's paying for this Bernard?"

"Did they ask you for a ticket at the door?"

"No."

"Then don't ask."

As we ate, Senator Bill Cohen regaled us with upbeat fisheries talk and reminders that we would have to "work together." After Cohen's speech Senator Olympia Snowe followed him at the podium, and delivered more amorphous, yet optimistic sounding messages. While their intent may have been sincere, they still could not serve two masters, their constituents and an economic dictate that targeted those constituents for removal from the industry. Neo-classical economics said there must be investment and growth within the industry, but economic growth could only manifest as an illusion created by allowing the stronger sectors to cannibalize the weaker.

Within that context, many environmentalist organizations acted as tools of the system.

"We speak for the fish," said a spokesman for the Center for Marine Conservation (later renamed Ocean Conservancy). "We're not getting involved in allocation issues."

"What about the wealth of knowledge we're losing when small-boat fishermen disappear in a consolidated fleet?" I asked.

"That can be replaced with technology."

"Replaced with technology," I repeated, realizing I was hearing the voice of hard-boiled ignorance.

In the late 1990s, champions of the fish crowded the media stage, often utilizing the glamour of high profile species and questionable science to garner support. Carl Safina wrote *Song for a Blue Ocean,* an eloquent treatise on the plight of the bluefin tuna. But in his book Safina supported the two-stock theory that divided the North Atlantic bluefin tuna stock into separate management areas. That political arrangement—based on the assumption that bluefin tuna in the western Atlantic seldom cross into the east—allowed Europe to quadruple its fishery to over forty thousand tons annually between 1981 and 1997, while US fishermen accepted equivalent reductions in their quotas, which dropped to eighteen hundred tons over the same period. Committed to saving the bluefin tuna, and unable to address EU overfishing, Safina called for deeper cuts in the US bluefin quota. Although the cuts would no doubt preserve some fish, EU fishers and pirates—flag of convenience vessels that offload their tuna at sea—would continue to plunder what many tagging studies have indicated is a shared resource.

Scientists such as Elliot Norse, of the Marine Conservation Biology Institute in Redmond, Washington, cited the damage done by dragging on Georges Bank and the Gulf of Maine. "Clearcutting" the ocean, they called it in their media campaign. He was right, massive damage had occurred, but the broad criticisms that scientists offered without ever setting foot on a dragger or talking to fishermen about places like Haddock Nubble, lacked credibility. They vilified and blamed fishermen rather than the economic system that was driving the madness.

Instead they proposed strengthening that system, and as a solution Norse and many others contended that Individual Transferable Quotas (ITQs), allocated to fishermen based on their previous catches, would allow more efficient harvest, and conservation, of marine resources. Out of work fishermen in Newfoundland, Canada, where ITQs existed in the northern cod fishery at the time of the 1992 stock collapse, agreed only on the first point.

"They caught all the cod very efficiently," said Bill Broderick, head of the Newfoundland Inshore Fishermen's Association.

World experience has demonstrated that ITQs act as economic tools: effective in creating cartels and allowing the market to manage fisheries, but not in conserving resources or the communities that depended on them. ITQs accomplished the goals identified in the Stratton Report, creating a small fleet of big boats. The boats that caught the most, the "efficient" ones, received the most quota. The boats that conserved the most, the fishermen who survived by alternating among several fisheries, got crumbs, making them more vulnerable to being bought out by the bigger players, or being regulated out of the fishery for non-participation during arbitrary control periods, as happened to Bernard.

If ITQs were the hammer, aquaculture leases became the anvil on which the small boat fleet would be smashed. Touted as the way to restore fishing communities, reclaim the productivity of inshore waters, help feed the world and create jobs for displaced fishermen, aquaculture, the farming of shellfish and salmon, found a warm welcome all along the Maine coast in the mid-1980s. After ten years however, it became apparent that the fast-growing salmon aquaculture industry had brought more economic harm than good to coastal communities.

A handful of activists, such as Greenpeace oceans campaigner Niaz Dorry, forged links with fishermen and struggled to help spread a grass-roots message that small scale operations harvesting wild fish offer the best hope for sustainability. Dorry and local activists such as Angela Sanfilippo of the Gloucester Fishermen's Wives Association organized to stop the use of factory trawlers in the region's herring fishery. They managed to retain local control of the resource, for a while.

The neo-classic economic model for development was not set up to register the value of local control; it measured only dollar values when looking at costs versus benefits. If something could not be assigned a value in that development model, it did not count in the decision making process. Community wealth, such as the memories of Bernard and other older fishermen, did not register in the accounting. The time would come when the powers behind global fisheries exploitation would recognize the value that millions of small scale fishermen held for local food security and global markets, but it was not in the late 1990s.

At the close of the twentieth century, "The Year of the Ocean," Saabs, Volvos, and SUVs have replaced old trucks along Main Street in Rockland. The schooners have returned; they set sail every week, carrying passengers on five-day tours of the Maine coast. Seldom-used yachts dance on moorings in Rockland harbor while the few remaining fishing boats unload at a public fish pier, which barely supports itself with landings fees.

In the newly renovated Farnsworth Art Museum, just off Rockland's Main Street, the paintings of N. C. Wyeth and his progeny depict the local scenery, and in their work one can see the changes along the coast. In an N. C. Wyeth painting, a lobsterman fishing from a dory holds a lobster trap he has hauled up by hand. In another, N. C. depicts a boat full of herring hauled from a weir. His son Andrew painted a relic dory stowed in a barn, and Andrew's son Jamie painted a rusting iron cleat bolted to a rock at the mouth of a large cove. The cleat, once used by stop seiners to hold their nets and trap herring in the cove, has become a curiosity.

Mid-water trawlers now dominate the herring fishery. The one-hundred-dred-foot-long high-powered vessels can target herring anywhere in the water column. They are equipped with the latest sonar technology, capable of producing an almost photographic view of the bottom, so that captains no longer need the ability to visualize the unseen. The few O'Hara boats still fishing out of Rockland are all midwater trawlers, mostly supplying bait to the lobster fishery.

Originally intended to harvest an allegedly bountiful herring stock in the deep waters of Georges Bank, the mid-water boats reported that the fish were not there, and one of the most technologically advanced fleets in US fisheries has been permitted to work close to shore where they out-compete traditional fishermen. While the numbers on the balance sheet indicate that mid-water trawling is more efficient because it enables fishermen to catch hundreds of thousands of pounds of herring in a night, the boats cost as much as $10 million to build, and burn more fuel per ton of herring landed than any other gear type used in the fishery.

Tourists filed through the quiet, carpeted rooms of the Farnsworth, admiring the two dimensional work and its subjects. Five miles away in Owls Head, Bernard worked in the barn, painting his new skiff. Two hundred miles away at a meeting of the New England Fishery Management Council in Danvers, Massachusetts, Brad sat slouched in his chair as a Gloucester fisherman kicked over a table. The police moved in to restore order and nervous council members struggled to regulate fisheries in what had become a war zone. When the dust settled, Brad had gone. He never went back to the meetings.

While the outbursts drew attention to the difficulties fishing families faced, screaming at regulators did little to stop the reallocation of resources to the more effective sectors of all fisheries. The mid-water boats, for example, outfished all other sectors combined. They took over the herring fishery in just a few years, and became the first New England fleet to lobby for ITQs.

Many levelheaded fishermen like Brad, those with a realistic view of the situation, vanished from the hot meetings. They saw themselves being played with, patronized for a political show while the wheels that had been set in motion with the Stratton Report thirty years earlier rolled over them. The meetings became gatherings of the usual suspects, where industry lobbyists and regulators often outnumbered fishermen.

At the Fishermen's Forum I had covered a tuna and swordfishermen's meeting and talked to Bernard about it afterward. "You wouldn't believe it, Bernard. I'm at this meeting taking notes and the most important person in the room walks over and introduces herself to me: 'Hi I'm Rebecca Lent, Chief of the National Marine Fisheries Service, Highly Migratory Species Division.'"

Bernard nodded, and remained attentive to his painting. "Did you tell her you was a wrinkle picker?" he asked.

"No."

"Why not?"

I laughed and let it go. "Did you hear about this 'Give Swordfish a Break' campaign?" I asked.

"We already went broke swordfishin'?"

In early 1998 the Pew Charitable Trusts funded Sea Web, and the "Give Swordfish a Break" campaign. "These people want to bring back the swordfish. They're calling for a boycott. They had a big thing in *The New York Times* telling everybody not to eat swordfish."

"Who's they?"

"The Pew Charitable Trusts."

"Well, I wish them luck. I'd be glad to see the swordfish come back; only thing is, what are they going to eat? There ain't no little fish around like there used to be, no more squid or butterfish. The swordfish can't come back if there ain't nothing to eat."

I wandered around the barn; looked at a model Bernard was building of the *Irene & Alton*. "Yeah, you got a point, but I don't think Pew could get the attention it wants with 'Give Squid a Break.'"

"No, I guess not."

"Plus the scientists say there's a lot of herring out on Georges."

"They're lying. And everyone knows it. All the mid-water boats went out there and they couldn't find'm. That's why they're fishing inshore here."

That conversation led to an article about the bigger environmental picture and what sustainable harvesting looked like. It ran in *The New York Times* that summer, illustrated with a photo of the *Irene & Alton,* decked out in her mast and pulpit. The article ended with Bernard's allusions to the breakdown of the food chain that supported the entire ecosystem, not just one fishery. "Ecological function," the scientists called it, and contrary to a long held belief, it did not always restore itself to the same balance it had before one species or another was depleted.

In an effort to safeguard biodiversity and a certain level of ecological function, the United Nations environmental consultant organization, the World Conservation Union (IUCN) launched a program calling for the formation of a global system of Marine Reserves that would safeguard parts of every ecosystem in the world's oceans. The Center for Marine Conservation became the most vocal advocate for MPAs in the US and in the Gulf of Mexico, where the poster child of MPAs began to take shape; fishermen strove to endure by forming partnerships with science.

Working on another article, I went down to the Dry Tortugas in the Gulf of Mexico and spent a week diving in the clear waters of a reef system destined to become the first designated MPA. Several CMC staff members and Florida Keys commercial fishermen had organized the trip with the goal of demonstrating the wisdom of protecting what CMC people liked to call ocean wilderness. "Protect half the reef, get twice the fish," they said. The idea sold well in the tropics, but not New England.

Back in Owls Head, Bernard pulled a gallon can of pine tar out from under a bench in the barn. Deep brown stains obscured the label, but clearly identified the contents. He handed me a pair of cotton gloves. "You want to get some coveralls?"

"Yeah."

He pulled a paint-splotched jump suit off a hook and handed it to me.

"Here, see if you can fit into these," he said. "Did you put your dive gear in the truck?"

"Yeah, I'm all set."

We drove down to the harbor, unloaded the truck, and dragged all the equipment to the end of the dock. Bernard hauled the dory in on its loop of rope, and like many times before, I caught it before it hit the granite blocks. He passed me my dive gear: a dry suit, fins, mask, forty-pound weight belt, two air tanks, regulator, and buoyancy vest.

"Didn't need all this down south did you?"

"No. It was amazing: 70 degrees at a hundred feet, didn't even need the wet suit except to protect you from the coral."

"Now what were you doing down there?"

"It's an area of deep water reefs. They want to make it into a Marine Protected Area. We anchored in 115 feet, and could see bottom. The first time we went down, we dropped through huge schools of fish, I never saw anything like it, you know? Coming from here where you can hardly see your hand."

"What kind of fish?"

"Silver snappers. They say you see more species of fish in ten minutes around a coral reef than in a lifetime in temperate waters. I can't even remember the names of half the ones I saw. But the fishermen aboard said that was nothing compared to what they used to see."

I bailed out the dory and Bernard climbed aboard. He started the small outboard while I untied the painter and shoved off. He put the engine in gear and we headed out to the *Irene & Alton*, weaving our way between the numerous lobster boats moored closer to the wharf. As we approached I saw *Irene* looked a bit weary, rust streaks marked her sides, and once aboard I noticed a big hunk of wood chewed out of the rail aft.

"What happened here?"

"Oh, the boys knocked that off bringing the doors aboard."

The boat felt tired and unkempt. "She don't look too good Bernard."

"We didn't haul her yet," he said. "Brad needed to use up his days at sea. Now all the schooners are on the rails, so we missed our chance. We'll haul her later and get her cleaned up."

I looked up into the rigging I had first tarred sixteen years before. "Where do you want to start?"

"Up to you, old son. Might be good to let the tar soak in while the sun's out."

"Okay. Where's the bosun's chair?"

"Down in the engine room where it always is."

It's been a while since the rigging has been tarred. "Nobody but you wants to do it," Bernard told me.

Gradually we recalled the process, and Bernard hoisted me into the rigging with my tar bucket. At one point, as I climbed up to tar the spring-stay, a wire running from the top of the mainmast to the top of the mizzen, I had to hang free over the deck one-handed, pull the bosun's chair up with the other hand, and hook it to the stay. A simple trick when I was twenty-five, but a bit different at forty-one.

"How you doing?" Bernard called up to me.

"Okay," I said, hanging thirty feet above the deck.

He let out some slack and I slid along the stay, periodically dipping a handful of tar from the bucket and working it into the steel strands of the wire. The wind blew and I felt my hair sticking to the freshly tarred wire. Hanging there in space listening to the breeze blow by, I paused to catch my breath and look out over the harbor, where I remembered watching Alton standing in his skiff, push rowing out to the *Osprey*—because of his bad hip he could not sit down and row. I could almost hear the voices of Georg and the rest of the gang getting ready to go swordfishing. I finished and Bernard let me down on deck.

"You okay, old son? I gotta go get Brad."

Brad stood on the wharf, and as Bernard headed in I climbed up the main mast again and tarred my way down the ratlines and the port side shrouds. Before I finished the dory arrived alongside. Brad came aboard and looked up at the tar.

"What're you doing up there?"

"Your favorite," I said, as a drop of tar dripped free and landed on Brad's shirt.

"Jeezus Christ."

"Man, it knows you."

I climbed down, and Bernard, one of the founders of the Rockland SCUBA Club, helped me get my dive gear together to check his mooring and clear some line out of the propeller.

"Now these MPAs," he said, reflecting on our earlier conversation. "Do they have any for fishermen?"

"No, just for the fish. Their thinking is that these closed areas will give populations a chance to bounce back, and provide fish for fishermen in adjacent areas."

Bernard nodded. "Father used to do something like that, he'd fish a place one day, but he wouldn't fish it out. He'd move to another spot the next day and leave a place alone."

"Try doing that today."

"Them places is all fished out anyway."

"Didn't he know what was going on?" I asked, wondering what Alton thought about as the fish disappeared from under him.

"Of course he knew. We knew the gear would hurt the bottom. But the scientists kept telling us it was okay, that we could never wipe out the fish, but we knew we would," said Bernard. "These fellows come over from the Mediterranean and told us what would happen, that the fish would get smaller and smaller, and the nets would tear up their last hidin' places."

"Why didn't you do anything?"

"I guess we was all thinking about how to catch more fish."

The contradictions in Bernard's thoughts illustrated his dilemma. He knew better, but he kept dragging. He had bills to pay and it was easier to believe the assurances that the resource could never be fished out than try to change the status quo.

Bernard looked over my gear, figuring it out. He clamped the regulator onto the tank and hooked the proper hose up to the buoyancy vest. "You need help to get this on?"

"Nah, I can pretty much take care of myself."

"Do you want to put it on here or in the skiff?"

"I'll just go right off here." I hefted the tank up over my head, let it slip down onto my back, and buckled it in place. Weight belt, flippers, and mask: all geared up, I flipped my legs over the rail, stepped off, and splashed into the harbor.

Below the surface at low tide the dappled summer sunlight reached bottom. I swam along beneath the keel of *Irene*'s familiar hull and worked my way down her mooring chain searching for the weakest link. Because things look so much bigger under water I carried a short ruler to measure. The chain looked good.

The Coast Guard had moved another of Bernard's moorings for a dredging project and he wanted me to see how it lay. I found it upside down with the chain wrapped around it in confusion.

"Like this," I said, back aboard the boat, drawing a picture with a pencil on a scrap of paper.

Bernard looked it over. "I see. Them fellas done quite a job."

"They won't come back and make it right?"

"No."

After I went back under and cleaned the rope out of the prop, Brad took Bernard in to keep a doctor's appointment, then came back to help me out of the water. Drifting off the stern of the *Irene & Alton,* I hung on the side of the dory while Brad idled the engine.

"Ain't the rope cutter working?" he asked.

"What're you talking about?"

"Didn't you see the rope cutter on the propeller shaft?"

"Let me look." I dropped back down below the surface and looked. I found a pair of jagged steel flanges on the propeller shaft, but nothing that looked like it would cut rope.

"Looks like it broke off," I said back on the surface.

"Broke off?"

"Yeah, it's gone."

"How can it be gone?"

"You want to check it yourself? Here, you can borrow my mask. You'll see when you haul out. It's gone."

Sibling rivalry. He took my weight belt and tank, and I climbed aboard.

In spite of reduced days at sea, and ever tightening restrictions, Brad continued to take the boat offshore. He had become a master of his trade with absolutely no foothold in the future. Bernard owned the boat and the permit. If he sold them, Brad would be unemployed with no benefits.

Limited entry created a quasi-privatized fishery, and compromised the common property view of the ocean. Limiting access to a fishery is a stepping stone towards privatization, but the coming of ITQs threatened to totally disenfranchise Brad and thousands of other captains and crew— with no benefit to fisheries conservation. For them, ITQ's represented nothing more than a cold-blooded stripping of their rights to the sea from which they had long earned their livelihoods.

Rural fishing communities in New England raised concerns that privatization of public resources would eventually strip them of access to the fish stocks on their doorsteps. The perils of individual fishing quotas were apparent in other countries such as Iceland and Canada, where harvest rights to fisheries had become consolidated in the hands of several large corporations operating out of urban ports, and many small communities had completely lost their fishing industries.

And once the juggernaut of ITQs got rolling it seemed impossible to stop. In Iceland, one of the first countries to use individual transferable quotas, a superior court judge ruled them unconstitutional after several disenfranchised fishermen took their boats to sea and caught cod without a quota. The Icelandic Supreme Court later reversed the decision and the fishermen were fined.

But large fishing constituencies still had a voice, and in 1996 their concerns about the social costs of ITQs compelled the US Congress to impose a four-year moratorium on the use of individual quotas. Senators Olympia Snowe (R-ME) and John Kerry (D-MA) succeeded in extending the moratorium for two years, but that extension expired on September 30, 2002.

For six years New Englanders succeeded in keeping ITQs out of the management toolbox, but the national tide of support for individual quotas overwhelmed the regions fishing interests. The National Marine Fisheries Service; the National Research Council (NRC); the chairmen of the regional councils, including Tom Hill of the NEFMC; several environmental groups, such as Environmental Defense; Senators such as Sen.

Ted Stevens (R-AK), and President George W. Bush all supported lifting the ban on ITQs.

With the handwriting on the wall, Sen. Snowe had introduced a bill, the ITQ act of 2001, which allowed individual quota systems under certain criteria. Kerry introduced draft re-authorization of the Magnuson Stevens Fishery Conservation and Management Act that includes similar language allowing ITQs.

But the Massachusetts Fishermen's Partnership (MFP), an umbrella group for most Massachusetts commercial fishing organizations, spoke for many New England fishermen in its refusal to welcome ITQs. "The Massachusetts Fishermen's Partnership remains fundamentally opposed to the creation of individual quota systems (IFQs, synonymous with ITQs) in New England because we believe that they are inequitable," said Al Farent, president of the MFP, testifying before Congress in May 2002. "They inevitably put the rights of individual fishermen in competition with corporate greed. The imposition of such quota systems in New England would do irreparable and unnecessary harm to the cultural makeup of fishing communities of the region."

"What bothers me," said Jim Kendall, head of New Bedford Seafood Consulting, "is that more people outside the industry than in want us to go this route."

Kendall, a veteran member of the NEFMC, acknowledged the appeal of ITQs. "It makes sense from a business perspective, if you've got a boat that's tied to the dock with only 120 days to fish, and ITQs could give you more days. And it makes management easier—here's your share. Go fishing."

But Kendall was far from sold on ITQs. "It's not so bad if you have an absentee owner dockside," he said. "But when a fishing vessel is being run from a corporate office a hundred miles inland, or overseas, you tend to lose control. All big business is looking at is the bottom line and I have some strong concerns about highgrading." Kendall claimed, as had many others before him, that quotas would lead to a high level of discards as fishermen threw back species they had no quota for in order to keep catching on higher value fish. Say a fellow had caught his quota for cod but not haddock. He would keep fishing, throwing the cod over the side until he caught his quota of haddock.

From an economic perspective highgrading makes total sense—sports fishermen with bag limits highgrade routinely; keeping fish in live wells, they return smaller ones to the water as they catch bigger ones, maximizing productivity within the limits. From a business point of view fishermen would be compelled to highgrade, but on commercial trawlers the fish going back in the water are dead.

In his testimony before the US Senate, Al Farent raised another important concern about ITQs. Initial allocations of individual quotas were usually based on a fishery participant's history. "It is imperative that historical fishing practices be taken into account in a way that does not discriminate against vessels who were unable to fish for various reasons," said Farent. Many others are also concerned that the "window of history," the arbitrary control dates used to establish who qualified for an initial allocation in a fishery, could shortchange fishermen who at some period or another, redirected their effort in the interest of conservation.

In spite of his efforts to improve Snowe's bill, Farent expressed little hope. "While we appreciate that there are well-intentioned efforts to create Individual Fishing Quotas with safeguards against transferability and consolidation," he said, "they are ultimately doomed."

Sitting on Bernard's front porch one afternoon after he had returned tired from the hospital, I tried talking to him about ITQs.

"Your business would probably be worth more," I said. "They would set a quota and you would get a share of the fish based on your past catch. Your quota would have a monetary value."

Bernard hadn't been following me; he was stuck on the first point. "Wait a minute," he said. "Nobody owns a fish until they catch it."

I sat there for a minute, realizing how easy it was to get caught up in a convoluted debate over an arbitrary idea that Bernard could point out the weakness of in one lucid sentence.

But the juggernaut of privatization through limited entry, ITQs, or their proxies had already rolled through fishery after fishery in countries all over the world, systematically taking control of resources out of the hands of human beings. Though not everybody took it lying down.

An important part of moving this agenda forward was the normalizing of the idea within the debate. Controlling the discourse was a vital part of moving ITQ's into New England. The work was subtle, but evident in a workshop held at the Maine Fishermen's Forum in 2001. Pat White, then head of the Maine Lobstermen's Association and I sat in a workshop called, "Individual Fishing Quotas: Benefits and Concerns."

"Doesn't that seem a little cockeyed," I said to Pat.

"What?"

"We're comparing tangible benefits to amorphous concerns rather than tangible costs. Seems a bit one-sided you know? I mean if you say 'benefit,' you should say, 'cost.' But they don't want to admit that there's costs, so we get "concerns.' It's bullshit."

He agreed, but nobody changed the workshop title, and those subtle manipulations of the conversation continued until fishermen found themselves boxed into quota management.

What would happen to those who offered significant resistance to the privatization agenda became evident in the summer of 1999. That year, the Canadian Supreme Court had handed down a decision on treaty rights that sent shock waves throughout Canada's Department of Fisheries and Oceans (DFO). The Court recognized the validity of a 1765 treaty in which three tribes, the Maliseet, Mi'kmaq, and Passamaquoddy, reserved for themselves the right to engage in limited commercial fisheries. The DFO knew that the most likely target of Native fishers would be the strictly controlled lobster fishery.

A few weeks after the decision, the Mi'kmaq of Burnt Church, New Brunswick, started setting lobster traps in the rich waters of Miramichi Bay. Neighboring lobstermen, French-speaking Acadians, descendants of the fugitives the Mi'kmaq had rescued from deportation two centuries before, came out in force, brandishing rifles and cutting the Native's traps. The DFO hauled Native gear and impounded it, citing the Mi'kmaq fishery as a threat to the limited entry lobster fishery, with its fixed season, and trap limits. By 2000, the situation had gotten heated

I went north to cover the story for *National Fisherman* magazine, and got back a week later. Talking to Bernard about the situation in New Brunswick, he did not make the connection between what the Natives called the systematic extinguishment of access rights that led to the conflict at Burnt Church, and the gradual disenfranchising of small boat fishermen in New England, including his own exclusion from the shark and scallop fisheries. He had also lost access to lobstering, which had played an important role in his family's survival.

"You can't have everybody fishing by different rules," he said.

"So why don't they all fish by Mi'kmaq rules then? The treaty came from 1765, long before the DFO existed, now the DFO wants to change the past to suit its version of the present."

Bernard did not say much.

"The Mi'kmaq plan sounds pretty reasonable," I said, and explained as best I could the Mi'kmaq fisheries management plan that used a version of ITQs, but solved the allocation and consolidation issues.

"Everybody in the tribe gets four trap tags. When you're born you get four tags. When you die, those tags go with you. If you don't want to fish, you can lease them; if you fish you have to lease enough of other people's tags so you can make it pay. Either way you can never lose access to the fishery. If the tribal population expands, the number of traps per person goes down, and vice versa."

The plan adapted old customs to a modern situation, but it had the drawback of only functioning well in a tribe, or a very tight knit community that felt it owed something to future generations. Even Bernard's family had failed in that regard. Either they never saw what was coming, or they felt powerless to change it; they may have believed that the system would work for them. The Mi'kmaq knew better.

The old diaries that Bernard had saved, Del's from 1898, and Alton's from 1930, reveal an entirely different world. They fished in a relaxed way, and while they recognized the limits of local stocks they apparently viewed the overall stocks as inexhaustible. Nonetheless, their progression offshore told a story of disappearing resources.

In 1898 Del made daily entries of fish and lobsters landed among the islands of upper Penobscot Bay. In his sardonic style he tells of working his sloop as far as Isle au Haut and Fox Island (North Haven), where among other things he "caught a big pout fish without an oath"—his mother was aboard with him that day.

In brief entries, nineteen-year-old Del documented simple joys in a rich world. Almost every day he found something to sell from "$25 worth of herring" to "80 cents' worth of hake." Other days, like Tuesday, June 8, he just had fun: "East wind tried to catch some cod-fish but they would not bite. We went ashore on Seal Island and saw some wonderful sights. I jumped across a crack in the ledge 100 feet deep and 7 feet across."

By the time Alton began running his boat, the *Ethel B.*, the family had moved down to Matinicus, the last island in the bay. At twenty-three years old he had started to range offshore in the summer, handlining and setting tub trawl around places like Haddock Nubble and the Falls. But he still caught the bulk of his landings near the islands, and enjoyed small pleasures.

January 13, 1930: "Today I set on Green I. ridge got six hundred cod, went to Vinalhaven, took in Movies. Stayed all night."

Like Del, Alton lived much of the time aboard his small boat, poking around the islands and working almost every day that the weather permitted. Reading about their daily activities, it would be hard to argue that their lives needed improvement.

But the improvements came. In another, incomplete diary from 1937, Alton jotted down measurements for his first otter trawl net.

"The men of my father's generation, the ones born at the turn of the century, saw the fishery go from all hooks to all dragging in the course of their lives," said Bernard. "And they saw it wiped out."

I pointed out that latest stock assessments showed cod and haddock were rebounding.

"They ain't rebounding here," said Bernard, and he wondered who decided what rebounding was. "They'll never make it the way it was because we don't know what it was. I never saw what my father saw, and he never saw what his father saw. Even if they did come back, nobody's got the permits to fish'm."

Despite the regulations intended to rebuild fisheries to historical levels, and spikes in some stocks, many scientists acknowledge that environmental degradation had put the ocean's long term health in peril. Most see pollution and climate change as the key factors. Ocean temperatures had risen 56°F over the last forty years, and some scientists predict possible increases of 2 to 4°F over the next century.

Dr. David Mountain of the Northeast Fisheries Science Center (NEFSC) in Woods Hole, Massachusetts, has suggested that climate related changes in phytoplankton productivity and composition might play an important role in determining groundfish abundance in the Gulf of Maine. "By influencing larval survival and recruitment, these bottom up effects could represent the most important pathway for changes in climate to affect fish resources," Mountain said.

While warmer water may jumpstart the larval development of several groundfish species, Mountain warned that a change in phytoplankton composition, from large diatoms to harmful dinoflagellates, could leave those larvae starving.

Rather than clean the environment, policy makers advocated more aquaculture to fill the void. Beginning in the 1980s the inshore waters—bereft of commercial quantities of fish—became host to a variety of aquaculture enterprises. Although the seafood farming industry promised to help out-of-work fishermen continue to earn their livelihoods on the water by farming mussels and oysters—investment soon focused on Atlantic salmon.

In the late 1980s several fishing families around Cobscook Bay in eastern Maine had acquired leases for salmon farming. With backing from Norwegian companies, they anchored sixty-foot-wide net pens in the deep waters of the bay, where tides rose and fell twenty-seven feet, twice a day, essentially flushing the toilet for the densely stocked pens.

After eighteen months the local farmers cashed in on fish that sold for over five dollars a pound. But by the late 1990s three foreign companies, Fjord Seafood, of Norway; Stolt Sea Farms, of Luxembourg; and Heritage Salmon, of Canada, owned over 90 percent of the industry in Maine. Production of farmed salmon peaked at a record 36 million pounds in 2000, compared to 28 million pounds of groundfish. But later that year, a viral disease, Infectious Salmon Anemia (ISA), ravaged the farms in Cobscook Bay The virus, which caused hemorrhaging of the fish's internal organs, had spread from nearby New Brunswick, where it had also infected wild salmon.

In an effort to eradicate the virus, the State of Maine ordered the bay cleared of all salmon. Towns like Lubec and Eastport, Maine, which had put their chips on the aquaculture number, found themselves losers. At the town wharf in Lubec, in the late summer of 2001, barges unloaded tons of rotting salmon—one local land owner made out alright by "composting" the disease-ridden carcasses on his back fields, and the smell of rotting fish filled the air for miles.

I saw a friend, Gene Blake, on the Lubec wharf, hoisting containers of dead salmon onto a truck. "What are you going to do now?" I asked.

"Go on unemployment," he said. "Or move. Ain't nothin' left around here."

US Department of Agriculture regulations allowed the companies to harvest infected fish that did not show clinical signs of disease, and sell them on the market. Through the efforts of Senator Snowe, the federal government provided a $16 million aid package for the three foreign-owned corporations that owned the bulk of the farms. The out-of-work salmon farm workers like Gene Blake collected unemployment for as long as they could.

A glut of farmed salmon on the world market kept prices low, and new environmental restrictions prevented the farms from bouncing back. The industry once touted as an environmentally friendly option for economic growth stalled for the same reasons the commercial fishing industry had: overzealous industrial growth that ignored the limits of the available common resource. In the case of salmon aquaculture, the common resource being exploited was relatively clean, disease-free water.

In Owls Head, Bernard had heard about the salmon debacle. "How's things Downeast?" he asked.

"Every house has a for sale sign out front and the out-of-staters are flocking in."

"How 'bout back home?"

"I just said . . ."

"I mean Pennsylvan-ee-a."

I thought about that for a minute as Bernard puttered in the barn.

"I was down there last Thanksgiving, went out to the farm with my uncles. The state took it by eminent domain in 1971. They were going to flood the land but they never did," I said. "We go out there and it's like a funeral; the apple trees are gone; the fields are all grown up. The old bridge is closed and they'll probably take that out soon. My brother said he tried to take his son out to Kerr's Pond, out to our old fishing hole, a few years ago, but the place was sold and they wouldn't let him on the land. Insurance, they said."

"Gettin' to be fewer places to go everywhere. Now we'll have your MPA-A-As, and ITQs, what's that going to leave us?"

"Did I tell you about open ocean aquaculture?" I asked. "They're selling it with the same tired old shtick that it's gonna create jobs for fishermen. It didn't give many jobs to fishermen Downeast. If we're lucky we'll end up like those folks in Burnt Church, fighting to get back our fishing rights. Unfortunately we don't have a treaty, and there's not many of us left to fight.

"Besides, you need food to run a revolution. We went through Valley Forge and I realized George Washington would have been shit out of luck if he had to rely on wild fish comin' inshore these days."

Bernard could not, or chose not, to imagine losing his right to the ocean; he was seventy-two, and his boat was still fishing. He changed the subject.

"Did you see the *Eva Grace* down in Eastport?"

Bernard had asked me about that old wooden boat several times since we reconnected in 1998; for some reason he could not get her off his mind. "Buff Bracket had her built down in New Harbor," he had told me. "She was the *Jackie B.*, he took her shrimping, he was one of the first, they give him ten cents a pound, and a kick in the pants. He sold her to Stinson's and they named her after one of their sisters."

"Yeah I saw her over in Eastport," I said. "She looks like hell."

"Well, next time you're down there see what they want for her."

"What are you going to do?"

"Brad can buy her and put the gear aboard her. I'll hold the permit and he can keep fishing."

"What about *Irene?*"

"I'll use her to carry stuff out to the islands. Maybe if somebody wants to be buried out there I can take'm out, or bury them at sea. Whatever they want."

"A funeral boat?"

"Sure, why give'm more of what they already got. Give'm something they never saw before."

All the time I've known him I never know what to make out of half what he says. If I wait long enough I find out what he means.

The fact is another NMFS buyback program, launched in 2002 and intended to reduce latent effort, aims to buy permits rather than boats. Fishermen could submit a bid for what they would accept for their ground-fish permits. If NMFS deemed the price reasonable, they would buy the permit and the boat could continue fishing for other species. Opponents of the $10 million plan said it would take access to the resource out of the small ports where fishermen had switched to lobstering during the groundfish crisis. If lobstering ever failed, those communities would not be able to switch back to groundfishing.

But for fishermen on the edge of bankruptcy, or with children disinclined to work on the water, the buyback presented a chance to cash in on their own misfortune. It offered them a stake to "pursue more productive work," according to Ralph Townsend, a professor of economics at the University of Maine.

Townshead vigorously advocated the dogma that economic efficiency must prevail, and that total net income from a resource offers the only measure of whether or not it is being wisely used. If the fish could be harvested by a fewer number of high tech vessels then that meant the excess effort could be put to more productive use in an infinitely expanding economy. "The less efficient fishermen can find other, more useful, employment," he suggested, but he did not say where. Most other natural resource-based industries have increased efficiency by downsizing. The need for funeral boats may be limited.

Bernard put a bid to sell his permit for $300,000—NMFS rejected it. He apparently was not meant to surrender, at any price.

Not so the *Sea Trek*. She met her end in 2002, fishing for slime eels. "I bought her back in 1996 for the permit," former owner Roy Enoksen said in the spring of 2003. "We transferred it to one of our new boats and then sold [the *Sea Trek*] to a guy in Gloucester. I don't know what happened to her."

The *New Bedford Standard Times* makes no mention of the *Sea Trek's* disappearance. The story went round mostly as a rumor, but the official Coast Guard report on the incident gives the details:

On November 13, 2002, at 2:44 a.m. Coast Guard Group, Woods Hole, Massachusetts, received a distress call from John Conneely, owner/operator of the *F/V Sea Trek*. Conneely reported taking on water about seven miles east of Nauset Beach, near the elbow of Cape Cod.

Chatham, Massachusetts, Coast Guard Station sent out a forty-seven-foot rescue boat, which succeeded in getting a pump aboard the stricken *Sea Trek* and pumping the water out of her. The Chatham boat and another forty-seven-foot Coast Guard rescue boat from Provincetown, at the tip of Cape Cod, escorted the *Sea Trek* to Race Point, where, according to the report: "Vessel master decided to return to homeport, Gloucester, MA."

Conneely and his two crewmen, David Lahey and Stephen MacElarnery, put Race Point astern and headed across Cape Cod Bay without an escort, thirty-eight miles to home. The wind blew out of the NE at 20 to 30 knots, with seas running six to ten feet; no problem for the ninety-two-foot vessel.

At 11:30 a.m., Woods Hole radioed the District 1 command center in Boston: "Vessel is dry—pumped out—no further distress—headed into Gloucester." Less than an hour later, more than halfway home, Conneely radioed the Coast Guard and requested pumps. The *Sea Trek's* generator and pumps had failed and she had begun taking on water again.

At one in the afternoon, the Coast Guard sent out two forty-seven-foot rescue boats from Boston, and a few minutes later a helicopter took off from Cape Cod loaded with pumps for the *Sea Trek*.

The Coast Guard helicopter succeeded in getting a pump aboard the sinking boat, but the intake hose did not reach the flooded area. The crew tried to set up the pump in the engine room, but waves broke over the stern and swamped them. The Coast Guard rescue boat #47259 put one of its crewman aboard the *Sea Trek* to help with the pumps, but to no avail.

At 2:13 p.m., rescue personnel reported that the pumps proved unable to keep up with flooding. The venerable old *Sea Trek* had three feet of water in the engine room and waves pouring in.

"Master was having trouble maintaining a steady course w/manual steering," says the report, "vsl [vessel] appeared to be settling gradually by the stern, and increasing smoke was observed from vsl stack. Decision was made for [helicopter] to hoist all F/V crew members and CG47259 crewman. . . . All subjects hoisted and delivered to Sta. Gloucester."

Although she was still afloat, the decision to abandon the *Sea Trek* meant the end of her. By 3:15 p.m., she had become a ghost ship. The rescue boat #47259 attempted to tow the dying vessel, but the *Sea Trek* began to list and the rescue boat cut the tow line.

By 3:29 p.m., Conneely and his crew had arrived by helicopter in Gloucester. The Coast Guard radioed a warning to mariners, a swamped vessel last seen at 42 29 N 70 31 W, a hazard to navigation.

As the Coast Guard boat left the scene on a raw November afternoon, the *Sea Trek* settled amid the gray waves, awash and alone. People like Roy Enoksen and Doug Anderson had pushed her to her limits for forty years. In her lifetime she had gone from the pride of the scallop fleet, to an unremarkable slime eel boat, to derelict hulk—a menace to navigation. The Coast Guard rated media interest as "medium," and few calls came in after a press release on the day of the sinking.

In his kitchen, Bernard picked up a bag of lobster shells and threw it in the garbage. "Joe Bray brought us a feed last night. Some folks remember the old ways," he said, referring to the days when fishermen fed their neighbors before sending the catch to market.

While Bernard holds his traditions by a thread, a new economic model has emerged to challenge the one that engineered the destruction of his way of life. "Ecological economics," pioneered by a former World Bank economist named Herman Daly, looks at social and environmental values as well as profit. In determining wise use of resources, eco-economics points out the impossibility of economic growth now that the earth's resources have become scarce. Daly advocates economic development to improve the quality of life, but calls for population control and a drastic reduction in consumption in order to achieve truly sustainable systems.

According to Daly, continued harvest of scarce renewable resources comes at a cost in the ability of those resources to regenerate. That depreciation of productive potential, says Daly, is not accounted for in the neo-classic economic model, which irrationally registers the depletion of fish stocks as income and an addition to the Gross National Product. What appears as wealth is actually debt, with increasing interest rates.

Daly points out what should be common sense: that an industry cannot outgrow the limits of nature. It may stretch those limits, but not forever. Fishermen and fish farmers who have destroyed themselves and their environment by ignoring those limits, are now in the payback period of the debt they created. But eco-economics offers some hope for a future that works for people and the ecosystem. It rests in the models used to guide decisions and finding ways to quantify human and environmental values that have long been ignored.

Ecological economics offers some hope for a future that works for people and the ecosystem. It rests in finding ways to quantify human and environmental values that have long been ignored, and include them in the models that guide decision making. Besides looking at what is gained, ecological economic models measure what is lost, and in more than just dollars. But because these often qualitative values are difficult if not impossible to assess, resources and cultures are regarded at worthless rather than priceless.

For centuries the fishing industry has been permitted to cascade down a declining ecosystem. Every time a new technology increases landings, the tangible value of those landings is compared to amorphous concerns about the welfare of the environment and coastal communities. Assigning a value to those things can at least enable their loss to be measured as costs, not concerns.

Smith, for instance, works to put Bernard's intrinsic values, such as self-reliance rather than reliance on expensive technology, and self-imposed limits on his harvesting capacity, into the equation that guides decisions on how best to use local resources. The fact that Bernard has survived so many years—albeit, subsidized by Eleanor's paychecks from the phone company—without the wealth of technology used by his peers, indicates that he holds something of equal or greater value. Something not accounted for in the Stratton Report.

Tyedmers looks at the ecological footprints of various production systems. In British Columbia, he gathered data on the energy consumption patterns of production systems for both farmed and wild salmon, and found that based on their respective ecological footprints, aquaculture proved less sustainable than all types of salmon fishing. Tyedmers and many others put a value on simpler harvest methods and the culture that commercial fishing supports. For thirty years that culture has been devalued by neo-classic economic models that regulators use to guide their decisions where everything is eventually subjugated to economic efficiency.

But in the eleventh hour, eco-economists are learning how to calculate what continued economic growth in fisheries—now taking place in aquaculture rather than fleet expansion—will cost.

Several studies performed by Smith's students indicate that aquaculture development by Norwegian and Canadian conglomerates operating in Maine does not compensate the state's coastal communities for the loss of local control over adjacent waters, or the resulting environmental impacts, such as the transfer of exotic viruses like ISA to wild fish.

Nonetheless, by the prevailing measures, finfish aquaculture still looks like a winner, and entrepreneurs eager to invest in aquaculture believe they have solved the problems that plagued salmon farming by moving to the new frontier: the open ocean.

Complete with rhetoric that sounds hauntingly familiar from the rapid expansion of the fishing fleet in the 1970s, open ocean aquaculture proponents trumpet the vast capacity of the offshore waters to support fish farming. Speaking in 1996 at an international Sea Grant conference on open ocean aquaculture, Jill Fallon, executive director of The Aquaculture Coalition, went so far as to call aquaculture "manifest destiny" and compare the fishermen to Native Americans. "This is not the time or the place to discuss the tragedy of the American Indian," said Fallon, in her racist diatribe. "They had to be removed, warred against, and eventually forced onto reservations in order to make room for settlers thirsting for land." In that same spirit, she urged, "We must open the Blue Frontier." If all goes according to plan, open ocean fish farmers and their allies in government would leave fishermen like Bernard with an ever-shrinking and damaged piece of the ocean. As had happened with the Native Americans, the Acadians, and now the fishermen, those with the technology and capital appropriated the resources from those without.

With help from Sea Grant, several commercial open ocean fish farms were already established by 2003. A company called Snapperfarm grew cobia in submerged net pens near Puerto Rico. Snapperfarm owner Brian O'Hanlon would later take his operation to Panama, where National Geographics Magazine described him of creating his fish farm "out of nothing, in the middle of nowhere." While ignoring the federal grants O'Hanlon had received, National Geo appeared to also credit him with powers of alchemy in his ability to create something "out of nothing, in the middle of nowhere." In New Hampshire, fishermen from the Portsmouth Fishermen's Co-op became participants in creating their own obsolescence. They joined a private company, Great Bay Aquafarms, of Newington, New Hampshire, and the University of New Hampshire, as leaseholders in an open ocean aquaculture project that will grow cod in submerged pens.

In spite of the fact that cod near Eastport, Maine, were identified as carriers of ISA, and that fish farms are known disease incubators, scientists with NMFS, the primary agency responsible for managing open ocean aquaculture, dismiss the risk of spreading disease to wild cod. "There is virtually no risk," said Linda Chaves, spokesperson for NMFS.

"We haven't even thought about it," said Chris Duffy, vice president of Great Bay Aquafarms. Like most fish growers, he focuses on what happens inside, not outside, the pens. Speaking at an aquaculture workshop in New Brunswick in the summer of 2003, Duffy predicted vast cod farms in the western Gulf of Maine. "I hope to see cod production on the level of chicken," he said.

In order to maintain healthy fish, however, cod farmers need to utilize the same productive waters that wild fish and commercial fishermen use, and cod in particular present more potential problems than salmon.

While disease often enters fish farms from wild carriers, the densely packed net pens offer more opportunities for viruses to mutate and shed into the surrounding environment. Cod school closer than salmon, and will probably be stocked at higher densities over longer periods of time. The spread of parasites from salmon farms has been blamed for the disappearance of salmon and sea trout from the rivers of Ireland and Scotland, and cod are extremely parasite prone.

Because of cod's comparatively low yield of edible meat per pound of body weight—40 percent compared to 60 percent for salmon—cod farmers in particular have a motive to jumpstart the breeding process by using genetic engineering to create larger, meatier fish. Inevitable disease outbreaks and efforts by some fish farmers to legitimize the use of genetically engineered fish—which most observers predict will eventually escape into the wild—further threaten wild cod and other species with biological and genetic pollution.

As with the expansion of the fishing industry thirty years before, regulators and entrepreneurs disregard warnings about the capacity of the environment to support open ocean aquaculture and the potential impacts of industrial growth on wild fish and ecological function. Most proponents contend that the emerging industry has hardly tapped the potential capacity, and that troubling questions can be ignored for the time being. They hope that the quantity of clean water in the open ocean will mitigate the problems of nutrient buildup and diseases that wrecked inshore aquaculture. If problems arise, industry advocates promise they will fix them with technology.

The probability of escaping fish contaminating wild stocks, genetically and virally, does concern them.

Eco-economists like Tyedmers struggle to prevent history from repeating itself on the open sea, with perhaps a greater impact on the world's food security. While Duffy points to a chart that shows global population reaching eight billion by the year 2025 and a seafood deficit of 120 million metric tons as a rationale for growing cod that will sell for five dollars a pound—hardly a product that will feed the masses in the developing world—Tyedmers points out the obvious: "There is only one reason to grow carnivorous finfish, which reduce the level of protein coming from the sea rather than increase it, and that is to make money. Don't tell me you're going to feed the world with farmed salmon and cod."

As with Maine's farmed salmon, most of the cod from New Hampshire will go into the fresh fish markets of New York, Boston, and elsewhere in the Northeast. Farmed product will continue to supplant wild fish in those markets and send confusing signals to consumers by driving down prices for the no longer abundant species.

A new faction of the environmental community has challenged the marine fish farming industry, often with the sort of exaggerated stories and misinformation Safina and Norse used against fishermen. But Tyedmers and other eco-economists strive to go by the numbers, and to that end they work to develop measuring rods for the heretofore unmeasured. By creating development models that put numerical values on things like social capital—essentially the value of having and being good neighbors with a common cause—eco-economic models aim to create a more complete picture of the world we live in. They provide decision makers with a tool to help them figure out how our culture can survive without economic growth, which Daly and his disciples believe has already exceeded the carrying capacity of the planet. Fishermen have seen the limits of the planet firsthand.

The level and complexity of the discussions, fused with advances in science and cooked in economic theory and an old debate on property rights, has become more than Bernard wants to digest. He has plenty to keep him occupied just maintaining the *Irene & Alton,* and does not dwell on the eco-economic models being designed to measure the values he has never doubted. He does not need eco-economics to explain common sense. But the eco-economists need him; he is one of the baselines for the models they want to create.

Being efficient in how he uses his energy, and getting the most he can from every fish he catches, have been instinctual for Bernard. He has bent to overwhelming forces reluctantly, compromising inch by inch on technological advances and destructive fishing practices. "You got to go with the times," he said to me one day, and I laughed out loud.

But I wonder if maybe his time has come.

Part V

CLOSING

Seventeen

TWENTY YEARS OF TAR

Bernard hauled his boat out late in 2003. It was mid-September when I drove down to Rockland for another day of tarring the rigging. At the house I pulled a heavy book out of my car, the paintings of Edward Hopper, and carried it in to show Bernard.

Seventy-seven years after Edward Hopper worked in Rockland, Bernard sat at his kitchen table, looking at a print of the artist's "The Bow of the Beam Trawler *Osprey.*" Bernard had never heard of Hopper, but he knew what he was looking at.

"What's this?" I asked, pointing to a tan splotch on the gallows.

"In them days they hoisted the net up to a block attached to the mast, and they put a piece of rawhide there to keep it from tearing on the gallows." He pointed to an apparently dislocated piece of steel. "That should be attached here," he said. "I guess the fellow that painted this didn't really understand what he was seein'."

"Hopper wasn't really a detail man."

Brad arrived, flipped through the Hopper book briefly, and closed it. Out in the barn Bernard rummaged around and found some old pine tar, and we headed over to Rockland where the boat sat on the rails.

I found the seat down in the engine room; the bosun's chair with old pine tar and paint on it from twenty-seven years of service, and we got started. I did the spring stay first, but couldn't muscle my way into the chair; had to climb up higher in the rigging and drop myself down in. I sat there breathless, hanging in space.

"Ready, old son?" Bernard called up to me.

We went through our paces, finished up, and the next morning I caught a plane out to Matinicus Island to write a story for *National Fisherman*.

Bernard's daughter lent me her cottage near the harbor and I spent a couple of days knocking around the island. Almost all the old timers I met out on Matinicus had a story about Del. He apparently made quite an impression on people, one way or another. "Old Del wasn't much for religion," said Ronny Ames, grandson of the man who reneged on his offer to sell his house to Del. "I remember when the *Sunbeam,* the missionary boat, first come out here. Del made up a little limerick or whatever you call it: 'Here comes the *Sunbeam,* she's a dandy little packet. But the fellow that's aboard of her makes an awful racket.'"

One afternoon I walked a mile across the island to the old homestead Del ended up buying. I recognized it immediately from the photos in Bernard's albums; it stood in a field of tall grass, and the door to the piazza was open. Chris and Mary Russell, who had bought the place in 1969 for the price of rigging the *Ruth & Mary* over for shrimping, still owned it; they happened to be there, and gave me a tour.

A door from the kitchen opened into the dining room. A chimney and a narrow stairway in the center of the house separated the dining room from the living room. Three bedrooms not much bigger than the beds they held, ran across the back. One had a small heart-shaped hole cut in the door. "They say that means a newlywed couple spent their first night together there," said Mary Russell.

The stairs led up to a long open room under the steep pitched roof— the loft where Bernard used to sleep. Old cardboard from Campbell's Soup boxes and newspapers from 1898 had been wrapped around the beams for insulation. Bernard had probably read them all.

We went back downstairs. Around back of the house, Chris opened an outside door into the big cellar where Del once kept his milk jugs and Ethel stored the canned goods she put up every year. Not much had changed, Chris told me. I looked around. Jars of fruit and vegetables that Ethel had canned sometime before 1969 still lined the back wall; the lids rusty, thick with cobwebs. "But probably still good," Chris said.

They invited me to come back, but I had offered to paint the mast on the *Irene & Alton,* and I needed to go. When I got back to Rockland the next morning I found Bernard at the fish pier. The boat was just coming in and I caught the lines.

Aboard, I climbed aloft to the top of the mast and started painting. As I brushed over the rust on the steel bands the topmast used to slide into, I wondered if they would still hold. I worked my way down to the crosstree and stopped to look around, and honest to God, an artist had set up his easel at the head of the pier. I watched him glancing back and forth from the *Irene & Alton* to his canvas, painting her picture. Down on deck Bernard worked as he always did, steadily, and meticulously: totally absorbed in his project. He had taken a worn piece of wood off of the rail and fitted a new one in place. I watched him from my perch, as he and Brad's crewman, Jimmy Weaver, drilled through the oak.

Relying on the continuity of his family's experience, Bernard had retained his own system, within but apart from the one aimed at destroying him. He built his boat, and the quality of his craftsmanship spoke for itself. He fished his way, and survived the perfect storm of federal fisheries mismanagement and environmental destruction. His continuing existence proved the fallacy of the images others created of him. The policy makers said he was obsolete. Far from it. He is a human being with a purpose, and the blessings of God.

Eighteen

BERNARD'S FINAL CHAPTER

We buried Bernard on a beautiful summer morning, July 17, 2013. Georg was there, Donald Pelrine, and a few others of the old crew. Eleanor asked me to speak and I can't forget the look of concern on her face when I began by quoting Ahab, from Herman Melville's *Moby-Dick:*

"Oh Starbuck! It is a mild, mild wind, and a mild looking sky. On such a day—very much such a sweetness as this—I struck my first whale—a boy-harpooneer of eighteen!"

The point I wanted to make is that we were all kids once, enamored with wooden boats and eager to get out on them. I was nineteen when Virgil P. McDowell hailed me from the deck of the *Kaynell,* and Bernard received his calling probably in the womb. We were all drawn to something in the sea and most of us did not make much money. We were able to, as the Stratton Report said, "eke out a moderate living," but we were accruing wealth far less corruptible than money.

Once upon a time in our lives, on such a day very much the sweetness of the day we buried Bernard, we would be setting out together for the swordfish grounds on the Northeast Peak of Georges Bank. We would be bound for an adventure on the ocean wilderness, and never any of us worried about anything when *Irene* carried us forth with Bernard at the helm.

I once lamented the passing of those days, but Bernard stopped me. "At least we were there, old son," he said.

Nobody can take those days away from us. We were blessed, and it seems fitting that these few years after Bernard's death, I am afforded the opportunity to write his final chapter.

Back in the day, I remember reading *The Perfect Storm*, and while it is a great read—I plowed through it in one sitting—I felt like it misrepresented fishermen. Junger made us seem like a bunch of divorcees and barflies, and while there are plenty of those in the ranks of fisherfolk, on the boats and on the docks—I was one of them for a spell—there are also many like Bernard; people with integrity and dignity, who remain guardians of their own heritage.

In the late 1990s, as New England fishing fleets declined, I wanted people to know that we were losing more than a bunch of losers; we were losing an almost mystic culture built on centuries of accumulated knowledge that technology will never replace.

I wanted my readers to understand the faith and brotherhood among Bernard's crew. The Rayneses always called us "the boys." And though we did not always get along, we would risk and probably give our lives for each other.

The *Irene & Alton* was the finest vessel I ever ventured out upon the ocean in, and she kept me and all of us alive. There is something of the sacred and maternal in the word vessel. It is the watertight womb that carries us safe in a dangerous environment. When my teenage children and I helped Georg move his sailboat from Maine to Connecticut in 2016, my son shouted, "Look, it's the *Irene & Alton*!" We all looked and there she was, still working as a lobster smack carrying bait to the islands and bringing back lobsters. It seemed a magic moment in many ways, Georg and I at sea together with the next generation, and that the image of the *Irene & Alton* had become so ingrained in my children's minds that they could spot her from a distance.

The worldview and the skills that created that vessel have largely vanished from the American coastline, relegated to an exclusive crowd of old timers and aficionados. Though I have traveled around the world and found wooden boatbuilding and a reliance on ancestral knowledge enduring among other fishing cultures in places like Melinka in the south of Chile, and among the Sea Gypsies of Koh Lanta in Thailand, the fishing industry in Maine and much of the USA is gradually losing ground to the privatization and consolidation advocated in 1969 by the Stratton Commission. In the years since *Doryman* was first published, the Maine groundfish fishery gave way to quota management advocated by a consortium of investors, government, and NGOs.

There are only a handful of small-scale draggers left between Portland and the Canadian border, and as I write, Maine Sea Grant has received a $20 million grant to privatize much of the coast as aquaculture leases. The non-governmental organizations that declare support for coastal communities as their mission are all on board with the privatization plan. Many are running programs in Maine schools promoting things like seaweed farming for environmental mitigation and health food, as the Department of Energy is proposing the creation of 18 million acres of kelp farms for the production of biofuels and chemicals.

While Maine's inshore fisheries licenses are non-transferable, and mostly restricted to owner-operators, Maine aquaculture leases can be sold, and there seems to be little heed to the fact that any entity with deep enough pockets can buy and consolidate large segments of that industry. Maine's salmon farms, for example, are now owned by one multinational company.

Many young people no longer learn the names of groundfish from their grandparents, and most do not know what a blackback or a dab is—they know them as "winter flounder" and "American plaice." Because of the strength of the lobster fishery, many young fishermen believe they can control development of other resources along the coast. All the policy papers and development initiatives I see indicate they are wrong, and that much may be lost in the coming years.

Many people are doing what they can to maintain solid coastal communities, and we may get lucky. To that end I offer this book. I want to give anyone who wants to know the story of what Maine's fisheries once looked like the opportunity to be informed by us, the people who lived it, even as I did, a bit of an Ishmael on the margins. Since I started working the docks in the mid 1970s I have seen the workings of the Stratton Commission's recommendations for fleet consolidation as the small boats vanish from the coast. I have had a front row seat to various acts of cultural genocide accomplished through implementation of the Magnuson-Stevens Fishery Management and Conservation Act. But I am fortunate. I traveled the coasts and soaked up everything I could from the people I was ready to die with on any given day, though none of them compared to Bernard. And I still ask myself, when confronted with a problem or a storm at sea, what would Bernard do?

APPENDICES

GLOSSARY

Barvil: a waterproof protective skirt with a bib front, worn by fishermen.

Cod end: also known as the "bag:" the end of a trawl net where the captured fish accumulate.

Combing: a band of wood rising above and inboard the rail of an open boat, or the decks of larger boats, to keep water out.

Dory: a hard-chine wooden boat built with sawn frames and the bottom planked lengthwise, usually with a narrow transom.

Double-ender: a boat that tapers, like the bow, on both ends.

Fo'c'sle: forward compartment below deck used as crew's quarters.

Handline: a fishing line wrapped around a frame and retrieved by hand without benefit of a rod or reel.

Haul-out: a loop of rope between an anchor in deep water and a point on shore (or a wharf). Used to haul a small boat away from the beach where it might become stranded at low tide, and to retrieve it, when needed.

High flyer: buoy with pole and radar reflector.

Hod: (clam hod) a rectangular of wooden basket made of lath, with a tall handle; used primarily by clammers.

Hookup man: crewman who works with winch man, hooking up the nets, dredges, etc., for hoisting.

Leadline: a lead weight tied to a line marked in fathoms, used to sound depth. The weight was cast overboard and the sounder counted off the fathoms until it reached bottom.

Lee: downwind, usually the "lee side" or protected side of an island, boat, or other object, except a "lee shore," which is downwind of a boat and threatens grounding.

Nubble: a rise, a bump in the topography.

Outrigger: a wood or steel pole projecting from the side of a boat.

Painter: a line tied to the bow of a skiff or dory.

Port: the left side of a boat when looking forward (trick for remembering: "port" has the same number of letters as "left").

Ragbag: Coleslaw.

Ripper: a short bladed knife used for gutting fish.

Skiff: a small rowboat or motorboat.

Sloop: a single-masted sailboat, with a main sail and jib.

Starboard: the right side of a boat when looking forward.

Stays'l: triangular sail rigged fore and aft, acts to steady the roll of a boat and to keep her pointed into the wind.

Tripper: a bronze trigger used to open the cod end or keep it closed.

Tub trawl: a longline strung with hooks and coiled in a barrel or tub.

Wheelhouse: pilothouse, cabin above deck housing the helm, or wheel.

Windward: upwind side of a boat.

FAMILY TREE

Francis Raynes   **Daniel LeBlanc**

Arrived in Falmouth, Maine, c. 1646   Arrived in Acadia 1646

Ninth Generation in North America   Ninth Generation in North America

Dalton Raynes, b. 1879, married
Ethel Brown, b. 1884, and had one child together,
Alton, b. 1908, d. 1990.

                                   Simon "Sam" LeBlanc,
                    b. 1876, married **Marie Lousie "Minnie" Bois,**
                        b. 1882, and had eleven children:
                               George, b. 1905, d. 1974;
                                 Joe, b. 1906, d. 1938*;
                               Irene, b. 1907, d. 1978;
                             Bernard, b. 1909, d. 1926;[8]
                             Burtman b. 1911, d. 1975;
                             Lamond, b. 1912, d. 1950;
                              Victor, b. 1914, d. 1926;
                               Tillie, b. 1917, d. 2001;
                              Betty, b. 1919, living;
                             Wilbert, b. 1921, d. 1967;*
                               Marc, b. 1922, d. 2000.

---

[8] Bernard's mother, Irene Leblanc Raynes, lost half her brothers, and two cousins either drowned at sea or were killed in the fishing industry.

Sam's brother **Michael LeBlanc,**
b. 1878, had two sons: **Lorenzo**, b. 1903, and **Thomas**, b. 1920.
Both died aboard the *Lynn* in 1951.*

Tenth Generation

Alton Raynes married **Irene LeBlanc** and had three children:
Bernard, b. 1932;
Patricia, b. 1937;
Sylvia, b. 1939.

Eleventh Generation

Bernard Raynes married **Eleanor Daniels** and had four children:
Deanna, b. 1957;
Dawn, b. 1960;
twins **Denise** and **Delisa**, b. 1962.

---

* Author's Note. After Bernard died I found that we shared a common ancestor, Rene LeBlanc, who died in Philadelphia in 1758. Bernard and I were very distant cousins and never knew it.

SELECTED BIBLIOGRAPHY
AND REFERENCES

In the course of writing *The Doryman's Reflection,* I consulted numerous books, science journals, and government publications, among them:

Anthony, P. D. "Cod Vision," in *Journal of Fish Biology,* Vol. 19 (1), July 1981: 87–103.

Arsenault, Bona. *History of the Acadians.* Montreal: Lemeac, 1978.

Bigelow, Henry, and William C. Schroeder. *Fishes of the Gulf of Maine.* Washington, D. C.: Smithsonian Books, 2002.

Crutchfield, James A. *The Fisheries: Problems in Resource Management.* Seattle: University of Washington Press, 1965.

Cushing, D. H. *Marine Ecology and Fisheries.* London: Cambridge University Press, 1975.

Daly, Herman. *Beyond Growth.* Boston: Beacon Press, 1996.

De Soto, Hernando. *The Mystery of Capital: Why Capitalism Triumphs in the West and Fails Everywhere Else.* New York: Basic Books, 2000.

Dewar, Margaret. *Industry in Trouble: The Federal Government and New England Fisheries.* Philadelphia: Temple University Press, 1983.

Finlayson, Alan Christopher. *Fishing for Truth: A Sociological Analysis of Northern Cod Stock Assessments from 1977 to 1990.* St. John's, Newfoundland: Memorial University Press, 1994.

Gibson, Charles Dana. *The Broadbill Swordfishery of the Northwest Atlantic: An Economic and Natural History.* Camden, Maine: Ensign Press, 1998.

Innis, Harold. *The Cod Fisheries: The History of an International Economy.* Toronto: University of Toronto Press, 1978.

Kurlansky, Mark. *Cod: A Biography of the Fish That Changed the World.* New York: Penguin Books, 1998.

Link, J. S., and L. P. Garrison. "The Diet of Atlantic Cod," in *Marine Ecology: Progress Series, Vol.* 227: 109—123.

McFarland, Raymond. *A History of the New England Fisheries with Maps.* New York: Elibron Classics, replica of 1911 edition by University of Pennsylvania, D. Appleton and Co.

McPhee, John. *The Founding Fish.* New York: Farrar, Straus and Giroux, 2002.

Melville, Herman. *Moby-Dick.*

Midling, K. "Calls of the Atlantic Cod," in *Bio-Acoustics Bulletin,* Cornell University, Vol. 12 (2/3), 2002: 233–235.

Polk, Marie, ed. *Open Ocean Aquaculture: Proceedings from an International Conference.* University of New Hampshire/University of Maine Sea Grant College Program, 1996.

Ross, Sally, and Alphonse Deveau. *Acadians of Nova Scotia: Past and Present.* Halifax, Nova Scotia: Nimbus Publishing, 1992.

Tacconi, Luca. *Biodiversity and Ecological Economics: Participation Values and Resource Management.* London: Earthscan Publications, 2000.

US Fisheries Reports, annual reports on the general health of fisheries resources and the industry, published originally by the Bureau of Commercial Fisheries, followed by the US. Fish and Wildlife Service, and the National Oceanic and Atmospheric Administration, 1931–2003.

Weber, Michael, *From Abundance to Scarcity: A History of US Marine Fisheries Policy.* Washington, DC: Island Press, 2001.

Whale, Rick. "Bycatch in the New England Multispecies Fishery," in *Northeast Naturalist, Vol.* 7 (4): 395–410.

ACKNOWLEDGMENTS

In creating the first edition of this book I drew on twenty-eight years of working in the fish business, six of them writing about the industry. In the years since *Doryman* was first published, I've added two more books and a trip around the world as a Guggenheim Fellow to my experience. Numerous interviews, lengthy research, and studying the journals of Bernard's father Alton, from 1930, and grandfather Del, from 1898, enabled me to push the limits of creative nonfiction in recreating the scenes of the Raynes and Leblanc families' history. I hope they will forgive me for any inaccuracies.

I wish to acknowledge all those who shared their memories and expertise with me, and those who helped in numerous other ways, particularly Bernard Raynes, his wife Eleanor, his daughter Deanna LaCombe, and his cousin and family genealogist, Elaine Box; fishermen: Doug Anderson, Ted Ames, Roy Enoksen, Jim Kendall, Ronny Ames, Glenn Lawrence, Georg Hinteregger, Donald Pelrine, Danny Ward, Peter Gladding, Don DeMaria, and all the others I have worked with, some of whom are mentioned in the book; economists: Stew Smith, Peter Tyedmers, and James Crutchfield; scientist, Rodney Roundtree; sometime fisheries regulators: Alan Christopher Finlayson and James Ward; Policy analyst, Mike Weber; environmentalists: Peter Shelley and Niaz Dorry; Acadian history buff, Soni Biehl; librarian, Jackie Riley at the National Marine Fisheries Service Library in Woods Hole, Massachusetts; Trish Clay at the National Marine Fisheries Service; the US Coast Guard; and everyone I have interviewed for a fisheries story in my writing career: you all helped shape my understanding of the situation one way or another. Many thanks also to the editors who opened doors for me: Bill Crowe, Susan B. Adams, and Jerry Fraser; my publisher John Oakes; and to the critics who read my drafts: Kathryn Belden, Katie Wilson, Ben Pasamanick, Dan Hoekstra, Earl and Joan Winderman; my old dorymates: Adam Pasamanick, Chris Scanlan, and Tom Hamilton; and my everlasting love, Regina Grabrovac; finally, thank you Oona and Asher, my patient children.